THE
THOMAS LAMONTS
IN AMERICA

The Lamont Coat of Arms

THE THOMAS LAMONTS IN AMERICA

by

Corliss Lamont
Edward Miner Lamont
Thomas Stilwell Lamont
The Reverend Thomas Lamont
Thomas William Lamont
Thomas William Lamont II
Margaret Lamont Heap
Francis T. P. Plimpton
Nathan M. Pusey

with Recollections and Poems
by
John Masefield

Edited by CORLISS LAMONT

SOUTH BRUNSWICK AND NEW YORK : A. S. BARNES AND COMPANY
LONDON : THOMAS YOSELOFF LTD

A. S. Barnes and Co., Inc.
Cranbury, New Jersey 08512

Thomas Yoseloff Ltd
108 New Bond Street
London W1Y OQX, England

ISBN 0-498-07882-5
Printed in the United States of America

To the Lamonts—
Past, Present, and Future

CONTENTS

LIST OF ILLUSTRATIONS

A WHO'S WHO OF THE AUTHORS

Corliss Lamont, editor of *The Thomas Lamonts in America,* was born in 1902, the son of Thomas W. and Florence C. Lamont. He is the author of *The Philosophy of Humanism, Remembering John Masefield,* and other books.

Edward M. Lamont was born in 1926, the son of Thomas S. Lamont and grandson of the Thomas W. Lamonts. He is Deputy Director, Office of New Community Development, U.S. Department of Housing and Urban Development.

Lansing Lamont, youngest son of Thomas S. Lamont, was born in 1930 and is the father of Thomas S. Lamont II. He is a journalist and Chief Canadian Correspondent for *Time.* He is also the author of *Day of Trinity.*

Reverend Thomas Lamont (1832-1916), a Methodist minister, was the son of the first Thomas W. Lamont and the father of the second Thomas W. Lamont.

Thomas Stilwell Lamont (1899–1967), son of Thomas W. and Florence C. Lamont, was a financier.

Thomas William Lamont (1870–1948), the son of the Reverend Thomas Lamont, was a financier and philanthropist, and the author of *My Boyhood in a Parsonage* and *Across World Frontiers.*

Thomas William Lamont II (1924–1945) was the grandson of Thomas William Lamont and the son of Thomas S. Lamont. He was a student at Harvard before he lost his life on a submarine in World War II.

Margaret Lamont Heap, born in 1930, is the daughter of Corliss Lamont. She is the wife of J. David Heap and the mother of two children.

John Masefield (1878–1967) was Poet Laureate of England and the author of many books of poetry, novels, and plays. He was a close friend of the Lamont family.

Francis T. P. Plimpton, lawyer and diplomat, was born in 1900.

He is a graduate of the Phillips Exeter Academy, Amherst College, and the Harvard Law School. From 1961 to 1965 he was a Deputy United States Representative to the United Nations with the rank of Ambassador.

Nathan M. Pusey, born in 1907, was President of Harvard University from 1953 to 1971. He worked closely with Thomas S. Lamont while the latter was a member of the Harvard Corporation.

PREFACE

by Corliss Lamont

Like my grandfather Lamont, my father, and my brother Thomas, I have a feeling of profound piety toward my forebears and family. My wife tells me that this attitude has much in common with Confucian ancestor worship. In an age when many traditional values have crumbled, I think it becomes all the more important to stress the significance of devoted and affectionate family life. Despite all criticisms, both justified and unjustified, of the family, it has shown great resilience as an institution and continues to thrive throughout the world.

In any case, I think that it is worthwhile to put into permanent form some record of the Thomas Lamonts and their ancestors going back to thirteenth-century Scotland. As the sole survivor of my original family, I feel a special obligation to do this. I do not, of course, attempt to give a complete summary or evaluation of the life of any Lamont; the emphasis is on the personal side and on relations within the family.

Clearly, there are hundreds of thousands of other families in the United States that could, if they took the trouble, trace back their genealogical tree over the centuries. The Lamonts were not unlike other families who came to this country two or three hundred years ago, who underwent hardships, killed or were killed by Indians, worked long hours, led lives of deprivation undreamed of by their present descendants—but who possessed riches rare today, such as clean air, pure water, and simple lives untrammeled by the bewildering complexity of a machine civilization.

This volume spans the lives of six generations of Thomas Lamonts: my great-grandfather, Thomas William Lamont (1803–1853), a merchant and farmer in Charlotteville, New York; my grandfather, the Reverend Thomas Lamont (1832–1916), a Methodist minister in upstate New York; my father, Thomas W.

Lamont (1870–1948), a banker of New York City; my brother, Thomas Stilwell Lamont (1899–1967), likewise a New York banker; his son and my nephew, Thomas W. Lamont II (1924–1945), a talented youth who sacrificed his life in the Second World War; and my grandnephew, Thomas Stilwell Lamont II, who was born in 1961 and is a schoolboy. Assuming that my grandnephew lives at least until 2003, there will have been an unbroken line of Thomas Lamonts for 200 years.

My grandfather Lamont and his son Hammond, my uncle, were the first members of the family to interest themselves in our genealogy. In 1913 Grandfather, then in his eighty-first year, wrote a brief history of our branch of the Lamonts in the United States during the nineteenth century. My father edited the manuscript and arranged for its publication in a small private edition in 1915. Much of that book is included here.

In his story of the Lamonts, my grandfather states that our first American ancestor, Robert Lamont, was born in Antrim, Northern Ireland (Ulster) in 1726 and emigrated from the nearby port of Coleraine to America about 1745 or 1750. During the summer of 1961 I took a special trip to Northern Ireland, flying from London, to try to find out more about Robert Lamont and to obtain some information as to when his ancestors came to Ireland. Making my headquarters at the capital city of Belfast, I drove several times to Antrim, Coleraine, and through the surrounding countryside—a green, undulating, agricultural land made lush by plentiful rain. I also took the longer route to Coleraine over the beautiful highway along the northeast coast from Belfast. From this road I saw splendid views of sea and cliff, and occasionally glimpsed Scotland across the Irish Sea.

Coleraine is a city of about 13,000 population and is situated on the small River Bann about four miles from its mouth. Ocean-going vessels come up the river from the sea to large wharves at Coleraine itself. Looking over the dock area, I reflected that perhaps this was the very place where Robert Lamont boarded his sailing ship back in 1750.

Delving into the matter of parish registries and other local records in Antrim and Coleraine, I found that such documents do not as a rule reach back much further than 1840. Moreover, almost all the records on Ireland in the hands of the British Government were burned in Dublin in 1922 by the Irish Republicans. For these reasons I was unable to trace with any assurance

the background of Robert Lamont's family. In the Public Record
Office of Northern Ireland at Belfast I did discover the names
of John Lamont and John Lamount on the 1663 Hearthmoney
Roll (a list of taxpayers to the Crown) for the town and parish
of Coleraine. Either of these gentlemen could have been a fore-
father of Robert Lamont.

It was after Queen Elizabeth's ruthless subjection of Ireland,
1599–1603, when large sections of Ulster became depopulated,
that the Scots, attracted by grants of free and fertile farm land,
began to emigrate in considerable numbers to Northern Ireland,
especially to the counties of Antrim and Down on the east coast.
Religious and political persecution in Scotland, and the fierce clan
wars (the big massacre of Lamonts by Campbells took place in
1646), were also important factors in inducing the Scots to cross
the Irish Sea.

Robert Lamont's forebears settled in County Antrim sometime
during the seventeenth century, but we do not know exactly where
or when. However, early in the eighteenth century economic conditions in Northern Ireland started to deteriorate, and many of
the Scotch-Irish decided to go to America to seek new opportunities
and a better life. From about 1718 to 1775 some 200,000 of them,
probably about one-third of the Protestant population of Ireland,
sailed to the New World. These included Robert Lamont, his
mother, and his two brothers. The large numbers of Catholic Irish
who emigrated to the United States during the nineteenth century
came for the most part from poverty-stricken sections of Southern
Ireland.

While I was in Belfast, I was bold enough to phone, completely
out of the blue, Mr. Andrew J. Lamont of Coleraine, one of the
forty-seven Lamonts in the Northern Ireland telephone book. I
said to him, "This is Mr. Lamont of New York, and I thought
you might be able to help me track down my Lamont ancestors."
Andrew Lamont was most cordial, told me he had some relatives
in the United States, and invited me to come see him at Coleraine.

When I met him a few hours later, he turned out to be a
handsome young man of perhaps forty, and a farmer. He took
me to his house to meet his wife and children, and gave me a
refreshing drink of vodka mixed with orange squash. Then he
drove me to the town's two oldest graveyards, in each of which
we looked at every single tombstone, hoping to discover a Lamont
name relevant to my search. But we had no luck. I am most grateful

to Andrew Lamont for his spontaneous kindness and cooperation.

I am also grateful to the Ulster-Scot Historical Society of Belfast and the Public Record Office of Northern Ireland for valuable assistance in my researches. The Public Record staff put me on to one of the best available books for background material, a Ph.D. dissertation by Robert James Dickson entitled *An Investigation into the Causes, Extent and Character of Emigration from the Northern Ports of Ireland to Colonial America*. The author also provides information as to why Scotsmen, especially in the seventeenth century, emigrated to Northern Ireland.

While my trip to Northern Ireland did not disclose all the historical data I had hoped for, I think that nonetheless it was most worthwhile. I not only acquired many facts relevant to the life of my ancestors, but also got a vivid impression of the sort of country in which they lived in Ireland. And I came away more keenly aware than ever that the Lamonts of the United States have their origin in both Ireland and Scotland, and that they are part of the great Scotch-Irish fraternity which has played such a significant role in American history for more than two centuries.*

At the back of this book I have appended a family tree in as simplified a form as possible. The charts do not bring out the fact that several Lamont ancestors, on both my father's and mother's side of the family, fought for the cause of independence in the Revolutionary War. For example, my great-great-great-grandfather, Elihu Corliss, took part in the Battle of Bunker Hill. Another interesting sidelight is that my mother, Florence Corliss Lamont, had as a lineal ancestor William Bradford, 1589–1657, who came to America on the *Mayflower* in 1620 and later became Governor of the Plymouth Colony. He was one of my grandfathers eight generations back, that is, a great-great-great-great-great-great-great-great-grandfather.† Mother's first Corliss ancestor in America was George Corliss of Haverhill, Massachusetts. He came to the New World in 1639, more than a century before my first Lamont ancestor arrived.

A current source of reliable information about Lamonts throughout the world is the Clan Lamont Society, founded in 1895 and

---

* For information, books, and historical documents relating to the Scotch-Irish tradition in America, the reader is referred to two organizations: The Scotch-Irish Foundation and the Scotch-Irish Society of the United States, both located in Philadelphia.

† See *Corliss, Parmelee, and Allied Family Histories, Genealogical and Biographical,* issued under the editorial supervision of Ruth Lawrence, National Americana Publications, Inc., 1942.

having its headquarters at 111 Union Street, Glasgow, Scotland. This Society, whose present Chief is Noel Brian Lamont of New South Wales, holds its annual business meeting during the winter and a gathering of a social character each summer or early fall. The Society also publishes the *Clan Lamont Journal* once a year. Any Lamont or person descended from a Lamont can join the Society by paying a small fee. Membership is also open to those belonging to one of the Clan Lamont Septs. A sept is a family group that is related by blood to one of the chief clans, or that has sought, and obtained, its protection.*

In June, 1970, I attended the two-day annual gathering of the Clan Lamont Society at Inverchaolain near Dunoon and Glasgow. It was a warming and happy experience. The many Lamonts who came for the occasion assembled for lunch, for tea, and for a special Clan Lamont Service in the Toward Church, where our clansmen had worshiped for 500 years. I was one of the two Lamonts from overseas. The other was attractive Brigadier Grace Lamond ("d" instead of "t" is a common spelling of the name) of the Salvation Army in New Zealand, dressed in her regular uniform. When I met her, she immediately said, "You look so much like my father." I replied, "Well, you look just like my daughter." When I returned to my hotel that evening, I looked in the mirror and decided that the person in my family whom Brigadier Lamond most resembled was none other than I. We even had the same sort of eyes that crinkle up when we smile and the same rather slender figure.

Although all living Lamonts may have had the same ancestors centuries ago, it was a strange and unique experience for me to find a Lamont of the female sex—and from far-off New Zealand— resembling me so closely. Jestingly, I started to concoct theories of reincarnation. Since my uncle, Hammond Lamont, had died about 1910, I said to Grace Lamond, "I suppose you were born in 1910?" She replied, "Yes, I was." She and I realized that two persons completely unrelated might by chance look like each other, but we agreed that it was probable that we had in common some distant Lamont ancestor, whose dominant traits, handed down generation after generation, played the main role in our resemblance. There can be no doubt that Lamont genes are powerful!

During the weekend of the Lamont gathering I stood in reverence once again before the Dunoon Memorial Stone erected to

---

* See Appendix II for list of Clan Lamont Septs.

The Dunoon Memorial Stone to the Lamonts massacred in 1646

the memory of some 200 Lamonts treacherously slaughtered by the Campbell Clan in 1646. Musing over this ghastly event, I wondered how any Scottish Lamonts survived at all, and felt thankful that my ancestors in that bloody seventeenth century had been wise enough to emigrate to Northern Ireland. The memorial shaft is of gray granite atop a small rock pile. A large Celtic cross is superimposed on the stone. A bronze tablet at the base of the monument reads:

> To the memory of their loyal forefathers who perished near this spot, the Clan Lamont dedicate this monument September 1, 1906. During the civil wars of the 17th century the Lamonts espoused the Royalist cause, thereby incurring the hostility of the neighboring clans who laid siege to the castles of Toward and Ascog. Sir James Lamont of that ilk was forced to surrender at Toward on 3rd June, 1646, when in violation of the articles of capitulation and indemnity signed by the besiegers, over 200 of the Lamonts were bound and carried in boats to Dunoon and there murdered. Among those who perished were:
> (Thirty names are then listed).

The detailed and authoritative work about the Lamonts is the 602-page volume, *The Lamont Clan, 1235–1935, Seven Centuries of Clan History from Record Evidence,* by Hector McKechnie (Neill & Co., Edinburgh, 1938).* To quote from Mr. McKechnie's first chapter: "The Lamonts were compact; they were not greatly isolated; they were law-abiding; they were colonists; and for these reasons they have made a mark upon the face of the earth out of all proportion to their numbers. They were a small and united body, which gives coherence to their history. . . . They took the world for their pillow, though often no doubt with a loch of tears beneath it when they thought of the heather at their father's door. . . . No clan of the size has the same record in colonisation."

Thus, sturdy Lamont folk migrated to many foreign lands, including America, the British Dominions, even the European Continent. This helps to explain why Shakespeare, in Hamlet (Act IV, Scene vii), refers to a French Lamont in a scene in which King Claudius and Laertes give high praise to a "Lamond" from Normandy. Laertes says: "I know him well; he is the brooch indeed and gem of all the nation."

---

* See pp. 86–87. The notes at the bottom of pages throughout this book are my own elucidations.

THE
THOMAS LAMONTS
IN AMERICA

PART I

The Lamont Family in the Nineteenth Century

by the Reverend Thomas Lamont

1
INTRODUCTION

More than ten years ago my children asked me to write something about our branch of the Lamont family in America. They knew that I had already given some attention to the subject. At the Reunion of the members of my father's family, held in 1876 at the home of my brother, George, at Bound Brook, New Jersey,* I read a brief sketch on the subject, which was afterwards printed for the members of the family. My children have always told me that I had a memory perhaps more than ordinarily retentive, and they have been anxious, before it was too late, to have me set down some of the remembrances of my childhood and of my talks with my aged kinsmen who were still living then. For instance, I well remember standing at his knee and listening to the tales of my great-grandfather, William Lamont, who fought in the War of the Revolution and whose own father, Robert, was the founder, about 1750, of our branch of the Lamont family in America.

It is curious to contemplate how many generations and what a long span of years such a connection covers. Here I am, revising these lines, with my little granddaughter, Eleanor Lamont,† playing near me. She was born in 1910 and as I look down at her I can readily hark back to the time when I was gazing up at my great-grandfather, born in 1756.

Of course to the present generation such a life as that led by my twelve brothers and sisters and myself, set down in a farming community many miles from the nearest town of any considerable size, must seem very tame in comparison with the eager, restless and complex life in and around New York in the present day. Yet,

---

* See pp. 77–83.

† The late Mrs. Charles C. Cunningham, my sister, who died May 22, 1961, at the age of fifty-one.

if the pursuit of happiness be considered not altogether ignoble, the life of our boyhood and youth was certainly a success. We lived in a beautiful country of high hills, lovely valleys, heavy forests and rushing brooks. The Summer heat was dry and seldom oppressive; the Autumns shone upon us in a blaze of color from the high hills; Winter, with its deep snows and bracing air, furnished far more of delight than terror. And our Scotch ancestors had evidently handed down to the most of us a tradition of thrift, hard work and good nature that, together, served to make my father's hospitable home a sweet and memorable abiding place for us all.

The accounts of my own school and college days will seem dull enough to my grandchildren, in the midst of their own more active times. But I know that they will be charitable and overlook the many imperfections of what is at best a hasty sketch, written at odd moments, with little recorded material available and with no attempt on my part—even had it been possible—to cast these pages in literary form.

I wish that I had been able, in the limits of this small volume, to include some extended account of the fine and useful lives led by my five brothers and seven sisters after their departure from the family home at Charlotteville. But I have thought it best to stop with the date of my own marriage in 1863.

I wish to say that the brief facts quoted in regard to the early Scottish history of the Clan Lamont, from which we are sprung, were collated by my son Hammond, when he was a Senior at Harvard,* from data which he secured in the Harvard College Library. I hope that some member of the family will seek an opportunity to search the clan records in Scotland so as to satisfy himself as to the date when our branch of the family went over to the North of Ireland, before coming on to America about 1750. A search of the vital statistics records in Coleraine, County Antrim, Ireland, might also prove of interest.

Englewood, N.J., 1913

---

* Hammond Lamont graduated from Harvard in 1886.

2
BACKGROUND OF THE LAMONTS

The original home of all the Lamonts that I know anything about was in Argyllshire, Scotland; and the Scottish annals contain frequent allusions to the clan of Lamonts or Lamonds, the name being spelled in both ways. All the annalists of Scotch history are agreed that the name Lamont or Lamond is derived from the Norse "lagamadr," meaning law-man or lawyer. But despite this Norse derivation the origin of the clan is said to be Dalriadic, and its founders came over to Scotland from Ireland, probably as early as A.D. 500. The following summary is taken from one of the numerous books written about the Scotch clans:

> The first of the clan (Lamont) of whom there is absolute historical evidence is Ferchar, who flourished about 1200. His grandson, Laumon, was the first to use the name which has since become hereditary; accordingly the latter is counted as the first chief of the clan.
> About 1238, Duncan, son of Ferchar, and this Laumon, son of Malcolm, son of Ferchar, granted to the monks of Paisley certain lands at Kilmun, at Kilfinan, and at Kilmory, on Lochgilp. Their possessions at that time are thus proved to have been of wide extent.
> The greatest blow to the Lamonts was dealt in 1646. The civil wars of that period gave a great opportunity for private feuds; and Ardkinglas, Dunstaffnage, and other Campbell leaders, acting doubtless under their chief's orders, ravaged the Lamont country, and besieged and took the castles of Toward and Ascog. They then carried their prisoners in boats to Dunoon, and massacred them to the number of about 200 on the Gallowhill. Thirty-six gentlemen of the name of Lamont were hanged on a single ash tree. Sir James, the Lamont chief, was hunted for his life, and the Campbells took possession of his lands till the Restoration. These deeds formed one of the principal

counts against the Marquis of Argyll at the trial for high treason in 1661, which resulted in his execution.

Following are the Clan Lamont mottoes, music, etc.:

Clan Pipe Music: Lament—"Cumha an Fhograich" ("The Wanderer's Lament"); Salute—"Mhic Laomainn ceud failte dhuit" ("A Thousand Welcomes to Thee, Lamont"); March— "Captain Lamont's March." Badge: Craobh-ubhal fhiadhain (Crab-apple Tree) or Machallmonaidh (Dryas). The coat of arms is thus: *Azure, a Lion rampant argent;* Crest, *A dexter hand couped at the wrist;* and for Motto, *Ne parcas nec spernas.** The supporters are *two wild men.*

In the further accounts of the clan and of the achievements of its leaders, the names most frequently appearing are John and Archibald. These two names must have been very numerous throughout the clan; and it is interesting to note that the three Lamont brothers who brought the family name to America, in about the year 1750, were named respectively, John, Archibald and Robert, this last being my great-great-grandfather.

The name Robert also appears not infrequently. One account says that "In 1463, Robert Lamont of Inveryne died, and his lands fell to the Crown by reason of non-entry and for ninety years were held of the Crown by his successors." Another Robert Lamont, the records show, was "on October 24th, 1688, gazetted Ensign in Col. Douglas's Regiment of Foot. He got his company next year, and in 1693 was present at the disastrous day of Landen, when the Allies under King William III were defeated by the French under the Duke of Luxemburg."

Our ancestors came not direct from Scotland but, about the year 1745 or 1750, from Coleraine, County Antrim, Ireland. How long they had been settled in Ireland we do not know, but certainly long enough for the family to come under the general designation of Scotch-Irish.

The Lamonts Come to America

About the time above mentioned, a widowed mother—tradition says she was the relict of one John Lamont—with her three sons, Archibald, John and Robert, settled in North Hillsdale, Columbia County, New York. The story is that Archibald, the eldest son,

* The best translation of this Latin motto is "Neither stint nor spurn," meaning "Don't be either mean or extravagant."

preceded the others in coming to America; that while but a boy he was enticed on board a vessel lying off Coleraine, and while, with boyish curiosity, he was inspecting the vessel she suddenly sailed away. When he begged to be set ashore to return to his mother, the heartless reply was: "It will be many a long day, my lad, before you will see your mother or home again."

So Archibald was brought to this country and sold to someone on Long Island to serve as an apprentice, and to furnish a profit to those who had kidnapped him, a not uncommon occurrence in those times. This boy was the magnet which drew the mother and the two other brothers hither. Other families from the North of Ireland settled about the same time in North Hillsdale, the Mc-Kinstrys among them. North Hillsdale was a newly-opened part of the country and land was cheap.

As to Archibald, he did not marry until he was almost sixty years old. When railed on remaining single he was wont to answer: "I am waiting for my wife to grow up; I have my eye on her." This seems to have been the fact, for the story has come down quite directly that Archibald was, in middle life, boarding as a bachelor with a couple named Smith who had a little girl called Abiah. Mrs. Smith, who looked upon Archibald Lamont with a kindly eye, used to say to him: "Archie, take good care of little 'Biah and you can have her when she grows up." So, as soon as she had "grown up" to be eighteen years of age, she married the fast-aging Archie. Archibald was a powerful man physically. His prowess was known throughout the countryside. One holiday he ran into a stranger who was a bit tipsy, but who evidently was a wrestler and a fighter. The ignorant stranger offered to have a bout with Archibald and boastfully said: "I can lick any man in the county but Archie Lamont!"

Archibald had several children, lived and died in Hillsdale. His descendants removed to the western part of New York State early in the last century and settled in the region about Lockport and Rochester. A grandson was graduated from Yale, became a lawyer, a member of the New York State Senate and a judge of the Supreme Court. One of Archibald's sons removed to Michigan, and a township in that State is named Lamont, after him.

Our Ancestor Robert Born in 1726

Coming, as I have said, with his mother to this country, in about

1750, to join his brother Archibald, Robert, our ancestor, was born in Antrim, Ireland, in 1726, and had three sons and a daughter. I do not know the order of their births, but their names were John, Archibald, William (my great-grandfather) and Mary. I have heard my grandfather speak of his grandfather Robert, whom he remembered well, though he was but a little boy. He said: "Grandfather was a short, thickset man, full of jokes and fun." It seems that Robert carried on a kind of weaving establishment. My grandfather said of his grandmother, the wife of Robert: "She was a real Irish woman," and added that she had a brother from the North of Ireland who visited this country when he was a very little boy.

Robert Lamont died July 26, 1789, only sixty-three years old, and lies buried in the little graveyard in North Hillsdale. His grave is marked by an old brown tombstone, with his name and age inscribed upon it. His wife survived him for some years, and came with her daughter, Mary, who had married John Gorse, to Fulton, Schoharie County, New York, where she spent her last days.

All Three Sons Revolutionary Soldiers

Robert's three sons were all old enough to be soldiers in the war of the Revolution, and they all served in the patriot army. Of Archibald's war record I have been able to find nothing. John served in the company of his Hillsdale neighbor, McKinstry, who had been a soldier in the old French-Indian war, and who was a commissioned officer. They were both captured by Brant, the Mohawk half-breed chieftain. McKinstry was a freemason, as was Brant, who had been educated in an academy in Connecticut. McKinstry gave the masonic sign to Brant, and was soon released or exchanged, but Lamont was carried away a prisoner to the Indian country. His captors planned to put him to death by torture, but among the spoils captured by them was a fiddle which John Lamont snatched up and on which he played so well as to charm the savages from their purpose of killing him. But they compelled him to run the Indian gauntlet, which he did successfully. John was then adopted into one of the Indian tribes and was assigned an Indian squaw for a wife. But watching his chance he made his escape, and in due time returned to his own people.

I have heard my father speak of this John Lamont, his great-uncle, as a rather eccentric character. His hard experiences were perhaps enough to make anyone eccentric. Nevertheless, he secured a wife and had one son, who bore his own name, John, and who went west and became a captain in the United States Army during the War of 1812 with England. This Captain John Lamont was treacherously shot while bearing a flag of truce to a British post. When the old father heard of his son's murder in this cowardly manner, he was so frenzied that he seized his musket and declared his purpose of going to the front to try to avenge the death of his son. I have no record of old John Lamont's death or burial.

The Old Graveyard at North Hillside

Twice I have visited the old burying-ground in North Hillsdale, where some of the Lamonts of the first generation in this country are buried. The graveyard is close to the Methodist church in North Hillsdale. I recall seeing on the stones the names of Archibald (the lad, you remember, who was kidnapped from Ireland, and who was the first of the name to reach America), and of another Archibald Lamont, his son; of Robert Lamont (the first Archibald's brother), our ancestor; of Phœbe Lamont, our great-grandmother and the wife of William, Robert's son. I think the latest death-date on these stones is 1796.

Close by the graves of the two old brothers, Archibald and Robert Lamont, is apparently another grave, somewhat sunken in, unmarked. I have always fancied that it must be the grave of their mother, who came with her two sons from Coleraine, Ireland, seeking Archibald.

I first visited this burying-ground in this wise: I had been told by a great-aunt, Mrs. Betsey Dibble, of Fulton, a sister of my Grandfather Lamont, that she had, when a little girl, visited her grandfather's grave, that it had a tombstone and that his face was cut on it. Of course she was mistaken—it was a little girl's fancy. The custom of course was frequently to cut a cherub on the tombstone to denote the blessed society in which the departed was presumably mixing. Aunt Betsey tried to make me understand where the graveyard was—"near four corners." But I got no definite idea beyond the fact that it was somewhere in Hillsdale.

In November, 1871, when I was pastor in Claverack, Columbia County (where my son, Thomas William, was born) I was called to officiate at the funeral of a woman in Philmont, five miles away.

After the sermon I was informed that I was expected to go with the family to the burial at North Hillsdale, ten miles away. This was more than I had bargained for. However, I made no objection, as the family was poor and in great trouble. After the burial a man asked me my name. Then he asked me whether I had any kindred buried in that graveyard. I told him I was not aware of any. He said that there were some Lamonts buried there, and he conducted me to the graves. I was glad to find the old brown stones with the names cut on them, and the rude carving of Aunt Betsey's cherub on her grandfather Robert Lamont's stone.

I copied the inscriptions from some of the stones. That of our ancestor, Robert, sure enough, at the top bore Aunt Betsey's cherub and read thus: "In memory of Mr. Robert Lamont who Died July 26th, 1789, in the 63d year of his age." Old Archibald's stone bore the following: "In memory of Mr. Archibald Lamont who Departed this life April 24th 1795 aged 71 years. For ye are dead and your life is hid with Christ in God." Great-grandmother's tombstone had as follows: "In Memory of Mrs. Phœbe wife of Mr. William Lamont who died June 12th, 1789 in the 38th year of her age. Be ye also ready."

Great-grandfather William Born in 1756

William Lamont, my great-grandfather, was born in Hillsdale in 1756, the son of Robert Lamont. He served as a soldier during a good part of the Revolutionary War, but not continuously. His name appears on the Revolutionary records as William Lemon, about as the name was undoubtedly pronounced by his own father and by his Scottish forebears. William never spelled it in any other way than Lamont. His military record is as follows:

A private in Captain Joshua Whitney's company, 4th Regt. N. Y. State Militia, Col. Kilaen Van Rensselaer. He served from October to December, 1775; then as a private in Captain Jonas Graves's company of the same regiment, eleven days in June (probably in 1776); as a private in Captain Joshua Whitney's company, 9th Regt. Albany County, N. Y. State Militia, Col. Peter Van Ness, from July to November, probably 1777. I give this year as the date of this particular service, for I heard a great-aunt say that her father served in the campaign against Burgoyne which led to his surrender in October, 1777, and was present at and witnessed the surrender of the Hessians as they laid down their arms.

His next service was in the same company and regiment from August to September, 1778; again in the same regiment under Col. David Pratt, in October, 1780, at Fort Plain, New York. William Lamont had been made a corporal at this date.

I confess that I have not much confidence in these old Revolutionary records, as they are notoriously inaccurate in many cases. In the New York State Militia men were enrolled and called into service as an emergency arose, served for a time and then were permitted to return to cultivate their farms until called out again, always holding themselves ready for such a call. This will explain the fragmentary character of my great-grandfather's service.

William Lamont, probably about the year 1779 or 1780, near the close of the war, married a Mrs. Phœbe Perkins, a widow whose maiden name was Gorse. She was an energetic, active woman, caring well for her household, deeply pious, a member of the Baptist Church. My great-grandfather bought a farm about three miles west of North Hillsdale, at the foot of the Cakeout Mountain, and built a house upon it, which is still standing. When I visited it I found a family by the name of Goslin occupying it. It had been held by the Goslin family from the time it had passed from the Lamonts.

On June 12, 1789, William Lamont's wife suddenly died. Just after working hard at her washing she sat down in a chair nearby, exclaiming, "How faint I feel!" and immediately expired. My grandfather, but a small boy then, was present, and related the scene to me with tears in his eyes. He spoke very affectionately of his mother and of her ability. She was buried in the same old graveyard at North Hillsdale.

My great-grandmother left a family of seven children, the eldest of whom could not have been more than about ten years old. Our great-grandfather married the second time a woman by the name of Rodman, and by her had three or four children. I never saw but one of them—Perkins Lamont, of Fulton, who sometimes visited us at Charlotteville.

The Lamont Clan Makes a Stand

At the close of the Revolutionary War the times were hard; there was a depreciated currency; there were arrearages in rent, and payments for land were overdue. The Van Rensselaers, who were large landholders in the region of North Hillsdale, tried to force collections. Archibald Lamont owned a farm on which the

Van Rensselaers had no claim, as it lay beyond the limits of their patent. The agents of the Van Rensselaers and the officers of the law came and demanded payment for back rents. Archibald Lamont denied the claim, affirming that his farm was paid for, and that he held a deed to it. The bailiffs said they would arrest him. With a loaded gun Archibald confronted the officers as they drew near, and said: "I will shoot and some of you will be killed. I, too, may be killed, but I will die before I will submit to such injustice."

They went away for the time, but one day returned unexpectedly and found Archibald without his loaded gun. They arrested him and threw him into the Claverack jail. Claverack at that time was the county seat of Columbia County.

William Lamont, our great-grandfather, got together a dozen or more men, and hastened to Claverack to rescue his uncle. With a blacksmith's hammer he succeeded in wrenching off the staple and lock of the jail door and burst in, telling his astonished uncle, "Go out and ride home!"

His uncle said: "Will, they will kill you for this."

"Never mind," Will replied, "we will attend to that later."

William was threatened by the county sheriff, Fonda, but was never arrested for his highhanded act. The probabilities are that the Van Rensselaers found that they were wrong in their claim.

About the year 1801 or 1802, having disposed of his farm in Hillsdale, Great-grandfather William Lamont removed to the west part of the town of Middleburg, afterwards set off as the town of Fulton, Schoharie County. His brother-in-law, Gorse, moved into the town about the same time. Here William Lamont bought a farm, largely forest, and began life again. He lived on this farm until his second wife died and his home was broken up, when he went to live with his children.

Great-grandfather and the Cucumber

I recall two visits he made to our family, one about the year 1842, the last in 1846, when I was fourteen years old. I remember the tenderness and respect shown him by my father, his grandson. Though bent with age, Great-grandfather was still fairly vigorous. He was rather stout, had a broad forehead, with eyes set far apart, gray in color. He was bald and had heavy, shaggy eyebrows. Always an active intelligent man, he still had a retentive memory.

He spoke of some of the battles of the Revolution he was in

and the whizzing of the bullets by his ears; of doing sentinel duty after fatiguing marches and of the difficulty of keeping awake. His aged appearance and conversation made a lively impression upon me. The last time he visited us he was with his eldest son, Matthew Lamont, my great-uncle, when he was about to go to Owego, New York. It was in August or September, 1846. Great-grandfather walked out into the garden, which was close by, picked a cucumber and, peeling it, called for a little salt, then ate it with a relish, showing that his power of digestion was still good. William Lamont died in 1852 or 1853, at the age of about ninety-six.

Let me mention here a reminiscence of the journey when my great-grandfather moved from Hillsdale to Fulton, told me by his daughter, my great-aunt Betsey Dibble. She said: "It was early in the spring and towards nightfall when we were driving through Vrooman's Land, not far from Middleburg, we came to an abrupt and lofty projection called 'Vrooman's Nose.' This precipice filled me, a little girl at the time, with wonder and I said to myself, 'An angel on the Day of Judgment will take his stand on the top of that mountain and blow his trumpet and hurl the rocks at the wicked below.' "

I, myself, have seen "Vrooman's Nose" a few times, and it would naturally excite wonder and awe in a little child.

William Lamont, junior, our grandfather, second son of William and Phœbe Lamont, was born in Hillsdale, New York, in 1784. In a rural neighborhood, at that time he enjoyed limited advantages for education, but he obtained all he could get, was fairly good in arithmetic and learned to write a good legible hand, fitting him for business. He was fond of athletic sports, once breaking an arm in a wrestling match. Later he was inoculated for and had the smallpox, though he bore no marks of it. He was for a while a clerk in the store of a Major McKinstry, a neighbor, of whom I have before spoken. This family was intimate with the Lamonts and visited them after our people had moved to Fulton.

Where the Stilwells Sprang From

At the age of eighteen Grandfather (William, Jr.) married Jane Stilwell, a maiden of about his own age. She was the daughter of Thomas Stilwell* of Greene River, a neighborhood near the

---

* This explains the middle name of my late brother, Thomas Stilwell Lamont, 1899–1967.

border of Massachusetts, not many miles from Hillsdale. Thomas Stilwell was of English descent. An ancestor of his was a member of that English Parliament which in Cromwell's time sentenced Charles I to be beheaded. Thomas Stilwell was born on Long Island, but moved from there to Dutchess County, and took up land in a region called "The Nine Partners." Thence he came to Greene River. He was of fair education for the times, and of considerable substance. He had a large family—seven daughters and two sons. I remember seeing five of the daughters—great-aunts of mine, and the two sons, one of whom, Samuel Stilwell, lived in Charlotteville.

My grandmother was a rather small woman with a pleasant face, kind, gentle, refined, and of a benevolent nature. This anecdote has come down concerning her: One black, stormy night, when she was a very small girl, someone said: "This is a good night for thieves to be abroad."

"How I do pity the poor thieves that have to be out such a night as this!" she exclaimed.

Soon after the marriage of this young couple they moved into the town of Fulton, whither Grandfather's father had preceded them but a short time, as I have said, in 1802. The younger William bought a small farm and set up his establishment in a log house almost in the wilderness. It is said that Grandmother, unaccustomed to the rude ways of pioneer life, nearly died from homesickness; that in the early years of her married life her father visited her and that on his departure she followed him for a considerable distance, walking and stumbling over the rough road. The life she was called on to lead in her new home was very unlike the one to which she had been accustomed near New England. In the winter after the birth of their first-born, named Thomas for his grandfather Stilwell, Grandfather drove them both in a sleigh from Fulton to Greene River, that Grandmother might visit her family and show her father his new namesake.

This union was blessed with a family of twelve children, all of whom grew up except one son, who died in infancy. There were seven sons and five daughters. I remember them all well, except, of course, the one who died young.

Charlotteville Becomes the Family Home

About the year 1806 my grandfather, having disposed of his

place in Fulton, moved to Charlotteville, Schoharie County. There he purchased a small farm. His father-in-law moved there about the same time, buying a tract of 700 acres, mainly forest. I have no doubt that this new move of old Thomas Stilwell's made my Grandmother contented, because she was near her own immediate kindred.

Charlotteville was situated on the upper part of the Charlotte Creek, a tributary of the Susquehanna River. The creek was named Charlotte in honor of a daughter of Sir William Johnson, whose grant of land included that region. Charlotteville at that time was little more than a black alder swamp near where four roads met. Soon after settling there Grandfather opened a small store, perhaps the first in that part of the country. He received in exchange for his goods little but barter. There was little money in circulation at that time in that region. My Grandmother Paine (my mother's mother) said she once had occasion to visit Grandfather Lamont's store, kept in a log house. Of his stock of goods she said: "I think I could have carried away with me all he had, or all I saw, except the barrel of whiskey."

A man by the name of Harman Mitchell, poor in those days, settled about the same time on a farm a mile or more further down the Charlotte creek, and came to the store to make some purchases, asking to be trusted, with the promise to pay in ashes in due time. Grandfather told him, "First bring the ashes, and you can then have the goods."

A little later, in company with a man by the name of Warner, Grandfather Lamont built a sawmill and a flour mill on the Charlotte creek near his house. These mills were probably the first of their kind in that immediate region. The sawmill has disappeared, but a flour mill stands on the same site where one was erected quite one hundred years ago. I have heard elderly people who had dealings with Grandfather in their early days say that he was strictly just in all his transactions, and very generous and kind to honest settlers who were in need. I heard one old man say: "He kept us from starving, letting us have flour from his mill and trusting us until we could pay for it."

William Lamont early became the land agent of Judge Smith, of Schenectady, who was the owner of a large tract of land originally included, it is said, in Sir William Johnson's patent. Grandfather soon acquired considerable land himself, buying partly improved farms that were for sale. He was elected Justice of the

Peace and appointed a captain in the State Militia, holding commission as captain during the war with Great Britain in 1812–14. His company was called by a draft to furnish a number of men. In my boyhood I heard an old man belonging to his company state how the draft was made. Captain Lamont called his company into a field and drilled it for a little time, then he ordered each man to load his gun. He then placed in his hat slips of paper for drawing by lot. Taking his stand on a little eminence he called the roll of the company, one by one. When a man's name was called he was to step forward and fire his gun in the air, then march up and draw. So the quota was filled. As the names were called some of the men marched very boldly, others were pale and trembling with fear. The men from this company were sent to Plattsburg, New York. My grandfather held himself in readiness to go when a draft was to be made for men holding a commission. I have heard my father, who at that time was only nine or ten years old, tell how the matter was talked over, and how they were dreading to have their father go off to war. But happily the war ended before the call came.

Captain Lamont a Born Leader

In my boyhood my grandfather was called Captain Lamont, and sometimes "Squar'" Lamont. He was considered well-to-do for that time and place. He was a large, portly man, with a fine ruddy face, a broad, high forehead, crowned with silvery hair. He had a stately, commanding air and would impress people as a marked character. Such he really was. He was born to lead, as others are to follow. The house which he built, and in which he lived for many years, is still standing and in good repair at the four corners in Charlotteville.

Grandfather took a deep interest in the politics of his day, generally acting and voting with the old Whig party. I think he never held any office higher than a town office, the party to which he belonged being generally in the minority in Schoharie County. He was a liberal supporter of the Methodist Church, a regular attendant when his health permitted, and his house was always open to the preachers. He was an invalid during the last few years of his life, a victim of diabetes. He died the latter part of September, 1847, about 63 years old.

My father always evinced great respect and warm filial affection for his father, showing him a great deal of attention. I have heard my mother say that never a day passed, when my father was at home, that he did not visit Grandfather and have some conversation with him. About the only time I can recall seeing my father weep was when he was told that Grandfather was dead.

Grandmother's Kind Ways

Grandmother (Jane Stilwell) Lamont survived Grandfather about seventeen years. She died during the dark days of the Civil War, towards its close. She was an excellent Christian woman, a member of the Baptist Church during her earlier years. When my father was converted and joined the Methodists, she withdrew from the Baptists and united with the Methodists, saying, "I can no longer belong to a church that will not allow me to commune with my own son, who is a better Christian than I am." The Baptists held to "close communion." She was exceedingly kind to the poor, giving rather indiscriminately. She would allow none to suffer if she had the power to relieve. I recall her gentle, tender ways, her laying her hand on my head and saying: "Dear little sonny!"

Grandmother was very careful of her family, never allowing any of them to work overmuch. Especially careful was she of her daughters, always keeping plenty of household help after her husband became a well-to-do man. She desired her grandchildren to become good scholars. Three of her grandsons, William Lamont Wood, William C. Lamont and Jacob P. Lamont, this last my eldest brother, were all of about the same age. She offered them twenty-five cents apiece as soon as they could repeat, without a break, the multiplication table. They all won the prize, which was something in those days when twenty-five cents counted for more than one dollar in these times. Grandmother Lamont must have been a fine looking woman when young, for she retained her good looks to old age. She had three married sisters living in Charlotteville, of whom she seemed very fond—Mrs. Jemima Van Buren, Mrs. Hannah Ryder, and Mrs. Charlotte Lincoln. I have seen the four sisters together, greatly enjoying one another's society.

The Reverend Thomas Lamont, author of The Lamont Family in the
Nineteenth Century

3

THE REVEREND THOMAS
LAMONT AND HIS TIMES

I write this sketch of a commonplace life, not that I think it worthy of record, but because I have been earnestly solicited by the members of my family to write it. I have no high estimate of my attainments or achievements; I can only say, as has often been said before: *"By the grace of God I am what I am."*

Birth of Thomas Lamont in 1832

I am the fifth child and fourth son of my parents, Thomas W. and Elizabeth Maria (Paine) Lamont. I was born on October 6th, 1832, in Charlotteville, New York, where my Grandfather had established the family home about 1806. It was my great advantage to be born in a thoroughly Christian home, in an atmosphere of warm, cheerful piety, in a family as well enlightened and as free from narrowness and bigotry as probably could be found in that region. The house in which I was born, and in which I spent the first two and a half years of my childhood, is still standing. It is in about the center of the village, on the south side, somewhat back from the street—an old red house, painted that color in all likelihood at the time it was built, almost a century ago.

The old, unpainted schoolhouse to which I was sent as a pupil when I was about three years old, was not far off. Perhaps there were so many of us little folks that it was thought I should be out of the way at school, being cared for by the teacher and the elder children. It was the summer term. One Sunday morning I started off to school as usual. One of my elder brothers brought me back, and I remember, after I got home, hanging my head and being very much ashamed of myself that I had so completely

41

forgotten the day. The teacher, Miss Rose Ann Rowland, was the one who taught me my alphabet. She afterwards married a Harry Boughton. In the wintertime, Charles Gorse was the teacher—a tall, strong man, a second cousin of my father. When I stood up close to him to spell my short words, as he was sitting down, I seemed to come only about up to his knees. He became a Methodist clergyman and for more than fifty years was a worthy member of the New York Conference.

Schoolboy Days at Charlotteville

I attended the district school both summer and winter until I was about twelve. The old schoolhouse, crowded right into the road, has long since disappeared. Another schoolhouse, not far from the old one, was built in 1842, much larger and more commodious, and said to have been, when built, the finest in Schoharie County. Though turned into a dwellinghouse, it is still standing.

I did not love study any more than the average boy; was as fond of play [as he] and was as glad when the teacher would say, "The boys may go out," when the noon recess of an hour arrived. We took a lunch from home to be eaten at this recess, usually of bread and butter, with a large piece of maple sugar between the slices, and some pie and cake. We played hard and by the time we reached home at night were as hungry as little bears, and went straight for the pantry to get something to eat.

The schools I attended were not made especially attractive. It was the time when there was unshaken faith in the virtue of the rod and ferule as aids in imparting instruction. My recollection, especially of the winter terms, is of seeing great big boys called out onto the floor for some breach of the rules, lectured and then whipped, in some cases unmercifully. The women teachers were, perhaps, as a rule, not quite so severe. Their pupils were small children and more easily managed, yet I have some unpleasant memories of being beaten with a ruler on my arms, legs and hands for simply looking off my book, and sometimes I did not even know the reason for this punishment. I recall one teacher who would frequently pass around with her ruler and strike us on the thighs. We got so that we would flinch when we saw her coming. She would then lay on the ruler, saying, "I know you must be guilty of something or you would not flinch so when you see me coming."

Brother Jacob Champions Little George

I recall one teacher who, as we stood up to spell just before the school was to be dismissed at night, had us call out our numbers, "first, second, third," etc., so that we might know our places in the class the next day. My brother George's number was third. He was only a little fellow and could not speak plainly, but did as well as he could. He said, "Thode." The teacher repeated: "Say 'third.'" He repeated "thode," getting as near "third" as he could. So two or three times, the teacher, believing in the efficacy of punishment, said, "Now if you say 'thode' again when I tell you to say 'third' I will whip you," and she stood ready with the rod. My eldest brother, Jacob, looking on with deep interest, sprang to his feet and went towards the teacher, saying: "Do not touch my little brother; he cannot speak plainly. He says 'third' as plainly as he can." The teacher did not touch him, but dismissed the class, nor did she say or do anything to Jacob. I think she was somewhat ashamed of herself. My eldest brother was a great defender and champion of his younger brothers and sisters.

There were from seven to eight months of school in the year. A young man taught the winter term and a young woman the summer term. The teachers boarded around in the families of the district, staying in each family a week or more, according to the number of pupils sent to the school. I had no special fondness for study in those days, but I was exceedingly fond of reading anything that interested me, this little trait perhaps in part inherited from my mother. I did once or twice win the prize offered for speaking, as did also some of my brothers and sisters. Indeed, I recall the close of one winter term when all the prizes came into our family.

From the age of twelve years I attended only the winter term of school, usually lasting about four months. Perhaps I had learned about all the young women teachers could impart to me. The wages, by the way, paid to the men teachers, were from $10 to $15 per month, and board; to the young women, from $1 to $2 per week, and board. Further, at about the age of twelve I was old enough to be quite useful in various ways on the farm.

So the winters passed until I was sixteen years old. I wrote a legible hand—much more so than I write today; had a fair knowledge of geography, American history, rhetoric, arithmetic, natural philosophy, and algebra to quadratic equations. From that time I either taught or attended some higher school until I was graduated from college.

Picture of the Lamont Household

The spirit of my father's family was one of industry, economy, kindness, cheerfulness, hospitality, liberality and godliness. My earliest memories of the farm are of driving with two of my elder brothers a herd of cows to pasture at some distance from the house, and then back to be milked at night; of bringing in wood and chips for the fire. In the summer there was a large open fireplace at which cooking was done. It made a very cheerful blaze in the cool nights of the spring and early fall. Baking of biscuits, etc., was done before this fire in a large tin baker. There was a large outdoor oven for bread and pies. A large cookstove was used in the winter. Wood was abundant, and large quantities were used, as there was no motive for saving it, since in clearing the forests what was not used for cooking and heating the house we burned up in the fields to get it out of the way.

About as good a picture of my mother as need be can be found in Proverbs, 31st chapter, where Solomon gives us a portrait of "an excellent woman." Mother never "ate the bread of idleness," and her children were early taught to follow in her steps. We were trained very early to be helpful in some ways. Large quantities of apples were cut and dried in the autumn. The drying was sometimes done by spreading the peeled and quartered apples on boards and exposing them to the sun; but generally by stringing the prepared apples on coarse linen twine, about five feet in length, by the aid of a large needle, and then hanging the strings of apples near the fireplace, or by laying them on flat poles overhead near the kitchen ceiling. In a dry room such apples would stay preserved almost indefinitely. Enough apples were often thus dried to provide a large family with apple sauce and apple pies for a whole year, or until the next season came around.

Also in the fall sweet apples were cut up and stewed in boiled cider made into a syrup, which would keep sweet through all the cold weather for perhaps six months. Mother would often fill a butter firkin with apple sauce thus prepared. Pumpkins were also prepared somewhat as apples were, by cutting them in large rings and stringing them on poles to dry overhead in the kitchen. Sometimes the pumpkin was boiled down into a thick paste and then spread out in large, thin cakes to dry, and thus was preserved for the family use. Soaked in warm milk or water it was soon ready for use.

In all this work of preserving fruit, apples and pumpkins for the family, we little folks early learned to do our full share. Wild berries grew in abundance on my father's farm, beginning with strawberries in June and ending with blackberries which continued to ripen until the frosts came in the fall. Mother had her children pick berries all through the season, going out after school was dismissed at four o'clock and on the Saturdays when there was no school. The berries not eaten immediately on the table or made into pies were dried for future use. Large quantities were thus often stored up for winter, giving us a fair variety in our winter food.

In my boyhood a shoemaker with his kit of tools would come to the house and make boots and shoes for the entire family, Father providing all the materials needed. Sometimes the cobbler would come more than once in the year. A seamstress or tailoress would come and spend weeks at our house in the fall and spring and make clothes for the whole household for the year. Homemade woolen cloth, fulled at the mill, was our winter clothing, and blue jean was the material for trousers in the summer.

Farm Work for the Youngsters

I early learned to do all kinds of work on the farm—to milk, to plant potatoes and corn, to hoe them and to dig the potatoes in the fall. When we were only little boys our work was to pick up the potatoes from the different rows. Father raised large quantities of potatoes, and sometimes, with the weather cool and frosty in the late fall, our fingers would get very cold picking them up. Big piles of potatoes were boiled and mixed with ground peas and oats and fed to the pigs in the fall to fatten them. A large kettle, built into an arch, the kettle holding five or six bushels, was the place where the potatoes were boiled. It was our business to fill the great "potash" kettle, as it was called, build the fire and boil the potatoes. This was not very hard work, but in doing it we made ourselves very helpful. In haying and harvest time we helped to rake the hay and stow it away when it was pitched up in high sheds, where the air was almost stifling with the dust, while the summer sun was pouring down on the roof, making the place almost like an oven. The grain was usually stowed away on top of the hay mow, or on a light scaffold overhead.

Later I learned to mow, but I never became an adept in cradling grain, though I did learn to rake up and bind the grain into sheaves after it was cradled. We learned to plow and to harrow. My brother, George, and I plowed a great deal in the fall, when he was not more than ten and I than twelve years old. He would drive the oxen and I would hold the plow. We learned to thresh with a flail, to cut and draw logs of wood to be cut up for fuel for the fireplace and stove. I recall one spring after school had closed there was quite a quantity of rye unthreshed in the barn, and Father gave George and me a "stunt," as it was called, to thresh fifty sheaves between us; then we could have the rest of the day to ourselves, until "chore time." We finished generally in a little more than half a day. The rest of the day we spent in reading Macaulay's *History of England,* just published and placed in the district school library. At another time I remember reading Josephus' *History of the Jews,* largely after my stunt was done.

We all had our share of the chores allotted to us, both in the summer and winter, caring for the horses and oxen, cleaning all the barns, and so on. I recall that for two or three winters it was my business to saw the wood and split it for the large cookstove. The wood had been cut the previous winter into four-foot lengths and was well seasoned. I worked on that woodpile before and after school. Saturdays, when there was no school, I would get quite a large pile ahead for Sunday and for emergencies during the next week. I have never forgotten how to saw and split wood, but have never had much success in making my own sons realize what excellent exercise it is for the whole body, and how great an aid to digestion.

Early Spring Among the Sugar-Maples

The making of maple sugar was the thing that kept us all busy in the early spring, beginning soon after the winter school closed and lasting for a month or six weeks. The south side of the farm had an abundance of hard maple trees. Two sap bushes, as they were called, were worked by us boys. One bush was allotted to my eldest brother, Jacob, and me, as assistant; the next bush was cared for by two other brothers, David and William. It was not very easy work. The sap had to be gathered and boiled down in large kettles until it was almost a syrup; then it was carried to the house and carefully strained through a cloth and allowed to settle, and then cleansed again before it was made into sugar. Some years 500 or 600 pounds of sugar were made. The sap was usually brought from the buckets or troughs into which it had run from the trees, in pails suspended from a sap-yoke worn on the shoulders. One of the compensations of attending a sap bush was that any one who cared for sweets could revel in them to his heart's content.

Another piece of farm work, attended to soon after the sugar-making was finished for the season, was to clear the stones from the fields that were to be mowed in the summer. Four of us boys, David, William, George and I, would work together at this task. We would have a yoke of oxen hitched to a stoneboat or sled and on it we piled the stones, going carefully over the entire field. Father would throw off the stones by the fence where a stone wall was to be laid. The greater part of the stone walls on the farm—and there were hundreds of rods of them—were made from the stones we boys picked up in clearing the fields. This was fine, open-air work, just suited to growing boys.

Spelling Bees in the Old Schoolhouse

The winters of my boyhood were not without their mild, innocent excitements. There were often spelling schools or "spelling matches," when two neighboring schools would meet and sides would be chosen. The two camps would stand up on opposite sides of the schoolhouse and spell against each other. When one person missed a word he sat down. The side that could stand up the longest won the contest.

There was usually a singing school during the winter, lasting from three to six months. It was held in the evening, gave the young people a good opportunity to get together and was greatly enjoyed. The Charlotteville and the Baptist Church neighborhood would sometimes unite and hire the same teacher, the schools being held on alternate week evenings in each neighborhood. We were very fond of the singing school. My sisters had naturally good voices and ears for music and learned to sing easily, but the boys of our family never learned music to any great extent.

Then there were debating schools held occasionally in the winter. There were two leaders in the debates, and each chose his own debaters. The judges were usually some elderly men of the community. Such questions as the following were often debated: "Should capital punishment be abolished?" "Which is the better team for a farmer to have on his place, horses or oxen?" "Which affords to us the greater pleasure, anticipation or realization?"

I have been told that my grandfather Lamont was very fond of getting boys who were at his house for an evening to debate. He would say: "Boys, I do not wish you to spend a stupid evening. I will give you some question to debate that may sharpen your wits a little, and I will decide which is the better debater." So he would give them some simple question to discuss, and the evening would thus pass pleasantly.

There were few holidays in my boyhood. The school was in session six days one week and five the next. The Saturdays when we had a holiday in the wintertime were spent in drawing and cutting wood or threshing grain; in the summertime, frequently in berry picking. New Year's Day was generally observed in some way, while little was made of Christmas. I recall, however, that in some winters the Sunday School gave an exhibition in the church on Christmas Eve, in which recitations, dialogues, singing, and the like were gone through in the usual manner. Nearly every pupil in the school took some part. Sometimes on New Year's Day the young people in couples would take a long sleigh ride of ten or twelve miles, get a supper and return sometime in the evening. I recall that occasionally we were all invited to Grandfather Paine's, with all our cousins, to spend the day.

The Fourth of July was also generally well kept in Charlotte-ville, by a celebration. All the Sunday Schools of the surrounding region would be invited to be present. All crowded into the church and there were singing and one or two addresses, then an inter-mission during which all the children marched, two by two, to the sound of a fife and drum, under the orders of a marshal on horse-back. The children were all treated to some cake and candy, then marched back to the church to listen to some patriotic addresses, and so the long, eagerly-looked-for day ended. The parents and elders on such occasions usually treated themselves to a specially prepared dinner at the village hotel, as did also the young men, each taking his favorite girl. Sometimes we would all drive to Summit or South Worcester to take part in such a Fourth of July celebration. These celebrations created a good deal of wholesome excitement, and were talked about long afterwards. It was a great deprivation not to be able to attend them. I remember once Mother wished to attend, but could not think of taking the baby with her. I was persuaded to stay at home and take care of the baby on the promise that I should go to Albany with my father the next time he went to "the city." I think the baby was my sister Katherine.

My First Visit to the City of Albany, in 1842

When I was not yet ten years old, my father, according to the promise, took me with him to Albany. It was early in September. A dinner-box, according to the custom of that time, had been prepared, filled with chicken, bread, cake and pie, for our lunches each way. The trip was to take four days. We arose some time before daylight and had breakfast. I imagine that I did not eat very heartily. We reached Summit, five miles away, by daybreak. We drove on through Fulton to Bryceville, near which place we stopped at the house of Father's Aunt Betsey, Grandfather Lamont's sister. She had, when a young woman, been Father's school teacher. After the horses had rested awhile and eaten some hay and grain, we drove on over what was called the Tegasabarrack hill, or rather mountain, and came down into the Schoharie valley in the region known as Vrooman's Land. The original owner of a large tract here was a Mr. Vrooman. It was a beautiful region, with broad, flat or bottom lands, very fertile, with fine buildings and large orchards loaded with apples, the finest I had ever seen. There was also that prominent peak, known as "Vrooman's Nose," jutting out from the mountain, that arrested my attention. We went down that beautiful broad valley to Middleburg, where we stopped for dinner and the rest of the day.

The Democratic Convention was to meet there that afternoon, and Father was a delegate from his town. The convention met and organized. I did not go in, as I was not interested. Father came out occasionally to look after me. I got up into the wagon and probably fell asleep, awakening sometime early in the afternoon, feeling very ill at my stomach. The food, the early rising, the hot sun and my continued gazing at the scenery had upset me. My father was called out of the convention and a very kind old colored woman, working in the kitchen of the hotel, brought me a preparation of some kind, with a strong taste of camphor, to drink. I swallowed it, my stomach was soon settled and I was all right for the rest of my journey.

After a supper at the hotel Father took me into the convention with him and I think I lay down in one corner on a lounge and slept all the evening. Later the convention adjourned and Father got out the team and we drove on down the valley through Schoharie village to a tavern then known as "Yankee Pete's," perhaps seven miles from Middleburg. The barroom or reception room presented a novel sight with a lot of slippers hung up on nails. The custom was for the guests, mainly farmers on their way to market, to pull off their boots and put on a pair of slippers and go to bed, leaving their boots behind. We went upstairs to a room with several beds, and I slept pretty soundly. We drove on the next day over the Helderburg mountain, through Quaker Street, Duanesburg, and then on the great Western Turnpike, as it was called, to Albany, arriving there early in the afternoon.

First Sight of a Railroad Train

From a high hill above the city, I had my first sight of a locomotive engine drawing some cars. It was on the line of the Albany & Schenectady railroad, the tracks having since been changed. Near the same place we were halted and a dozen men swarmed around, asking what produce Father had to sell. They were then called "runners," and were the agents of merchants in the city. Father had inquired along the road the going price of the things he had for sale, and so was in a position to trade intelligently.

Entering the city I was completely amazed, and gazed with open-eyed wonder at the Court House, the old City Hall, the Capitol and all the fine houses we passed as we drove to the place where our goods were to be delivered. Such fine houses, and so compactly built together, I had never dreamed of.

By the time we were unloaded and the settlement for Father's produce had been made it was night, and Father drove back to a hotel on Washington Street, kept by a Mr. Loucks, an acquaintance of Father's, where we got supper and remained for the night. The next morning Father did a great deal of shopping of one kind or another. He took me into what was then called "The Museum," showed me over a steamboat, and I saw any number of canal boats and sloops, for sloops were still largely employed in carrying freight on the river. These were all entirely new sights to me, a little country boy. We started homeward after dinner and drove as far as Central Bridge, staying overnight there. The road to Albany at that time had plenty of hotels or taverns, as they were then called, scattered all along the way.

We returned by way of Cobleskill instead of Schoharie. I remember the long climb of five miles from the valley of the Cobleskill creek to Summit. We had quite a load, so Father walked up the hills and I drove the team. We did not reach home until some time after dark on the fourth day. I was a very tired, sleepy boy by that time and glad enough to get to bed. I had seen a great deal and had enough to talk about for months afterwards. A new world had been opened to me. Seventy years have rolled around since that memorable trip, yet I can remember the events of those four days as if they had been only yesterday.

Current Literature in 1840

We all had at least the average boy's fondness for reading, but of course books for children in my boyhood were not very numerous in the region of Charlotteville, or anywhere else for that matter. There was a post office in the place, established a good while before I was born. There was a weekly mail, carried sometimes on horseback, but generally in a one-horse wagon. Not many weekly papers were in circulation. My father always took the Methodist Church paper, *The Christian Advocate and Journal.* In it I found little to interest me. Another paper my father took was the *Weekly Albany Argus,* which I read eagerly for its general news. It was a strongly partisan Democratic paper, advocating the election of James K. Polk as against Henry Clay, and the annexation of Texas and the righteousness of the Mexican war. Of that war I read all the news that came to hand.

There also came into our family, by way of exchange with some of the neighbors, *The Philadelphia Saturday Courier* and *Neal's Saturday Gazette.* These two papers were mainly filled with cheap stories by T. S. Arthur, Caroline and George Lippard, who wrote "Legends of the Revolution," Lee Hents, and the like, but they were very interesting to me. Then there was the *Sunday School Advocate,* which began to be published early in the Forties, which I also eagerly read. There was also a scanty Sunday School library. Then, too, there was the School District library, provided by the State, from which only one book might be drawn by a family at one time.

From this library I became quite familiar with the *History of the United States, Life of George Washington, Colonial and Indian Wars, History of the Jews,* by Josephus, *History of England,* and Fox's *Book of Martyrs.* Not many monthly magazines were published. Occasionally I saw *Graham's Magazine,* published in Philadelphia. I do not recall any other.

Lawlessness in the Rent Riots

In my boyhood, from the years 1843 to 1845, there was carried on what has since been called the "Anti-Rent War." Charlotteville was not the theater of this war, but was in that region, and our village shared in the general excitement. Farms had been purchased in Albany, Schoharie and parts of Delaware Counties, subject to an annual lease or small rent. The agitation began for the purpose of getting the lands with a clear title, encumbered no longer with a lease and yearly rent. This object was perfectly legitimate, but the agitation degenerated into forms of lawlessness and disorder. Bands of armed men in the disguise of Indians were present at the anti-rent meetings.

We boys attended one such meeting in the Dugway meeting house about two and one-half miles away, where large numbers of disguised men were present, hooting and yelling after the Indian fashion. There was no leased land about Charlotteville, but some neighbors joined in the anti-rent movement, hoping in some way, perhaps, to escape paying their indebtedness on the lands for which they had contracted. The excitement continued until a deputy sheriff, by the name of Steele, was shot in the town of Andes, Delaware County, where he was trying to force the sale of a man's cattle in order to compel him to pay his debts. The whole region was greatly agitated, hundreds were arrested in Delaware County, which was declared by the governor to be in rebellion and was placed under martial law for a time. There were a great many criminal trials at Delhi; several were convicted of murder and sentenced to be hanged. These sentences were changed by the governor to imprisonment for life. The men were pardoned after a few years, none serving a full term.

About four miles from our place, a deputy sheriff was tarred and feathered in the wintertime, while attempting to serve some papers on a delinquent landholder. The scene for several years was called "Tar Hollow." After the criminal proceedings in Delhi the excitement died down. A law was passed forbidding the wearing of disguises. The landlords also came to be willing to sell their land and give a clear title.

I recall that during this excitement John Jeffers, a loudmouthed talker in my father's employ, was caught one day by a band of the so-called Indians who threatened him and made him leap up and down, shouting: "Down with the rent!" The Lamonts about Charlotteville had no sympathy with this lawless movement. My Grandfather Lamont, to whom was due not back rent but back payments for land purchased from Gerrit Smith, whose agent Grandfather was for that region, was threatened. When the old man, then in poor health, sat on his porch one day and a load of disguised men rode by, whooping and shouting and holding up a tar bucket, he shook his cane at them, saying: "Be off, you calico devils!"

Charlotteville, in my boyhood, was a very religious community. There was the Sunday School organized by my father, to which I was taken, I cannot remember how early. Then the Church catechism was taught in the home as well as at church. We were expected to learn and recite at least six new Bible verses each week. I was in a class of four or five boys, among whom was my brother George. Our teacher, David Morris, offered a new jack-knife as a prize to the boy who would recite the most verses in a given time. I won the knife. There was always the Sunday morning preaching service in the church which we attended, even when very small boys. Then there was a Sunday afternoon or Sunday evening prayer-meeting, usually led by my father; also a week-evening prayer-meeting on Thursday night, held in the schoolhouse or in some home. My earliest recollections are of one held in our house, right opposite the church; of the loud singing in which Charles Gorse, the schoolteacher, took a leading part.

Plenty of Preachers Right at Home

My father's house was always the temporary home of the itinerants, that is, the traveling Methodist ministers. I recall one, O. G. Hedstrom. He would, almost as soon as he entered the house, walk back and forth in the room singing very heartily and rubbing and clapping his hands. When we were outdoors playing, his hearty singing would announce to us little folks his presence. Then there was the old-fashioned "Quarterly Meeting," when the house would be crowded to overflowing for a night or two by those who had come from a distance. Sometimes, to make more room for these guests, we little people were taken to Grandfather Paine's to stay for a few days, which pleased us very much. Such was the open-hearted and open-handed hospitality of my father and mother that it led one of my father's neighbors in those days to say to my grandfather Lamont: "Mr. Lamont, those Methodists will eat your son Thomas out of house and home; you would better caution him." Whether my grandfather cautioned Father or not I do not know, but my father spoke of it pleasantly in after days, saying: "I have kept on in my old way, but never yet have wanted for a house and home."

Four of us brothers had advanced in our studies as far as we could in the common school during the winter of 1848–49. We all felt that we should like to teach, as the custom was then for young men of fair attainments. What was called a select school was kept in Charlotteville in the fall for a few weeks by William Gorse. A number of youths attended, for he was a superior teacher. Among his pupils were the four of us. We worked hard and brushed up our studies in the common English branches so as to be able to pass examinations and receive school certificates. My brother David secured a school in Jefferson village, about seven miles from home; my brother William secured my brother Jacob's old school in the Harnacker valley in Worcester; my brother George, only fifteen years old, a little later was sought as a teacher in the same town in a neighborhood called Briar Hill. I will say to his credit that, young as he was, he was quite as successful as any of us.

My brother Jacob secured for me a school on Davenport Hill, about two miles south of his home, at the rate of $10 per month and board. I was not seventeen years old when the school was engaged for me. In October I was examined as to scholarship and fitness to teach by the school inspector, a Mr. Metcalf. He gave me a certificate which is somewhere in my old papers today, dated in October, 1849.

I began work about November 1st of that year. The schoolhouse, which was an old, unpainted structure, stood at four corners. I remained there as teacher for about four months, it being the winter term, with no great amount of satisfaction to myself, however it may have been with the patrons of the school. It was what may be called a "hard school." There were about forty students, many of them boys and some of them older and larger than myself. The trouble was not in the teaching, for I was quite at home in all I was required to teach, but in keeping proper order. But I managed to get along in some way and get through, using the rod very sparingly.

Vicissitudes of Boarding Houses

I boarded around the neighborhood; always slept in cold rooms and in some very poor houses—in some cases log houses. My lunch was always brought to me with the children's dinner, and it usually consisted of rye bread and butter, cake, pie, and sometimes cold pancakes! I kindled my own fires and the wood was always unseasoned. Each family furnished a load or two of wood, according to the number of pupils sent from that home, and sometimes the wood supply would get very low.

I suffered greatly from homesickness that winter among strangers. In order to wash I always had to go out into the kitchen or woodshed—sometimes outdoors. Of course the water was always cold and the soap was "soft" and homemade. I was glad enough at the end of the week to walk over the hills to spend the time until Monday with my brother Jacob's family. I never can be sufficiently grateful to my brother and his good wife, who always made me so welcome in their home. It seemed almost like a paradise.

About the first of November, 1850, the New York Conference Seminary at Charlotteville was opened for students. The school, as I have said before, was overcrowded, enrolling in all not far from 250 or 300 students. The opening of this school marked an epoch in my life. Large numbers of young men of about my age in the region of Charlotteville entered as students during the first term. Five were enrolled from our family—David, William, George, Elizabeth and myself. I believe we were all eager to make the most of our opportunity. During the first term of twenty-two weeks I studied higher algebra, geometry, Wayland's moral philosophy, Latin and rhetoric, though not all of them at the same time. The next term I added Greek and in Latin read Caesar. I remember my brother George was in the geometry class with me. I do not now recall any other classes.

The school was divided into four sections. A literary society called "The Wesleyan Association" was formed, which I think we all joined. This was helpful to me in some ways, especially in learning to debate. Sometimes every quarter, and at least once every term, a public debate was held in the chapel, sometimes in the church, to which the public was invited. In one of the later terms, perhaps the second year, my brother George was president and I had the oration, such as it was. Another time I recall a public debate in which I was assigned a leading part. The question was: "Is a republican or a monarchical form of government the better for mankind?" I supported the republican position.

In the summer of 1852 Father erected a much larger building to care for his growing business under the firm name of "Lamont & Sons." He was also appointed postmaster in the spring of 1853. Towards the end of May he prepared to go to Windsor to look after his land in that town, and to visit some of his uncles and cousins who had settled in the neighborhood of Owego, New York. Mother accompanied him on his journey.

The Death of My Father

Well do I recall the morning they started. I was just starting for the Seminary as they were getting into the carriage. Father said, "Good-bye, Thomas; look after things while I am away." On the morning of June 3d he had transacted his business in Windsor and was driving westward on a highway near the tracks of the Erie Railroad, about ten miles from Binghamton. A hand-car came along the track, and Father's horse, unaccustomed to seeing cars of any kind, took fright and tried to run away. By a good deal of exertion Father succeeded in stopping him after a little time. He then alighted to adjust something about the harness that had gotten out of order. Mother, too, got out to pick up something that had fallen out a little way back while the horse was running. When she returned she noticed that Father was leaning against the horse, looking pale. He said: "I feel faint." Mother said: "Lie right down on the ground." He did so at once. She went to him and found that he had ceased to breathe. She felt his pulse, and it had stopped beating. She could discover no signs of life. He must have died the instant he reached the ground.

Mother found his knife and tried to bleed him, but when she opened a vein the blood would not flow. The conviction was forced upon her that her husband was dead. In speaking of the scene at that moment Mother said: "I could feel the angels' presence there:

they had come to take him to the heaven for which he had been preparing and ripening for years."

A singular thing was that the horse, so unmanageable a little while before, seemed by instinct to know that something unusual was happening, for all this time he stood perfectly still.

Mother was entirely alone during this fearful ordeal. Seeing some men working on the railroad nearby, she hurried towards them and called for help. They came at once and the lifeless body was carried to a house perhaps a·quarter of a mile away. A doctor was sent for, and he pronounced Father dead. A coroner was summoned. After careful inquiry into all the circumstances he decided that death had come from over-exertion in stopping the runaway horse—exertion that had ruptured a blood-vessel of the heart. Mother sent at once to Binghamton, ten miles away, for an undertaker and all else that was needed to bring Father's body home. A cousin of Father's, a Mrs. Messereau, living a few miles away, having in the meantime heard the sad news, came to offer her sympathy, which was all she could do.

Finally all things were ready for the return. Mother hired a man to drive her alongside the hearse, and about evening time she started on her sad journey homeward. She was at least a hundred miles from home. She rested for a little time during the night at a hotel on the road to feed her horses, but she could not sleep. They pushed on early the next day and after dark that night reached my eldest brother's (Jacob's) home, about three miles east of Oneonta. It was heavy news to him, a great shock, for Father and Mother had stayed all night with him on their way out only a short time before.

A Melancholy Homecoming

Long before daylight Mother started to cover the final twenty-two miles of the journey. A neighbor of Jacob's, Dexter Brown, who had once lived in Charlotteville, was sent on in advance of the sad procession to break the news to us. That morning I was in the cowyard milking. Mr. Brown rode up and halted. I stepped to the road to see him.

"Your father took a journey not many days ago, did he not?" said he.

"Yes," I answered.

"I am very sorry to tell you that he is dead and that they are coming with his remains a little way behind me."

The sad news soon spread through the household, and by that time Mother, with the procession, had arrived.

We all preferred to remember our father as we had last seen him, in health and strength; and so, with little further preparation, we laid him at rest that same afternoon in the Lamont burying-ground. That was on Saturday. The funeral proper, as the custom was at that time, was held in the church on Sunday morning, the Rev. David Buck, the newly appointed pastor of the Church, officiating. I have always regretted that the Rev. Harvey Brown, an old and lifelong acquaintance of my father, who was visiting the place, was not invited to preach the sermon. He would have been able to do greater justice to the occasion. He only made a few remarks. The reason he was not invited was a fear that Mr. Buck, the regular pastor, might in some way consider himself slighted. Mr. Buck's sermon was generally regarded as quite unequal to the occasion.

A Few Observations about My Father

My father was a man of fine presence, of about medium size, with a pleasant face, a ruddy countenance, a high, broad forehead, black hair just beginning to be sprinkled with gray, large bluish-gray eyes, large front teeth and a very pleasant smile. He was a man of much natural dignity—few would be inclined to take undue liberty or use undue familiarity in his presence. He impressed people favorably—it was his unconscious influence speaking through his whole personality. He was a man of good, well-balanced intellect and sound common sense; an excellent judge of human nature. He had excellent business ability, better than anyone else of his father's family.

He was a public-spirited man and favored with heart and hand whatever was for the general good. He took an interest in the political questions of his day, though not a zealous party man. On national and State elections he voted the Democratic ticket. Twice before he was forty years old he was elected supervisor of his town. His advocacy of any candidate greatly helped, if it did not actually secure, his election to any town office.

He was ardently attached to the Church of his early choice. He was regular, devout and constant in his attendance upon the Church

The first Thomas William Lamont, 1803–1853

services. The prosperity of the Church was his joy; her decline, his sorrow. It was his influence and earnest advocacy that secured the building of the Methodist church in Charlotteville in 1832, before I was born. He was a generous contributor towards its construction. The church is still standing. He was a generous giver in his day and according to his means for the support of the Church and other benevolent causes. I have no doubt that year by year, on an average, he gave at least a tenth of his income to the Church and other benevolences.

In the fall of 1852 I was invited to take charge of the Stamford Academy, an institution perhaps ten years old, twelve miles south of Charlotteville. I was twenty years old when the term opened about the middle of October. My brother George drove me over to my place of work. There were fifty pupils—too many for me to teach properly and I secured as my assistant my cousin Kate E. Lamont, afterwards the wife of Bishop Hurst. Cousin Kate taught the smaller pupils and I had charge of the elder ones. I taught almost everything from higher arithmetic, algebra and philosophy to Latin. I was at Stamford about five months. My salary was $20 per month and my board.

I enjoyed teaching in Stamford much better than in Davenport Hill. I went home occasionally, usually walking five miles over the hills to Jefferson where someone from home would meet me and I would drive the remaining seven miles, always getting back to Stamford in time to open the Academy on Monday mornings, by starting from home about three o'clock, long before daylight. It was a long, cold drive in the winter time. Brother David took me over at one time and Austin at another.

A Trip to Faraway New York City

In the fall of 1853, when my brother William went to New York to purchase a stock of goods for the store which he and David were running, I went with him. It was the year of the "World's Fair," as it was called, the great Crystal Palace Exhibition in New York City. The newspapers had been full of it and I had a natural desire to see it. We took a night steamboat from Albany, my first ride in a boat of that kind, and it seemed like a floating palace. Owing to fog we did not reach New York until nearly noon the next day.

I had at this time become somewhat familiar with Albany, but New York seemed very unlike it—so full of noise and bustle. We stopped at a hotel downtown at which Father used to stay. The next day I went to the Crystal Palace, riding up on the horse cars recently introduced into New York. It was a long ride—the Palace was that time considered away uptown if not out of town. There was a long stretch of country not built up at all between the Palace and the city proper. I need not dwell upon the exhibition; it was very interesting to me, but of course vastly inferior to many held since.

We also visited Barnum's Museum, one of the great attractions of New York at that time; saw the play *Uncle Tom's Cabin*, then very popular, having a run of many weeks. The book had been published only a year or two before and had created a great sensation. On Sunday we attended the John Street Methodist Church, which was near our hotel.

My brother George had entered Union College, Schenectady, N. Y., in September 1953 and I decided to follow in his footsteps. I took the examinations in the fall of 1954 and did not find them a very difficult ordeal. In the classics it was found that I had read the requirements for the second term, junior year. I was then required to read certain passages from Latin and Greek authors. The Latin was easy enough under Professor Newman, and I was equally fortunate when I came before Dr. Taylor Lewis in the Greek. He called on me to translate some passages from Euripides, then handed me Homer's *Odyssey,* marking two or three places for me to read and translate; then he asked me to parse some and give the derivation of some of the words. I was quite at home in these authors as I had but recently read them, and he immediately gave me a certificate that I had passed a satisfactory examination in his department.

Brought before Professor Jackson of the Mathematical Department, I said I had understood that Conic Sections were regarded as an equivalent to Spherical Trigonometry. He said he could not accept that but passed me in everything else, conditioning me in that study, which I duly passed later on. I called on the president, the venerable Dr. Nott, at that time eighty-four years old. He treated me very kindly, calling me "my son." He gave me a note to the registrar and I was enrolled as a member of the Class of 1856.

At that time Union had an attendance of about 300 students. It was the most popular college in the State, and in New England only Harvard and Yale exceeded it in members. Just contrary to what it is today, the senior class was usually the largest and the freshman the smallest. The class I entered numbered about 100, and about ninety were graduated. There were some elective studies, especially in engineering and the sciences, but there were very few elective studies in the regular classical course which one must complete to receive the degree of A.B.; the others secured the degree of C.E. or B.S. The majority of the students were in the regular classical course.

College Customs in the 1850's

The examinations were held at the end of every term and were generally written. Daily prayers were held in the chapel morning and evening, except Saturday and Sunday mornings. The morning prayers were at seven o'clock both summer and winter; the evening prayers at five o'clock. In the winter at the time of the morning prayers it was hardly light. The young men would scamper across the campus from the North College to the South, where the prayers were held, hurrying into their coats as they ran. Dr. Hickock usually conducted the morning prayers, Dr. Nott the evening. There was no music of any kind, only the reading of a chapter from the Bible and prayer. We had a recitation immediately after morning prayers and before breakfast. The rule of the college was very strict as to attendance at prayers and the roll was usually called. We all had our seats—the two higher classes on the first floor, the two lower upstairs. When the roll was not called we were marked by a tutor. The absentees were then called the next evening to visit the president and give their excuse, if they had one; to be admonished and fined if they had none.

Absence from recitation was also a serious matter. Fines of from five to ten cents were inflicted for these absences with a strong caution against repetition. When the name of someone who had been absent was called out in chapel at evening prayer, he usually made light of it, saying: "I am invited to take tea with the old Prex tonight." We could choose our church, but if at times we attended elsewhere it was regarded as no offense. On Monday a professor or tutor made inquiry of every student as to his church attendance the preceding day and marked him accordingly.

All the leading Churches were represented in Schenectady, the two strongest and most popular being the Reformed Dutch and the Presbyterian. The majority of the students attended these two. While Union College was undenominational, most of the professors and their families attended one of these two churches. Dr. Nott was a Presbyterian minister and stood high in the councils of that Church. The prevailing tone of the college was Presbyterian.

Before the Craze for Athletics

There were, properly speaking, no "athletics" in my day in

Union College. The students got their exercise in walking, bathing and swimming in the Mohawk in the summer, and in the old-fashioned football on the campus between the two colleges—North college against the South. I was always glad to take part in this game; while it was spirited it was not rough or dangerous, nor did it require great skill. We took our places on each side at a point halfway between the colleges and by the toss of a penny decided which side should have the first kick at the ball. The side that drove the other back to its college was the victor. All the students of the two colleges were invited to the play; each to help his own college. I do not remember that any one ever received an injury in the game. We would get very healthfully warmed up. Repeated games were played the same afternoon.

There were two literary societies in the college to one or the other of which the majority of the students belonged. I joined the Adelphic, whose rooms were in the North college. It had quite a large library. I took my turn in the debates and other exercises when appointed. Then there was the "Senate," made up of the members of the two upper classes. Its business, debates and the like, was supposed to be conducted like that of the United States Senate. The public political questions before the country at that time were about the only questions discussed. There was greater interest displayed in the discussions of the "Senate" than in any other discussions in the college. The Crimean war, the attempt to force slavery into Kansas, the repeal of the Missouri Compromise were burning questions. Mutterings of the Civil War were also beginning to be heard distinctly in those days.

Then there were the Greek letter societies. I joined Alpha Omicron. We had debates and discussions of various kinds. Henry A. Butz, a sophomore from New Jersey, was a member of this society. He was not in very good health, and left Union to recuperate for a year or two, then entered Princeton College, completed his course and received his A.B. degree. He became a prominent member of the Newark Conference of the Methodist Church and has been for a good many years a professor and president of the Drew Theological Seminary. After I was graduated the Alpha Omicron was absorbed into another Greek letter society called the Delta Upsilon, of which society I know very little beyond the fact that all the former members of the A. O. were created members of it.

There was also the Theological Society, in which purely Biblical and theological questions were discussed. This society was made up chiefly of young men who had the Christian ministry in view. I was at one time the president of this society.

Book Canvassing in Old Virginia

My college vacations were spent at home on the farm, in the hay and harvest fields, recuperating my health and getting rid of indigestion. It seems to me I never slept more soundly and more refreshingly than in those vacation days at home. My fall vacation before my last winter term was spent in Virginia. My brother George and some other students, just before the term closed, had gone South to canvass for a popular map of the United States published by a New York house. George was succeeding, as he usually did in everything he undertook. I had no relish for the canvassing business, but I had a great desire to see something of the South and slavery, about which there was so much being said and written. I took the agency to canvass Frederick County, Virginia. Winchester was my headquarters. I did the best I could, but found canvassing no easy work. I did enough to pay all my traveling and other expenses, which was about all I could expect, and I had the advantage of a little wider view of the great world.

I was not greatly enamored of the South; being a Northerner I was looked upon with suspicion, and I kept a pretty close mouth. I saw something of slavery—saw a company of Negroes handcuffed, put on board a train and started for distant Southern States. They had been bought at slave auctions in the neighborhood of Winchester. I attended several services in the colored church where the slaves worshiped, was much impressed with their singing and their very lively and active way of conducting their worship, also the earnestness but doleful ignorance of their preachers. Some could not read at all and always misquoted their Bible texts.

About this time I received a license as a "local preacher" of the Methodist Church. I was much urged to this step by the Reverend Mr. Chipp, the pastor of the Church in Charlotteville. I was examined and received my license in a Quarterly Conference held in Fergusonville during one of my college vacations. Professor Newman often urged me to go to a schoolhouse about two miles from Schenectady, where there was a Sunday School, and speak. It was in the town of Niskayarra. One evening I walked out, accompanied by my cousin, Wellington. For the first time in my life I spoke to a congregation in the way of giving an address. The schoolhouse was well filled. I had comparative freedom. I was invited to come again and did so occasionally while I remained in college. On one occasion I preached in the Methodist Church in Schenectady, and once or twice in one or two of the missions in the city and in the colored church.

Before the close of my last college year in 1856 I was elected to membership in the Phi Beta Kappa society, nine others being elected out of a class of about 100. It was an honor highly prized, being conferred, as it is today, as a badge of scholarship. I hardly expected an election, as I had entered the class so late.

Graduation from Union College

I had been invited to teach in Charlotteville, and taught in the Seminary there a good part of the spring term before I graduated. The graduating day came late in July—a very warm day. I was given to understand that I could have a place on the program, but declined as I had been absent so much of the term. After the close of the speaking we received our degrees at the hands of Dr. Nott, as he repeated the words, *"Perseverantia omnia vincit nec non gloria ducit."*

I did not go back to receive my second degree, A.M., which was conferred upon me two years after graduation. And I found that I soon had so many more pressing duties and expenses that it seemed to me almost out of the question to attend my class reunions.

I paid my own expenses through college. I gave to my father $100 that I saved in Stamford, and to his estate nearly $200 that I saved in Fort Plain. All the expense of graduating and all the last term's bills I paid from my salary as a teacher in Charlotteville. I think my brother George met the greater part of his college expenses in much the same way. I presume our college expenses were about the average. The whole country was much poorer fifty years ago than it is today; far less money was in circulation.

In February of 1857 my sister Elizabeth, who had gone west with my brother Jacob a year or two earlier, was married to the Reverend W. F. Cowles, a prominent member of the Iowa Conference. He was a widower and considerably older than my sister. My sister was a beautiful young woman, perhaps the most beautiful of my sisters, and very bright. It was no wonder that she had many admirers. She died a good many years ago, leaving two clever boys who have grown up to be successful men, one, Lamont Cowles, a lawyer, and the other, Gardner, a successful banker.* This dear sister died at the early age of thirty-six. She was worn out with the hardships of a Methodist itinerant's wife in the West of her day.

Teaching Is Not My Calling

I decided that I would leave the Charlotteville Seminary at the end of the winter term in 1859, and take regular pastoral work in the New York Methodist Conference. I did not feel that my calling was to be a teacher. I had taught for three years and, on the whole, had had a pleasant time with agreeable associates. But I was far from being contented and I left with no thought of ever returning to teach in the Seminary. The Conference of 1859 was held in Kingston early in May. I drove with the Reverend Aaron Rogers, the pastor at Charlotteville, to the Conference.

We were four or five days in getting to Kingston. I passed in all my studies as a probationer and was recommended to membership in the Conference, and to receive deacon's orders. I was ordained deacon by Bishop Janes, in the Rondout Methodist Church, of which thirty years later I became pastor. In the afternoon Dr. Daniel Curry preached the ordination sermon. His theme was "Divine Providence." I was received into the Conference as a full member.

The session of the Conference was quite protracted; the slavery question was up for a long discussion. All were agreed as to the evil of slavery, but just what the Church could do more than it had already done was the matter under discussion. Some wanted a rule passed absolutely prohibiting slavery and expelling everyone who held slaves. The more conservative wanted the rule left as it was, saying: "Slavery is a great evil and we are as much as ever opposed to it, advising our people to keep from it and emancipate their slaves as fast as it is practicable." Dr. McClintock, a strong man, was a speaker on the conservative side; D. W. Clark, Dr. Crawford, B. M. Adams on the radical side. Of course we could settle nothing—only express our opinions. My recollection

---

* My grandfather's nephew, Gardner Cowles, was of course my father's first cousin. He gave up banking during the second part of his life to become president and publisher of the *Des Moines Register and Tribune*. Two of his sons, Gardner, Jr., and John, have also made their mark as newspaper publishers.

is that when the vote was taken the radicals were in the minority. Bishop Janes had recently returned from holding a Conference in Barham, Texas, where he had been threatened by a mob because of his being a Northerner, holding well-known views on the slavery question.

My First Pastorate at Fishkill

The Reverend Matthew Van Dusen, a former pastor on the old Charlotte Circuit, was a guest at the same home in which I was entertained. Mr. Van Dusen had known my father well and seemed much interested in me on my father's account. William Van Wyck of old Fishkill Village visited the Conference in the interests of the Methodist Church. He was making inquiry for a young man for their Church, and Mr. Van Dusen mentioned my name to him, I was told. At any rate, when the appointments were announced I was read off for Fishkill. Fishkill was a very old Dutch village, about five miles back from Fishkill Landing on the Hudson. There had been a church organization of the Dutch people there for nearly 200 years. An ancient brick church in the village had been erected some time before the Revolutionary War. The older, wealthier and more influential families were all connected with that Church, as I found out a little later.

After returning to Charlotteville for a day or two I hastened to Fishkill as soon as I could get ready, which did not require much time. I was now to leave my dear mother and home, and I started with not a very light heart. I was to embark on a calling that I had long felt was to be my life work. I had only a small trunk for my clothing and a box of books. Mr. Lape kindly volunteered to take me to Canajoharie, from which place I took the New York Central railroad to Albany.

I arrived in Fishkill towards the latter part of the week, was very cordially received by Mr. Van Wyck, and was told that the arrangement was for me to board with him at the rate of about $2 per week. I was twenty-six years old, and it was with no little trepidation that I waited for the first Sunday. A "Quarterly Meeting" was held on Saturday at which the Reverend L. M. Vincent, my Presiding Elder, presided. Here it was voted that my salary was to be $300 a year. It was thought at that time to be quite a generous salary for an unmarried Methodist preacher. Anyone can see that after paying my board, buying books, periodicals, and paying traveling expenses, I could not have a very large balance left. But it was as much as I could expect and I was content; in fact it was more than some Methodist ministers who had families to provide for were receiving at that time.

First Sermon in My New Pulpit

Mr. Vincent preached in the morning and I was to preach in the evening. I have a vivid memory of my feelings before delivering this first sermon in my first pastorate. I found the church well filled; my text was, "If any man will come after Me let him deny himself, take up his cross and follow Me." Mr. Van Dusen, who was stationed at Johnsville, about four miles to the east, and who seemed to feel a deep interest in me, treating me as kindly as he would a son, was present that evening. After the sermon he spoke encouragingly to me, and doubtless I needed encouragement.

I was to preach twice on Sundays and lead a prayer-meeting in the middle of the week. There was also a Sunday School before church which I generally attended. "Class meeting" was held on a week evening. All this obliged me to study diligently. My library was limited, made up largely of the Methodist standard books of that time and what was needed in my regular Conference studies. I usually selected a text for my Sunday morning sermon by Tuesday morning and worked at it as faithfully as I could, getting it in some shape before night. On Wednesday I usually decided on my Sunday evening discourse, and I worked on both sermons all the rest of the week. Monday was rest day, devoted to reading and sometimes to my Conference studies. The habit of beginning to prepare my sermons early in the week I have always followed despite many interruptions. After studying during the mornings and a part of the afternoons, I walked out and made pastoral calls, but rarely took a meal away from my boarding place.

The Methodists had a somewhat inferior social position in the place. Dr. Kipp had been the pastor of the influential Dutch Church for twenty-five years. He was pleasant and called on me, but always had a kind of patronizing manner. Our Church had for its congregation day laborers, the servant class, some clerks and mechanics and a few fairly well-to-do families. But there was little social life for me in the congregation. I did the best I could and had reason to believe that I was fairly acceptable to the congregation. The most that could be done was to hold our own and try to keep a vigorous Sunday School.

On the whole I was happy in my work—happier and more contented than I had been in teaching, for I believed I was in the line of duty, which is everything. George Esray, pastor in Glenham, a bright but poorly balanced young man, called on me quite often. He could preach well, but beyond that he seemed to fail. He withdrew from the Conference some years later and entered journalism. I visited my mother during the summer and spent nearly two weeks with her—a great privilege. I kept up the habit of visiting her, always once and more often two or three times a year, as long as she lived.

The Joys and Sorrows of Donation Parties

During the winter in Fishkill an old-fashioned donation was made for me at Mr. Van Wyck's, which netted about $50. I did not enjoy that way of raising money for a pastor and never have enjoyed it. There were some bickerings and jealousies connected with the donation, not on my account but owing to some old feuds existing before I became pastor of the Church. These were unpleasant. In the Conference held about the middle of April in St. Paul's, New York City, Bishop Scott presided. I was invited to be the pastor of the Charlotteville Church, with the understanding that I should act as principal of the Seminary. At this Conference there was a long debate on the slavery question, but nothing could settle that question except the war which was fast approaching.

The summer and fall of 1860 were a time of great political excitement in the country. Abraham Lincoln had received the Republican nomination for the presidency. The Democratic party was split into two factions, with two nominees—Stephen A. Douglas and John C. Breckinridge, thus making certain the election of Lincoln. I voted for Lincoln, as I had four years earlier voted for Fremont.

Meanwhile, the Southern States were seceding from the Union, one after another. President Buchanan was showing great weakness and the members of his cabinet were resigning to join the Confederacy. Peace conferences were being held to try to compromise matters, without any success, and altogether the outlook for the country, the church and the school was not at all encouraging. Reports came of the failure of a plot to assassinate Lincoln

in Baltimore on his way to be inaugurated as President. Then came
the inauguration and things seemed to be drifting on for a few
weeks, but not towards peace, no one knowing what would happen.

Breaking out of Civil War

About the middle of April I was driving with my brother William, in his carriage, towards Albany, when we met Henry Smith
of Cobleskill, a lawyer whom we knew. He halted us, telling us
the news of the firing on Fort Sumter by the Confederates and
the capture of the fort. The war had actually begun! In Albany
all was excitement. Loyal people were putting up their flags and
the purpose to maintain the Union was unmistakable. Then followed immediately the call for 75,000 volunteers from President
Lincoln—a call quickly responded to.

The Conference that spring was held in Poughkeepsie. The
spirit of patriotism was at the boiling point. A patriotic meeting
was held, addresses were made and resolutions passed pledging
the Conference to sustain the Government in its efforts to put down
the rebellion and preserve the Union. I speak of this to show the
state of feeling among the ministry and in the churches. If there
was any sympathy with the rebellion it was overawed—at least it
dared not as yet show itself.

Pious Comment upon the Death of an Enemy

The New York Methodist Conference for 1862 was held in
April in Peekskill, Bishop Ames presiding. During the session the
terrible two days' battle at Pittsburgh Landing took place. A telegram was brought into the Conference telling of the battle and
of the final result, including the death of one of the leading Con-
federate generals, Albert Sidney Johnston, at which Bishop Ames
coolly remarked, "The will of the Lord be done!"

The hard times had resulted in a great shrinking in the work
in the Conference; in some cases two charges were united into one.
I was beginning to learn some of the uncertainties of a Methodist
Conference, for I found myself appointed to Ridgebury, a place
of which I had never heard. In due time I arrived there and found
an old decayed village which had once been fairly flourishing but
had lost all of its prosperity because of its location, five miles away
from the Erie railroad. I found myself in an almost purely rural

community, the greater part of the congregation being farmers who made butter or sent their milk to New York.

I was expected to board with a farmer, a dairyman, Nathaniel W. Bailey. A little later it appeared that there had been some little jealousy as to where the pastor should board, two or three families seeking that doubtful honor. Mr. Bailey and his wife always treated me with great kindness. They were always up early in the morning; had their breakfast both in the summer and winter at six o'clock. During the butter-making season I would hear the rattling of their churning machine right under my window at about five o'clock in the morning. I did not mind the early breakfast in the summer, but in the winter we had to eat it by lamp light. Mrs. Bailey and her helper would be up and finished with the Monday washing before breakfast, but she really gained nothing by such strenuousness, for she was so tired that after dinner, which always came at twelve o'clock, she could do nothing in the afternoon but sleep in her chair as she tried to sew. They had two nice little boys, who seemed quite fond of me.

I Am Called a "Black Republican"

The summer of 1862 was one of continual fighting in the Civil War. It has sometimes been called the "bloody summer." Those were days when ministers needed to be extremely careful in their pulpits about allusions to any political questions. I made no secret of my sympathy with the national Administration in its efforts to crush the rebellion and save the Union, and I made it a habit publicly to pray for our rulers, our country and our armies. Some members did not like it. They said: "The Dominie is a rabid black Republican." I was accused of "preaching politics" when I had no thought of doing so. Once I was preaching about the slavery of sin, the thralldom of bad habits. I compared the man under their power to a slave, one not his own master. One man took his children from the Sunday School and said he would not allow his children to attend a Sunday School where the minister "preached politics" and against slavery.

Another time a prominent member of the Church arose and walked out of the church at some allusion I had made to the national events that were then happening. It was during this summer that General McClellan was driven back with great loss from before Richmond, and Lee invaded the North. It was the year of inflated paper currency and the suspension of specie payments; of General Burnside before Fredericksburg and the first Emancipation Proclamation. The general aspect of affairs was not bright, the Confederates having scored a good many successes.

In August, I visited my youngest brother, Austin,* who was practicing medicine in Hyde Park, Dutchess County, New York. After having taken his degree as a graduate of the University of Michigan Medical School, he had begun practice there a year or two before. We took the long drive from Hyde Park to Charlotteville. The first afternoon we drove to a point on the Hudson River opposite Catskill. We arrived too late to get the last ferry and were obliged to sleep in a farmhouse where, before the night was over, we had the discomfort of finding that we were not the first arrivals. From Catskill we drove on over the turnpike and spent the night in Prattsville. We reached Charlotteville the next afternoon. We had found the roads rough and my brother's horse nothing extra as a traveler.

Opportunities for Reading and Walking

Ridgebury, while in many respects pleasant, was not and is not to-day a promising field religiously. There was too little harmony in the Church. It may be seen that Ridgebury was a rather lonely place for me. My boarding place was a mile and a half from the church and two miles from the post office. I read considerably, including at that time Gibbon's *Decline and Fall of the Roman Empire,* and Hume's *History of England.* These books had long been in my library but I had never had leisure to read them. Those were the days when there was no specie in circulation and sticky postage stamps were given to make change. A little later business men issued little fractional printed notes, called "shin plasters," by way of making change. Then the Government issued fractional currency of the denominations of 3, 5, 10, 25 and 50 cents.

It was in Ridgebury, I remember, where there was an unhappy custom of inviting the dyspeptic pastor to a dinner party with a lot of the neighbors, where the chief dish was a roast pig. My salary was to be $300, but the Church was exceedingly slack in paying it. They resorted to church sociables, held in different neighborhoods, to try to raise the money. I was expected to be present

---

* My late brother Austin Lamont (1905–1969) was named after our great-uncle and, like him, became an M.D.

at every one and I confess I did not greatly enjoy that method of making up the minister's salary. An old-fashioned "donation" was made for me in the fall at Mr. Bailey's, but at the end of the year there was still a deficiency of more than $50 on my salary, which of course was never paid. From the $250 received I had to pay my board and all my other expenses. However, all the people were kind to me and I do not complain.

On April 9th, 1863, I married Caroline Deuel Jayne, at that time in Fergusonville with her aunt, Mrs. Jane F. Henry. I will not now speak of all she has been to me in my work for over fifty years; a peerless wife in all respects, given to me by a wise and loving Heavenly Father.

4

THE JAYNE FAMILY

My wife, upon her father's side, is descended from pure English stock. The first of her name to come to this country was William Jayne, her great-great-great-grandfather, who arrived here in 1678. This William Jayne was of an ancient Norman family. His earliest ancestor in England was Gardo (called also Guido) de Jeanne who, formerly a general in the French army, accompanied Henry of Anjou across the channel and was with him when, as Henry II, he was crowned king of England. As a reward for his bravery and military prowess de Jeanne had allotted to him the manor of Kirtland, still said to be the English seat of the de Jeannes. This was in 1154.

William Jayne's own father was Henry de Jeanne, a graduate of Oxford and afterwards a lecturer there on theology and divinity. He moved to Bristol and there on January 25, 1618, his son William was born, and, as the records show, was christened fifteen days later. According to the family tradition this William went to Oxford and while a student there, because of his dissent from the established church, was expelled from the University. This was in 1642. He became a Puritan preacher and at the time of the Civil War, a few years later, became one of Cromwell's chaplains. After the restoration and coronation of Charles II in 1661 this William de Jeanne, on account of the religious persecution to which he was subjected, changed his name to Jayne and after living for some years in Llewellyn in Monmouthshire, where the name of Jayne is still common, emigrated to America in 1670. He was already a man long beyond middle life and was a widower, leaving sons behind him in England.

William Jayne Comes to America

Not unnaturally he came direct to New Haven, Connecticut, where years earlier, about 1634, his father's brother, William de Jeanne, after whom he was named, had settled with the New Haven colony and had long been the town clerk. Here the younger William met Annie Biggs, who was afterwards to become his wife; and in 1675, after purchasing a tract of land in Brookhaven township, Suffolk County, Long Island, he came back and married her. He was then fifty-seven years old and she only twenty-two. By her he had four sons. After her death in 1692, he married a third time and had three more sons, the youngest of whom, Stephen, was born in 1700, when his father was still a virile old man of eighty-two.* Practically all the Jaynes in America today trace their descent from some one of these seven sons.

William Jayne was now quite an old man, but the same Puritan, religious fervor that had attracted Oliver Cromwell and that later, under the gay Charles II, had drawn religious persecution down upon him, led him to become Dominie of the little Presbyterian Church at Setauket, Long Island. Here he busied himself in good works during an hale old age, and died March 24, 1714, when he was ninety-six years old. He was buried at Setauket and his old tombstone still bears this legible inscription:

Here lyes y body of
William Jayne
Born at Bristol Eng.
Jany 25th, 1618
Dec'd March y 24th, 1714

A Family of Ancient Mariners

The old Puritan church records at Setauket supply many dates of the family record. The place where William Jayne first settled was still, at last accounts, in the hands of his descendants of the sixth generation and all the old records are remarkably complete. It appears that not a few members of the family engaged in seafaring and in shipping. My wife tells me that in her childhood there was much talk of the old sea captains of previous generations of the family; and as recently (comparatively speaking) as the will of her grandfather, Peter Jayne, who died in 1813 (just a

---

* Cf. p. 161.

hundred years ago) there are bequests made of his sloop *Teaser of Smithtown* and the sloop *July Ann*.

In the War of the Revolution the Jaynes furnished almost a company of soldiers for the Continental Army. This company was under the leadership of Captain Timothy Jayne, who was a great-grandson of the original William Jayne. Captain Timothy's eldest brother was killed in the assault on Fort Washington, and in the battle of Long Island two other brothers, Isaac and Ebenezer, were officers in the same company. Tradition is that there were fifty-eight members of the Jayne family in this company, but probably that is exaggeration. Many of them were captured by the British in a block house; the officers were exchanged and privates were sent to the prison hulks in New York Harbor. There is still in existence in the family the parole of Samuel Jayne of Brookhaven, given when he was released from the prison ship on September 1, 1778.

Walter Peter Jayne, my wife's father, was born at Islip, Long Island, on January 18, 1810, and died at his home in Williamsbridge, New York City, on January 27, 1894, at the ripe old age of eighty-four. He was a man of quick, keen mind and charming disposition.

PART II
A Lamont Reunion in 1876

5

REPORT

by the Reverend Thomas Lamont

At the beginning of his Introduction (Part I) Thomas Lamont referred to a Lamont family reunion that took place in November 1876 at the home of his brother, George La Monte, at Bound Brook, New Jersey. The George La Monte family spelled our surname in French style, as did Thomas Lamont during a considerable part of his life.

Thomas Lamont was chosen Secretary of the Reunion and published a brief report about it, including some historical material about the family and two poems read at the gathering. Below is his short "Account of the Reunion of the Descendants of the late Thomas W. Lamont."—Ed.

A call for a reunion of the members of the family of the late Thomas W. Lamont was issued in October 1876 by George La Monte. The time named for the meeting was November 22, 1876, place, Bound Brook, N. J. The call was repeated, until a favorable response was received from every surviving member of the family.

At the time named, there assembled at the home of George La Monte, Mrs. E. M. Lamont, the widow of Thomas W. Lamont; her six sons and five surviving daughters, together with their wives, husbands and children—nearly all the living members of the family—making a company of forty-two persons.

The arrangements for the entertainment of so large a company were on a generous scale. Though there was some sadness at the thought of the two deceased daughters, Elizabeth* and Hannah†

---

* Elizabeth Lamont, the wife of the Reverend William Fletcher Cowles, a Methodist minister, died at Hamilton, Illinois, August 3, 1873, aged thirty-six. Cf. pp. 65–66.

† Hannah Lamont, the wife of Wesley G. Hartwell, died at Leroy, New York, December 14, 1872, twenty-eight years of age.

—the occasion, on the whole, was thoroughly enjoyed by all.

A chronicle of the Lamont family was read, and two poems recited, both of which, by unanimous request, were submitted for publication.

An organization for the holding of future reunions of the family was formed, of which George La Monte was made President, Thomas Lamont, Secretary, David S. La Monte, M. A. Ruland and Simeon Lape, Executive Committee.

The company closed their pleasant reunion on the morning of November 24, to meet again at the call of the President and Executive Committee.

6

TWO POEMS READ AT THE REUNION

Manly A. Ruland of Brooklyn, New York, who married Jennie Lamont and was my grandfather's brother-in-law, wrote the following poem and read it at the Reunion.—Ed.

A TRADITION

Long years ago, so the old folks say,
The family of Lamonts kept festal day;
There was great-grandmother, the oldest of all,
And forty-one children and grandchildren small.
At the head of the table sat George her son,
A round robust man, full of frolic and fun,
The generous host of that occasion,
Was a host in himself in any station,
Good looking, interesting, a man of parts;
He won by his wit the way to men's hearts.
As an offset to this peculiar bundle of fun
Was Thomas, the serious, the next older son,
Whose calling and election he strove to make sure
By preaching the gospel to rich and to poor.
His manner was grave, his hair was gray,
He was wisely chosen the historian of the day.
Another son, Austin, younger in years,
So noted for making good use of his ears,
And keeping his tongue, yet much of a wag
Who would drop a sly word when conversation would lag
That would rouse up the guests with roars of laughter,
And keep them aroused for long hours after.
There was Jacob the oldest, not like Jacob of old,
Of whom such a story of deception is told;
This one was frank, he knew no deceit,
Not a shred of dishonesty from his head to his feet;

He had garnered a fortune by his long years of toil,
And was proud to be reckoned a son of the soil.
The twin brothers, David and William, were there,
No two more alike could be found anywhere;
One alone by himself you would claim was the other,
And their wives to distinguish them had much of a bother:
And, no doubt, out of this fact, the story grew
That they both courted Mary—and married her too.*

Now *these* were not all, these six noble men,
Who trace to the Huguenot their noble origin.†
Five daughters as well—there late had been seven—
But the Angel of Death had snatched two to heaven;
And the chairs that were now vacant, most eloquently plead
That the living would kindly remember the dead.
The dead! Nay, the living who live evermore,
And beckon us onward to the bright shining shore;
And a voice from Elizabeth and Hannah seemed to say,
Be prepared for Death's coming, ye know not the day.
In silence sat Julia, whose heart had been riven
By great sorrow, and its tendrils were stretching to heaven,
Toward a bud that had drooped in her garden of love,
And had been transplanted to the garden above;
Though the pang was severe, yet her heart was serene,
When the love of a Father in this chastening was seen.
Close by her, Maria, the youngest of all,
The bitterest of bitterness, Mara they call.
Oh mother why named you me Mara? Oh, why?
Must my life be bitterness till the day that I die?
There was Catharine, cheerful in the midst of great sorrow,
Hoping happiness would drive away woe on the morrow;
Not giving away to "It might have been,"
While the dawn of a brighter life, through the clouds could
be seen.
There was Lucy, great hearted and generous and true,
Unselfish as Mary—and like Martha too,
Devoted to friendship, to family, to God,
Walking prayerfully the path that her father had trod.
If ever were joined the divine and the human,
'Twas in Jennie, the modest, housewifely woman;
No purer affection in wife or in mother,
Was ever matured in the heart of another.

Time would fail to mention the names of the others—
The husbands of the daughters, the wives of the brothers,

---

* The twin brothers both married young ladies by the name of Mary.
† This reference is based on the erroneous idea that. France was the original homeland of the Lamonts.

The children—some infants just standing alone,
And others to manhood and womanhood grown;
And surveying all with a loving pride—
The good Grandmother. Save two that died:
These were her only jewels. She had prayed
That in the better land there might be made
For all of hers, a grand reunion. She little thought,
That to her on earth would come, unsought,
So bright and holy a vision as this,
So blessed a foretaste of heavenly bliss.
The guests arose; each went his way,
Some saddened in heart, and others gay:
But this fearful thought stung each soul with pain—
Not all of these friends will meet again.

*Mr. Ruland's little son, Arthur, aged six years, recited the lines
below.*

SALUTATION

There was a young lady lived up on a hill,
And, if nothing had happened, she'd be living there still.
A young man, named Tommie, would a-wooing her go,
And coaxed the young lady from her mamma, you know.
Of course, they got married, and of children they bore
Seven girls and six boys, no less and no more.
Now the girls are big women and the boys are big men.
And by all getting married the number doubled again;
So that husbands and wives make two bakers' dozens,
And their children, we little folks, number twenty-six cousins.
Uncle George and Aunt Bec having bidden us here
With the warmest of smiles and the greatest good cheer,
Rejoicing we've come to the welcome call.
Long live Auntie Bec, Uncle George, and all!

The second Thomas William Lamont on an ocean voyage in 1931

7

COMMENTS

by Thomas William Lamont

One of the Lamonts present at this family reunion was my own father, who in 1876 was a small boy of six. Many years later, in 1943, he arranged for the reprinting of the Reunion brochure which his father had prepared. My father wrote the following special Foreword for the new edition.—Ed.

I have had reprinted in its original form for my children and my few remaining Lamont cousins a brief informal account of the Lamont family in America as prepared and read by my father, Thomas Lamont, at a reunion of the family of my grandfather, Thomas William Lamont (after whom I was named), in late November 1876. The family gathering was held in the large and pleasant home of our Uncle George in Bound Brook, N. J. Of the six brothers (my father had five brothers and seven sisters) George had always been the outstanding financial success.

I dimly recall this reunion of 1876. I was just turned six years of age. My two chief recollections are first of the entire family assembled in the large drawing room or parlor of the Bound Brook house at the time my father read aloud the historical sketch of the family. My other recollection is of a big bedroom with any number of mattresses on the floor, made up into beds, and the whole room turned into a dormitory for us boy cousins, of whom there must have been about fourteen. Our grandmother Lamont at that time, having been born in 1811, was sixty-five years old—a very vigorous, intelligent person, always dressed in black silk so heavy and stiff it could have stood erect by itself, keeping a watchful eye upon her many children and grandchildren, and full of friendly

85

anecdote. I recall too how, at the end of the reunion, a good many of the family, including my father and elder brother Hammond, journeyed to Philadelphia to view the great Centenial Exposition (a World Fair we should call it now). To my intense disappointment I was considered too young to go, and I recall even now the bitterness with which I reflected upon the inevitably faulty judgment which parents exhibit!

It will be noted that in this account of the beginnings of the Lamont Clan my father accepted his family's traditional, though mistaken, belief that their ancestors originally came from France. Later, however, in his *Brief Account of the Life of Thomas William Lamont and His Mamily,* published in 1915, my father corrected that error and pointed out that from the records that had become available to him since 1876 it was clear that the original home of all the Lamonts was in Argyllshire, Scotland. In fact, the Clan Lamont Society of Edinburgh published in 1938 a complete and voluminous History of the Lamont Clan from 1235-1935 (Seven Centuries of Clan History from Record Evidence) by Hector McKechnie, a well-known advocate of Scotland and historian of note, who had taken five or six years to compile this volume. It was dedicated to myself and to the late Harry A. Black, one of our distant kinsmen, because between us we had provided the funds for the compilation and publication.

Mr. McKechnie's Chapter I tells the story of our origin: "The Lamonts were always a namely people, descended from the Lamon mor of tradition, the Sir Laumon of history, the benefactor of Paisley Abbey." "They were," says Mr. McKechnie, "lords of all Cowal in the days when it was virgin forest" (Cowal being in general the region covering the lower part of Argyllshire with Loch Fyne on one side and the Kyles of Bute and Firth of Clyde on the other). But McKechnie adds rather sadly that "never after the Wars of Independence did they bulk so large as the MacDonalds, the Campbells, or the Mackenzies, who all straddled several counties, had many branches, and were definite political forces."

Mr. McKechnie speaks of the "hereditary feud with the Campbells" which oppressed the Lamont Clan for so many generations. And in my father's larger volume of which I have spoken, he mentions the siege which the Campbells carried against the Lamonts, cooped up in their Castles Toward and Ascog in Argyllshire; of how the Campbells on a promise of safe conduct persuaded the Lamonts to surrender; and then, when they and their wives and

children marched out from their two strongholds, how the Campbells fell upon them and after a brief interval cruelly hanged
"thirty-six Lamont gentlemen" on one ash tree.

The way McKechnie describes it is this: "What happened is
generally known. In short, the Lamonts were treacherously seized
and bound; a similar capitulation was obtained at Ascog; both
castles were reived and burnt; the estates were scoured and
scorched; a number of women and children were murdered in cold
blood; thirty-six prominent clansmen were hanged in Dunoon, and
many others were dirked just after; the chief, and his brothers
and some of the cadets were carried to Inveraray, where they were
robbed, imprisoned, and threatened, and young Ascog and Aucha-
goyl judicially murdered; and finally their whole lands and pos-
sessions were taken over by the Campbells, except such as had
already been attached by the creditors."

All this is known as part of the Dunoon Massacre. When I took
my family to Scotland in the summer of 1937 and rented Sir Iain
Colquhoun's estate, Rossdhu, on the west shore of Loch Lomond
with a beautiful prospect of Ben Lomond across the water, I
motored over to Dunoon to see the shaft erected there long generations ago as a memorial to those who were killed at the Massacre
of Dunoon. And there, lettered on the tall shaft, were many Lamont names, including those of Archibald, John, and Robert, men
who must have been the nearby progenitors of the very three
brothers bearing these identical given names who emigrated to
America about 1750 and started the Lamont family on its way in
the New World.

Well, we need go back no further. Following the family reunion
at Bound Brook in 1876, there was another somewhat less numerous one held in the family seat at Charlotteville, Schoharie
Co., N. Y., in the summer of 1879. From that date on no formal
attempt was ever made to get all the family together, although
for years up till the time of Grandmother Lamont's death many
of her children and grandchildren visited her at Charlotteville
every summer. The David La Montes, who lived in Albany, made
a practice of spending a good part of the summer there and not
infrequently my own father and my Uncle George went up together.

The last visit I ever paid to Charlotteville was about ten or
fifteen years ago when, with my sister Lucy Gavit and her husband,
I motored over from Rensselaerville and spent a day with them
in the Charlotte Valley: a brief visit in the morning to Ferguson-

ville where my mother had attended school under the tutelage of her uncles, the Reverends Samuel D. and Sanford I. Ferguson; and then eight miles up the valley to Charlotteville where we had a picnic lunch and spent the rest of the day visiting the Lamont graves, with the tall marble shaft marking the grave of my own grandfather, Thomas William Lamont. The village had changed very little. There was Uncle Simeon Lape's general store with the big house opposite in which he and our Aunt Lucy lived and died. The by-ways and the whole village were filled with ghosts. Lamonts had come, had seen, and had conquered, and then had all gone, leaving only memories behind them.

PART III

Thomas William Lamont and Florence Corliss Lamont

Corliss Lamont

8

A MEMOIR OF MY FATHER AND MOTHER

by Corliss Lamont

In his book, *My Boyhood in a Parsonage* (Harper's, 1946), my father, Thomas W. Lamont (1870–1948), gave a delightful account of his early youth as the son of a Methodist minister and of his years at Phillips Exeter Academy and Harvard College. In a substantial posthumous work, *Across World Frontiers* (Harcourt, Brace, 1951), Father told of his first job as a reporter on the New York *Tribune* after he graduated from Harvard in 1892, and then went on to describe his work as a banker, especially in J. P. Morgan & Co. The greater part of this volume, however, he devoted to his experiences abroad on various financial and economic missions in Europe and the Far East.

Father had intended to write a more complete and detailed history of his far-flung adventures in international affairs. But his serious heart ailment starting in 1943 and his death in 1948 prevented him from transposing into consecutive, readable form the enormous amount of material in his files and the vivid memories in his mind. It would have been most interesting, for instance, to learn from him at firsthand more about his trips to Mexico—in 1919 and in 1921—to carry on negotiations with the Mexican Government for the adjustment of its debt to foreign investors. If I remember correctly, *Life,* then a humorous magazine, ran a drawing of Father entitled "Mr. Fix-It" in reference to this Mexican Mission.

My mother, Florence Corliss Lamont (1872–1952), wrote wonderful letters throughout her life to her children and friends; but her only written work that appeared in book form was a delectable diary, originally penned with no thought of publication, that gave a day-to-day account of her trip to Japan and China with Father in 1920. In that year he went to the Far East on behalf of the International Consortium for the Assistance of China, a bankers' organization, to try to work out equitable financial arrangements with the Chinese Government. Mother's little book, *Far Eastern Diary,* which I edited, was privately issued in 1951. If she had had the time and inclination, she too could have written a fascinating autobiography.

I can state without qualification that Father and Mother were the two most enterprising world travelers in the history of the Lamonts. Their trips to Europe became more frequent after the United States entered the First World War in 1917. Father went to England and France in November of that year as an unofficial adviser to President Woodrow Wilson's U. S. Government Mission headed by Colonel E. M. House. During this period Father had important conferences with, and came to know, Lord Reading, later British Ambassador to Washington; Montagu Norman, Governor of the Bank of England; John Buchan, later Lord Tweedsmuir and Governor General of Canada; Prime Minister Lloyd George of England; Premier Clemenceau of France; and General Pershing, Commander of the American Expeditionary Force.

When Father talked with General Pershing at the town of Chaumont in northeastern France, there was present an old friend, General Charles G. Dawes (later a Republican Vice President of the United States), who was Pershing's top aide in charge of the procurement of supplies in Europe for the U. S. Army. At the end of the conversation General Dawes turned to Father and said: "Tom, I want you to stay over here and become the active scouting officer for the procurement division. You know all the people over here. You are a business man. You can save millions of dollars for the Government. We need you."

Father answered that he would accept such a position without hesitation if he did not think his work in the United States would help the Allied cause more. He added that anyway his old friend Jeremiah Smith, Jr., a classmate at Exeter and Harvard, could do the procurement job better than he because Smith had had legal training. Generals Dawes and Pershing immediately accepted this advice and forthwith sent a cable to Jerry Smith commissioning him captain and asking him to come to France as soon as possible. He promptly accepted this assignment. Jerry Smith, who later accompanied Father to both Mexico and Japan as his legal adviser, was not only a brilliant attorney but also had a charming personality and a wry sense of humor that made him one of the most delightful people in the world. Father called him "the most entertaining man, I think, that I ever met."

During his 1917 trip abroad, Father worked with his old friend from Phillips Exeter days, Colonel William B. Thompson, head of the American Red Cross Mission in Russia, in an effort to bring about better relations between the new Soviet government and the Allies. At a luncheon with Lloyd George in London, Thompson and Father convinced him that limited cooperation with Lenin's regime could help keep the Soviets in the war against Germany. Returning to New York on Christmas Day, 1917, Thompson and Father within a few days went to Washington to persuade President Wilson to join Lloyd George in the cooperation plan. But Wilson refused even to see them and continued his hostile policy toward the Soviet Republic.

The result was that in April, 1918, Wilson ordered an American expeditionary force to Soviet Russia. This force joined the armies of Britain, France, and Japan in a far-flung campaign to overthrow the Communist regime. Commenting on this invasion in *Across World Frontiers,* my father wrote: "Of all the essays that sober statesmen have ever been guilty of, that of attempting in the spring of 1918 to overturn the Soviet Government (which by that time had control over vast millions of Russians and of the regions they occupied) was, as we look back, the maddest."

In January 1919 Father and Mother sailed for France, where Father was to serve for five months as a representative of the United States Treasury at the Paris Peace Conference. Until the end of June, when the Treaty of Versailles was signed, he worked hard over the economic problems facing the Conference, especially those concerned with the controversial subject of German reparations. At the same time Father and Mother extended their acquaintance among figures prominent in international affairs, becoming friends, among others, with Lord Robert Cecil, one of England's most stalwart defenders of the League of Nations; Philip Kerr, Lloyd George's secretary and later Lord Lothian; and General (later Marshal) Jan Christiaan Smuts, Premier of the Union of South Africa.

Father came into close contact with most of the leading diplomats at the Paris Peace Conference. He saw a great deal of President Wilson and became a strong believer in the League of Nations.

In the 1920 elections, when the Democratic candidate for President was Governor James M. Cox of Ohio and the Republican candidate Senator Warren G. Harding of the same State, Father broke away from the G. O. P. ticket for the first and only time in his life, casting his ballot for Governor Cox and his Vice-Presidential running mate, Franklin D. Roosevelt.

In a public statement explaining his position, Father declared: "My chief reason is, of course, that Cox is for the League of Nations and Harding is against it. The League is admittedly not perfect. But it is the most practicable instrument yet offered for the prevention of future wars. . . . There is a call upon America to render high service to the world and to herself. To this call Harding answers No, let us turn back. Cox answers Yes, let us go forward. That is why I vote for Cox."

Till the end of their lives Father and Mother remained faithful to the central League principles of international cooperation and of united action by the peace-loving countries against aggressor governments—usually known as the concept of collective security. They actively supported the League of Nations Association and the Foreign Policy Association. When the League went out of existence and the United Nations replaced it after the Second World War, Father and Mother wholeheartedly backed the U. N. and the American Association for the United Nations. They also were interested in Clarence Streit's Federal Union, the aim of which was to unite the democratic nations in an inclusive political federation. No causes were ever dearer to my parents' hearts than those of international peace, worldwide disarmament, and understanding between the peoples of the earth.

During the First World War, in 1916, when John Masefield, later Poet Laureate of England, came to the United States to lecture about his country in wartime and to arouse sympathy for the Allies, Father and Mother became acquainted with him. That acquaintance quickly grew into a strong and lasting friendship with Masefield and his wife, Constance. In 1918 Masefield dedicated his book *The War and the Future* to my father. Until my parents died (my father in 1948, my mother in 1952), the Masefields remained the closest of their foreign friends. Whenever Father and Mother visited England, which was at least every other year, they saw the Masefields and often stayed with them. The Masefields also joined them on several trips abroad. Meanwhile, a voluminous correspondence developed between the two couples, and sometimes I was privileged to read letters from Mr. or Mrs. Masefield.*

My parents, with their special affection for England and its people, added to their circle of English friends Professor Gilbert Murray, eminent Greek scholar and supporter of the League of Nations, and his wife, Lady Mary; Julian Huxley, noted biologist (later knighted), and his wife, Juliette; novelists St. John Ervine, John Galsworthy, Charles Morgan, Henry W. Nevinson, H. G. Wells, and Francis Brett Young; dramatists John Drinkwater and Robert Nichols; and poet Walter de la Mare.

Father and Mother made these enduring friendships not only because they were charming and considerate hosts, but also because, as my late brother Austin put it, "They were intelligently and enthusiastically interested in ideas and their expression. Hence they naturally were attracted, and attractive, to people who had ideas and who were expressing their ideas, whether it was Cecil and the League, or Wells and his novels, or Masefield and his poetry." My parents entered with animation into the life of the mind, both giving and receiving constant intellectual stimulus. And in their four children—Thomas S. (1899–1967), Austin (1905–1969), Eleanor A. (1910-1961),† and myself—they kindled a zest for knowledge and a liking for the best in literature, music, and the arts. Often after supper on a Sunday evening the entire family gathered around for poetry reading, each of us reading aloud a poem of his own choosing. To this day I can almost hear my father reading in a tone of suspense his two favorite Kipling poems, "Gunga Din" and "Danny Deever." ("O they're hangin' Danny Deever in the mornin'!")

When the friends from foreign lands whom I have mentioned visited America, they would very likely appear at my parents' dinner table or stay at their New York residence. Their first house in New York, at 49 East 65 Street, my father and mother rented in 1915 for several years from Franklin D. Roosevelt when he was Assistant Secretary of the Navy in the Wilson Ad-

---

* After my mother's death in 1952, more than 2,000 letters from John Masefield to her and Father were presented by their children to Harvard's Houghton Library, which houses special collections. These letters have the release date of January 1, 1978, for scholars and writers. This Masefield Collection also includes a number of Masefield's published books inscribed to Mother, as well as some of his original manuscripts and a portrait by Charles Hopkinson.

For further details concerning the relationship between the Lamont and Masefield families, see *Remembering John Masefield* by Corliss Lamont, Fairleigh Dickinson University Press, 1971.

† The late Mrs. Charles C. Cunningham.

Austin Lamont

ministration. Roosevelt's mother, Sara Delano Roosevelt, lived next door. I used to browse in F. D. R.'s big library on the second floor of his house. Then in 1921 my parents moved into a spacious house of their own which they had built at 107 East 70 Street.*

This beautiful residence gradually became a sort of International Inn, with George Metcalfe, the incomparable Lamont butler, watching carefully over the welfare and comfort of every guest. Metcalfe was born in England, fought in the Boer War, and emigrated to the United States while still a young man. In the employ of my parents for more than thirty years, from 1914 till his death in 1944, he became their chief household aide and a true friend to everyone in the family. Hard-working, exemplary in all his duties, Metcalfe was one of the most considerate and understanding persons I have ever known, always ready at any time to sacrifice convenience and leisure to perform some service for a member of the family or a visitor. Over six feet tall, he was blessed with a robust physique and, just as important, a fine sense of humor.

While we were growing up, we young people were frequently given the opportunity to listen to and participate in conversations and arguments on public affairs and international questions of every kind. These discussions built up into an informal education of inestimable value. I recall quite clearly, for example, dinner-table conversations with the John Masefields, with H. G. Wells, and with General Smuts in the solarium on the fourth floor of our New York home. Father and Mother ate most of their meals in this small dining room, often with sunlight streaming through the windows. Both Mr. and Mrs. Masefield were most interesting conversationalists, roaming over the whole history of literature and art in stimulating fashion. "H. G.," with his squeaky little voice, was a convinced socialist and undoubtedly the most radical of my parents' foreign friends; and he would argue with them good-naturedly on the subject of differing economic systems. Occasionally my young sister Eleanor crashed a big party at 107 East 70th by dressing as a waitress and serving throughout the entire meal.

In a letter to my mother in 1942 General Smuts said: "There is no doubt that your house is an international meeting place, and an influence for good, for international understanding and con-

---

* This house has become, according to the terms of Mother's will, the headquarters of the Visiting Nurse Service of New York.

ciliation, second to none in the wide world."* Smuts had a vigorous military bearing and gave the impression of great alertness and precision, both physically and mentally. His far-ranging abilities covered not only the art of government and the field of international relations, but also the sciences and philosophy. My mother and I used to have deep-delving philosophical talks with him. In 1936 my parents went by boat all the way to South Africa to visit General Smuts, and he took them high up on the veldt on a memorable camping trip through the Kruger National Park.†

In the winter of 1928 Father and Mother traveled to Egypt, saw the Sphinx and the pyramids, visited several of the famous royal tombs and sailed up the Nile. With my parents on this Egyptian tour were the John Masefields and their daughter, Judith, and John L. Tildsley, Associate Superintendent of Schools in New York City, and his wife, Bertha, Mother's beloved classmate in Smith '93. When Father and Mother made trips to distant countries, they were more than likely to persuade a small group of congenial friends to go along with them.

Thus, in the spring of 1931 when they went to Greece, they had in their lively party the Walter Lippmanns and Gilbert Murray, and at Athens, Mr. and Mrs. Masefield joined the company. Professor Murray proved the best possible interpreter for bringing into focus the ways of ancient Greece as revealed in the unsurpassed relics and ruins on every hand. During that trip Mother wrote her children one of her superb descriptive letters. It was one which my brother Tommy and I both relied upon in our respective visits to Greece more than twenty-five years later. Here is what Mother said in that typical letter:

Nauplia, 1931

My dears,
It cannot be described. It is too utterly lovely. Eye hath not seen, neither hath it entered into the heart of man to conceive, the beauty of Greece. I am in a sort of daze of ecstasy most of the time.

Well, to begin with, Father has written you about our landing.‡ Too terrible. "The friend of King Constantine" and the Governor etc. etc. all came to meet us, and had arranged a

---

* General Smuts's letters to my parents are preserved in the Smuts Archive at Capetown in the Republic of South Africa. Complete photostat copies of them are to be found in the Houghton Library of Harvard University.

† Cf. p. 120.

‡ The landing was from the Italian liner *Saturnia* at the port of Patras on the Western coast of Greece.

A.TAVOLA.NON.S'INVECCHIA

The Thomas W. Lamonts and guests on board the S.S. Saturnia, *en route to Greece, 1931. First on left, Henry James, son of the philosopher William James; fourth on left, Professor Gilbert Murray; fifth on left, Mrs. Lamont; at head of table, Captain Stuparich of the* Saturnia; *fifth on right, Mrs. Faye Lippmann; fourth on right, Mr. Lamont; second on right, Walter Lippmann.*

special tender to take us ashore. Metcalfe did not know this, so half our luggage (42 pieces for all!) was on the common tender and half on the special, and Metcalfe and Josephine almost in tears, and all the other passengers glaring at us with hate as we made our quick getaway. When we landed, Father said in a lordly way, "Let us go on to the hotel," and the poor Lippmanns obediently followed only to find at 11:30 P.M. that two trunks and two bags were missing. I am sure Father has written you of his heroic and frantic efforts to rescue these things from a tender in the middle of the Gulf of Patras at 1 in the morning. It really was awfully educational for Father, but was hard at the time.

The trip to Olympia was great and glorious. I got a tremendous kick out of it. I have never thrilled so over sculpture in my life.

The Greek landscape cannot be described. It is surpassingly lovely. The light is unlike any in the world; a sort of unearthly radiance shines over everything. The mountains and the sea are everywhere, always, the sea an intense blue, the mountains snow crowned.

I think that Delphi is without doubt the most beautiful place in the world, up and up on the side of Parnassus. It would be very easy for me to believe in gods and nymphs living there. The automobile ride to Delphi takes about ten hours, very fatiguing as the roads are like those shelled by the Germans in the war. You go from one deep hole to another, and why the cars stand up under it, beats me. Parnassus dominates the landscape for hours: we got nearer and nearer to this glorious snow-capped peak and finally climbed up its side to Delphi, with the blue sea at our feet and range after range of blue mountains glowing in the beautiful light. It has been wonderful having Gilbert Murray with us. He has made Greece live for us in a remarkable way.

When we are in Athens, we try to go to the Acropolis twice a day, once in the morning sunshine, and again at sunset. It is one of the great places in the world.

I am writing this letter from Nauplia where we are spending two nights in order to see the Peloponnesos (Corinth, Mycenae, Tirynthus, etc.), all the Argive plain. It has been a wonderful trip down here. Mycenae thrilled me to the bone. To see the great, though ruined, palace of Agamemnon, and to see the line of mountains that Clytemnestra knew by heart and probably saw as she hurled the dagger at Agamemnon, all this is very exciting. We almost always have a picnic luncheon because the hotels are most of them so bad. We sit in the sun and read poems about Greece after luncheon. Walter Lippmann gave me a little book called "The Englishman in Greece" containing all the good poetry ever written in English about Greece.

Well goodbye my dears. I think of you all a lot and pray for all good things for you. I hope everything is going well and that the babies are well.

Dearest love to you,

from Mother

In a letter from Athens dated April 17, 1931, Father gave *his* version of the historic debarking at Patras. It was, he wrote, "like an Anthony Hope novel, or a light opera—better than the one that Kit Morley wrote and produced. The Governor of the Province, the Captain of the Port in full gold braid, a representative of the Greek Cabinet, the American Consul and Vice Consul—all came dashing out to the steamer in a special tender, lined themselves up in formal array in the saloon and tendered us the welcome of Greece. They insisted upon sabotaging all the steamer's landing arrangements—despite our earnest entreaties—and in landing us and our 36 pieces of luggage before anything could happen. It was a struggle between the Governor and Metcalfe as to who should carry your mother's bottle bag and hat box. . . . The Governor marched us up the quay to the hotel, where they gave us a very decent and entirely informal dinner. They proposed one toast to us—calling themselves the descendants of the ancient Aegeans.

"After dinner it was discovered that two trunks were missing. Metcalfe was invisible. So I sneaked away from the Government officials and had myself rowed out in the midnight darkness to a lighter out in Patras Harbor. It was loaded with a thousand trunks and loose bed springs, which acted as traps to catch you as you searched with matches through the swaying trunks. But I located the missing ones and got back undiscovered."

On several occasions Father and Mother took the whole family to Europe. I remember as far back as 1908 when we had a cottage during the summer at Seaford on the English Channel. Our English landlord was fond of referring to the Lamont boys as "them three imps." When Father and Mother went traveling on the Continent, they left us in charge of Grandfather and Grandmother Lamont.

In the summer of 1913 my parents took a cottage, the Villa Roche Blanche, at Paris Plage on France's Channel coast. We enjoyed the splendid swimming, and all went well until one day when I rose suddenly from a wave and bumped accidentally against our tutor, Mr. Strickland, knocking out two of his front teeth with my head. On this same European trip we drove through the lovely hill towns of northern Italy, and while in Florence had a leisurely tea with Bernard Berenson at his Villa I Tatti just outside the city. Then we spent two weeks in the Alps, at Mürren and Chamonix. We hiked up the mountain trails and took exciting walks out onto the face of mighty glaciers such as the Mer de Glace, where we were able to look down into the very depths of the crevasses.

The good friends whom Father and Mother had in Europe, especially England, were always most kind and hospitable to the Lamont children and helped to pave our way when we traveled abroad on our own. After I graduated from Harvard in 1924 I went to study at New College, Oxford, and my parents made arrangements for me to live at the home of the Julian Huxleys on Holywell Street. During term time I often rode my bicycle up Boar's Hill from the city to have tea or supper with the Gilbert Murrays or John Masefields. Sometimes after supper on a Sunday evening Masefield read from his poetry. I recall, too, driving out to John Buchan's for a meal, going for Sunday lunch to Lord and Lady Astor's at Cliveden, and spending a weekend with H. G. Wells. For all these most stimulating contacts I had Father and Mother to thank.

My parents roamed far and wide not only in the world at large, but also in America itself. In 1914 they took the family to the Flying D Ranch (altitude, over 5,000 feet) near Salesville (now Gallatin Gateway), Montana. Our cabins were only a stone's throw from the swiftly flowing Gallatin River. All summer long we rode horseback, fished, climbed, and went on pack trips. I used to go trout fishing with my father, both of us wearing high hip boots, in the nearby streams. The views of the jagged Spanish Peaks from the ranch were superb.

In the summer of 1915 we all went out to Oregon and stayed at White Pelican Lodge on the edge of Klamath Lake, named after the nearby Indian tribe and at the base of the Cascade Mountains. There we did most of our trout fishing by trolling from boats on the lake. The flat meadows along Lake Klamath were marvelous for riding, and we usually galloped our horses over them in high glee. Both in 1914 and 1915 there came with us to the West a most congenial family, Dr. and Mrs. John H. Huddleston and their three children, Margaret, Carrol, and Jean. With a physician along, we were well prepared for any serious accident or illness, but nothing of the sort came our way.

These two summers in the heart of the West gave the Lamont children a lasting appreciation of outdoor life, of America's rugged mountain scenery, and of our splendid National Parks. At the end of the 1914 trip Father and Mother took us through Yellowstone National Park, with its unusual geysers, hot springs, and brightly pigmented canyon, and through Glacier National Park in northern Montana. In 1915 we not only visited the unique Crater Lake National Park, which was not far from our Lodge in Oregon, but also went north into the Canadian Rockies and took a week's camping trip on horseback from our base at glorious Lake Louise. From Canada we traveled to San Francisco, the most beautiful and dramatic harbor in North America, to attend the World's Fair of 1915 (Panama-Pacific Exposition).

Father and Mother consistently chose most beautiful places to live in or travel through. For a permanent summer home they experimented with Easthampton, Long Island, where the sand beaches and surf bathing were unsurpassed, and then tried Northeast Harbor and Islesboro on the Maine coast. Finding the social life in both of those Maine resorts too formal and demanding, they finally settled down on the island of North Haven in the middle of Penobscot Bay. After renting houses for two or three seasons, my parents finally bought some property on the north shore of the island and in 1920 built there a large, sprawling, informal dwelling that merged several small houses into one.

Their place, called Sky Farm, was only a short distance from incomparable Pulpit Harbor, the entrance to which is marked by a rocky pile topped by a fish hawk's nest. Father and Mother provided comfortable cottages in the same vicinity for each of their children. The big house on Sky Farm, now occupied by my sister-in-law, Mrs. Thomas S. Lamont, stands on a bluff more than 100 feet high and looks across West Penobscot Bay, with its islands, to the Camden Hills. The views and sunsets from Sky Farm are a joy to behold. Its main flower garden, tumbling down a hillside toward the sea, has been celebrated by Evelyn Ames in a poem that is dedicated to my mother:

MAINE GARDEN

There is something almost magic about these flowers:
Their size, their perfectness; the way, in fog,
The colors ring and rock and clash together
Outraging every garden catalogue.
Calendars they ignore; whatever hours
Feel like summer, they use (knowing how weather
Observes the seasons) and since between cold and cold
Are not too many days of outright sun,
Dahlias lift autumn heads beside Sweet Peas,
And Bleeding Heart, which ought to have begun
Bleeding in May, has clearly not been told
To stop by August. To these inclemencies
Add the few inches that there are of loam
Between this shelf of granite and the sky—
A flower's a miracle on such a coast,

And yet—no more than any who defy
The rock and fog we're born to and who bloom—
The more superbly for hardship being their host.

For more than fifty years the Lamonts have made their summer
headquarters at North Haven, with its active, informal life of
boating, sailing, tennis, golf, and berrying. Father and Mother
did not themselves do much sailing, but preferred to explore
Penobscot Bay and its innumerable islands in their motor yachts,
of which I remember with most pleasure the *Reynard,* given by
Father to the United States Government at the outbreak of World
War II, and its successor, the *Little Reynard.* These fine craft
were skippered respectively by Captains Christensen and Hansen,
both Norwegians.

Not infrequently we went off for a whole day in one of these
boats, sometimes on a deep-sea fishing expedition, but more often
landing on some lovely island with a far view of hills and sea.
We would swim, explore, and take our ease while enjoying the
beauty all around us. Occasionally after lunch we would climb a
high hill, as at Isle au Haut, now part of Acadia National Park.
A favorite trip was to Seal Island, a bare and rocky outthrust at
the edge of the ocean, where it was thrilling to watch the foaming
waves rush unrestrained upon the reefs and dissolve in tumultuous
spray. There, too, it was fun to stand by Squeaker Guzzle, where
the sea gushes up into a deep and narrow cleft to make a weird,
whistling sound.

The Lamonts became especially enthusiastic over Hurricane
Sound and its cluster of pink-white granite islands. For picnics,
big Hurricane Island* was always a wonderful place, with its fine
sea views, its walks through woods and alder bushes, and its abandoned granite quarries to roam and clamber over. The Vinalhaven
poet, Harold Vinal, has immortalized this island in the verses of
his Maine Coast chronicle, *Hurricane,* describing it in the early
years of this century when it had a prosperous granite industry
and a good-sized village. When we first landed on Hurricane Island
in the late 'teens, many wooden frame houses and two churches of
the deserted village remained standing.

Half a mile from Hurricane is the outermost White Island,
which has high granite cliffs on the west and south, a thick ever-

* In 1965 Hurricane Island became one of the main headquarters for Outward
Bound, a national organization that trains youth to be self-reliant and physically
rugged.

green covering intersected by a path or two, and dramatic views on every side. The Lamonts fell in love with this fascinating little island, and finally Father bought it. Actually, Lamont ownership has made little difference, since everyone is in any case welcome to its shores for picnicking, camping, swimming, or climbing over the huge boulders.

Father and Mother had another beautiful home, high up on the edge of the Palisades, at Sneden's Landing, New York, just north of the New York-New Jersey State line. They moved there in 1929 from Englewood, New Jersey, where all of us children had been born and brought up, as was our mother before us. Englewood was an attractive suburban town sprawling out along the broad slope down from the top of the Palisades. It was a congenial place to live in because it had a real country atmosphere, with woods and cliffs nearby for walking and riding, and because we all had many good friends in the town. I have happy memories of Englewood.

My family's place at Palisades was named Torrey Cliff and had breathtaking vistas north to Hook Mountain on the west bank of the Hudson River. Our property extended some distance into the woods, where pine-needled trails took you across an exquisite brook, with leaping cascades, to the sheer 400-foot wall of the Palisades. From high lookouts at the summit, there were magnificent panoramas of the river and the countryside beyond. On a clear day you could see all the way to Long Island Sound. For some twenty years my parents gave their children and grandchildren marvelous weekends of rest and recreation at Torrey Cliff.

Toward the end of her life Mother gave all the buildings at the Palisades estate, and much of the woodland, to Columbia University to serve as a headquarters for its new Geological Observatory. When she officially handed over this property in 1950, Dwight D. Eisenhower, who was President of Columbia at the time, came down to the 70th Street house in New York for a brief ceremony of acceptance. After my mother had presented to him the deeds of ownership, he made a few appropriate remarks. The Lamont Geological Observatory,* under the leadership of its Director, Professor Maurice Ewing, an able geologist, built up a nationwide, and indeed a worldwide, reputation.

In her will, Mother set aside about twenty-three acres of woodland and cliff from the Palisades estate and left this section to

* In 1969 renamed the Lamont-Doherty Geological Observatory.

Florence C. Lamont hands over the deeds to her Palisades estate in 1950 to Dwight D. Eisenhower, then President of Columbia University.

my brother Austin and me, stating that the property should be preserved permanently in a wild and natural state. Approximately twelve miles from the George Washington Bridge and bordering the Palisades Interstate Park, the Lamont Sanctuary offers hikers and nature lovers a fascinating network of trails, constant glimpses of birds and wild life, and rare beauties of forest and cliff. Columbia University is now the official custodian of the Sanctuary.

In this essay I have stressed Father's and Mother's international contacts and interests. At the same time they had a host of devoted American friends from almost every walk of life, many of whom we children came to know and appreciate. I think especially of Chester Aldrich, the architect, and his sister, Amey; John Corbin, the author, and his wife, Amy; Eleanor Robson Belmont (Mrs.

August Belmont), well-known as an actress and as the guiding spirit behind the Metropolitan Opera, and Mrs. Helen Rogers Reid, former President and Board Chairman of the *New York Herald Tribune*; Robert Frost and Walter Lippmann; Judge and Mrs. Learned Hand; Mr. and Mrs. Pierre Jay; Arthur Lockett, another of Father's classmates at Exeter and Harvard, and his wife, Olie; Dwight W. Morrow, a Morgan partner with Father, and his wife, Betty; Dr. Alvin Johnson, President of the New School for Social Research; President and Mrs. William Allan Neilson of Smith College; Mr. and Mrs. Lewis Perry, he the Principal of Phillips Exeter Academy for more than thirty years; and three persons I mentioned earlier: Mr. and Mrs. Tildsley, and Jeremiah Smith, Jr.

On one occasion my father and Mrs. Morrow, both excellent dancers, proposed that the two families give a dance together. My mother and Mr. Morrow were rather unenthusiastic over this idea. But Father and Mrs. Morrow decided to go ahead anyway, and sent out the following invitation:

Mrs. Dwight Morrow
and
Mr. Thomas Lamont

Request the honor of your company
At a dance given in honor of

Mrs. Thomas Lamont
and
Mr. Dwight Morrow

The party proved to be a great success.

In the business world Father was, of course, particularly close to his partners in J. P. Morgan & Co. Besides Mr. Morrow, to whom I have just referred, these were Henry P. Davison,* Russell Leffingwell, George Whitney, Arthur M. Anderson, Thomas Cochran, and J. P. Morgan himself. Other bankers whose friendship my father greatly valued were Norman H. Davis, financier-at-large; William C. Potter, Chairman of the Board of the Guaranty Trust Company; Seward Prosser, President of the Bankers Trust Company; and Myron C. Taylor, Chairman of the U. S. Steel Corporation.

---

*In 1933 Harper's published Father's biography of Mr. Davison, entitled *Henry P. Davison: The Record of a Useful Life.*

The Huddlestons, the Morrows, and the Tildsleys all had children of an age with the Lamont progeny, and this happy circumstance made for much extra pleasure and merriment when the Lamonts foregathered with one of these other families. The Huddlestons, as I have said, we got to know intimately during our two summers in the West. The Morrows we saw a great deal the whole year round, especially because they lived near us in Englewood and had a summer place at North Haven. Ever a delight were the four Morrow children: Elisabeth, later Mrs. Aubrey N. Morgan, who died at the age of thirty; Anne, later Mrs. Charles A. Lindbergh; Constance, the second Mrs. Aubrey Morgan; and Dwight W. Morrow, Jr., who became a teacher.

The Tildsleys had a vacation cottage in Maine, first at Buck Harbor and then on Little Deer Isle. Both places were within two hours by motor boat from the Lamonts at North Haven. Every summer "the Tildsley picnic," when the two families met on some enchanting island in Penobscot Bay, was a high point of the season. Often, after we had finished the delicious Tildsley fish chowder, the sandwiches, and the hard-boiled eggs, the family elders read favorite poems aloud to the group.

After one of the first Tildsley picnics, in the vicinity of Eggemoggin, the Lamont motor yacht, *The North Wind,* ran onto a reef in a thick fog that, almost before we knew it, had blown in from the southeast. Some of us were playing bridge in the dining saloon when the crash occurred. The captain put the engines into reverse, but the boat was stuck fast and did not budge. So we lowered the auxiliary motor launch and made our way through the fog to take refuge with the Tildsleys at Buck Harbor. During all this excitement my brother Austin continued calmly to read one of Masefield's novels of adventure. The next day a tug came over from Rockland on the mainland and pulled *The North Wind* off the rocks at high tide. The yacht was only slightly damaged.

In these reminiscences I do not want to overlook the important role that some of our relatives played in our family circle. Very close to my father was his brilliant elder brother, Hammond, a teacher of English at Harvard and Brown Universities who later became Managing Editor of the *New York Evening Post* and then Editor of *The Nation*. Uncle Hammond's house was just a step from us on Beech Road in Englewood, and his liberal views on public affairs had a significant influence on my father. He died in 1909 at forty-five, at the height of his career, after an operation from which he never recovered consciousness. It was a prime example of the tragedy of premature death.

Father's elder sister, Lucy, married John Palmer Gavit, another liberal and a most capable newspaper man who became Chief of the Washington Bureau of the Associated Press and Managing Editor of the *New York Evening Post* several years after Uncle Hammond left that position. He also wrote *Americans by Choice,* a book about immigrants to the U. S. A., *College,* and *Opium.* Aunt Lucy and Uncle Jack combined a great interest in the sciences with an unwavering belief in Spiritualism, stimulated to a considerable extent by the early death, at twenty-one, of their promising son Joe.

Aunt Lucy herself purported to be a medium of sorts and thought that she was in regular communication with the spirits of the dead. For my twenty-first birthday she presented me with a poem supposedly dictated to her by Joe from "the other side." It was called "A Man Thou Art Today." On another occasion she claimed she was talking with the late J. Pierpont Morgan (the elder) and that he gave her an important message for my father. The message was: "Tom, you are doing a fine job." Father was not impressed and Mother was scornful. Despite these goings-on, there is no doubt that the Gavits, with their broad knowledge in science, journalism, and international affairs, contributed much to the education of the Lamonts.

On my mother's side of the family were her elder brother, Charles, a successful business man, and his wife, Anne Parrish, a well-known American novelist and author of *The Perennial Bachelor, Golden Wedding* and other delightful books of penetrating satire. One of her finest achievements was *A Clouded Star,* a historical novel about the escape of Negro slaves from the South to Canada through the underground railway. Aunt Anne had a keen and sensitive mind.

Uncle Charles was the only complete conservative among our close relatives. In 1898 he and my father had founded the wholesale firm of Lamont, Corliss & Co. My uncle became head of the business five years later when Father left to become associated with the Bankers Trust Company. Lamont, Corliss & Co. were distributors for such well-known products as Nestlé's Chocolate, Peter's Chocolate, Pond's Vanishing Cream, and O'Sullivan's Rubber Heels. In the early thirties, the Soviet Government suggested that Lamont, Corliss & Co. take over the entire concession for Russian caviar in the United States. But my Uncle Charles, a man of unswerving anti-Communist principles, turned down this lucrative offer. He later explained to me that he would have nothing to do with "a gang of robbers."

Of my four grandparents, the one who was nearest to us was Mother's mother, Mrs. Wilbur F. Corliss ("Mimi")—affectionate, lively, gossipy, and at times amusingly caustic. She and Grandpa Corliss lived in Englewood, and we were constantly visiting back and forth. Mimi died in 1939 at the grand old age of ninety-six. She spent her last years at Atlantic City, where we went to see her occasionally.

The Gavits, the Charles Corlisses, and my grandparents, together with other relatives and guests, came frequently to the big Lamont gatherings at Thanksgiving, Christmas, New Year's, and Easter. Those parties were always enormous fun for everyone who attended. At the great Christmas banquet there were always at least three generations present, and the young people as well as the grown-ups displayed their histrionic talents between courses, reciting poems and singing songs. When we had finished dinner, we would go into the drawing room where we often separated into two groups for acting charades.

Here is a letter that Miss Amey Aldrich wrote my mother after our Christmas celebration in 1948: "I really cannot tell you what it was to me to have last evening with you all. That table full of laughing children, the sweet young voices, the genuine love and friendliness made it something to remember always with a glow of joy. . . .

"I was much impressed by the delightful ease and eagerness with which each child liked to play its part, and the spontaneous courtesy, down even to the littlest ones, that didn't let me feel an outsider for an instant.

"Bless you, beloved Grandma of so united and happy a family, for letting me share in that real feast of Christmas love. I went to bed feeling so happy to live in a world full of light and warmth and love."

At one of Mother's last Christmas dinners, I toasted her with these words: "There are many Generalissimos, but only *one* Generalissima." She was not displeased.

From the time he entered J. P. Morgan & Co. in 1911, Father, except during the First World War, habitually took two or three months' vacation every year. In my opinion this was a major reason for his unfailing good health (until he was seventy-two), for his unceasing good humor, and for his calm and reasonable approach to whatever problems confronted him. I almost never saw him angry or over-excited; and one of his mottoes, stemming originally from his golf game, was "Easy does it." To me he always seemed the most amiable of men. And I well understand what Jerry Smith meant when he said that Father's 1920 mission to Japan was successful because "he simply outsmiled the Japanese."

As a banker, Father was preeminently successful and moved continuously in the mainstream of American life. His chief side interests were journalism and education. He bought the *New York Evening Post* in 1918 and owned it for several years, and helped to launch *The Saturday Review of Literature* on its independent and successful career. Father was President of the Phillips Exeter Board of Trustees for more than a decade, served as a Harvard Overseer for many years, and was a Trustee of the Carnegie Foundation for the Advancement of Teaching and of the American School of Classical Studies in Athens. At Union College he established a Lamont Professorship in memory of his father, at Brown a Lamont Professorship in honor of his brother Hammond, at Harvard another Professorship in honor of Hammond, and also a University Professorship in Political Economy.

In addition, Father's generosity was responsible for the Lamont Infirmary at Phillips Exeter and helped to make possible this school's Lamont Art Gallery, founded as a memorial to Thomas W. Lamont II, his oldest grandchild and namesake. His gifts were the predominant factor in the building of Harvard's Lamont Library, designed especially for the use of undergraduates. Father was also a Trustee of the Metropolitan Museum of Art from 1935 until his death. The beautifully remodeled south wing of the Museum is dedicated to him and bears his name.

My mother's interests were likewise far-ranging, and frequently of a liberal nature. When she was only twenty-one she made a first-rate address, as Ivy Orator for the Smith Class of 1893, about the need for greater democracy in the College and the nation. She supported not only several organizations concentrating on international affairs, as I noted earlier, but also birth control, civil liberties, the American Association for Labor Legislation, Russian War Relief, the Women's Trade Union League of New York, poetry societies, and various educational institutions. Through a bequest in her will, Mother enabled the Academy of American Poets to institute the annual Lamont Poetry Award.

She also bequeathed large sums to seven outstanding women's colleges in the United States: Barnard, Bryn Mawr, Mount Holyoke, Radcliffe, Smith, Vassar, and Wellesley.

Mother had a genuine flair for philosophy and took an M.A. in that subject at Columbia University in 1898. Her Master's essay was entitled "A Criticism of Browning's Dramas, from the Aristotelian Point of View: A Study in the Philosophy of Literature." In obtaining her M.A., Mother worked under Professor F. J. E. Woodbridge of Columbia, a brilliant teacher and one of America's leading naturalist (or Humanist) philosophers of the twentieth century. She and Father soon became friends with the whole Woodbridge family. Mother had originally intended to go on with her philosophy work at Columbia and to get a Ph.D. degree, but she dropped this plan in order to give more attention to her young children.

Nonetheless, she maintained an active interest in philosophy. She became a Trustee of *The Journal of Philosophy,* contributed handsomely to Columbia's acquisition of the greatest Spinoza collection in the world, and often attended lectures on philosophy at Columbia and other institutions. Her acquaintance among professional philosophers was wide, and she numbered among her close friends not only Professor Woodbridge, but also Professors William Ernest Hocking of Harvard and William Pepperell Montague of Barnard.

Mother's lifelong concern with philosophy was, of course, a significant factor in influencing me to pursue studies in the same fascinating field and to take a Ph.D. at Columbia. I likewise had the privilege of doing my research work under the direction of Professor Woodbridge. In 1951 I dedicated my book, *Humanism as a Philosophy,* "To My Mother, Discerning Companion in Philosophy."

Until the end of her life, Mother continued to disagree with me in philosophy, retaining her allegiance to a liberalized and modernized Christian faith. But over the years we repeatedly discussed in a friendly spirit the basic philosophic problems, and these conversations were both stimulating and helpful to me. In fact, the Lamont family circle early became a lively open forum where we debated freely and frankly most of the main issues in philosophy, religion, economics, politics, and international affairs. Father and Mother, innately affable and tolerant, took pleasure over the years in listening to the offbeat ideas of their children. One of my books

I inscribed to my father in this way: "To T. W. L., Father, creator of us all, and, like God, sometimes astonished at the results." My parents' enlightening educational influence extended eventually to their grandchildren. Here, for example, is a 1939 entry in the diary of my nephew Tommy, then fifteen years old: "Had lunch with Grandma Lamont. We had good political conversation."

A lengthy volume, at least, would be required to render an adequate account of the lives of my parents—of all their travels, achievements, friends, interests, recreations, gifts, and activities in their chosen fields of concentration. Both of them left a vast accumulation of letters and diaries. A second stout volume, then, would be needed to publish the best from my parents' letters and records.*

In this brief sketch I have obviously not tried to fill in for the autobiographies that Father and Mother might have written; nor have I attempted to develop all the manifold memories of them that have come to mind. For example, I have said very little about their long and happy years in Englewood where they lived for more than three decades and enjoyed the companionship of a most genial and attractive group of neighbors. It was there they belonged, with the Morrows and others, to a Shakespeare Club that devoted an evening once a month to the reading of a Shakespeare play, with each member present rendering an assigned part. Again, I have not mentioned my parents' many vacation trips to southern climes such as Bermuda and Nassau, Florida and the Carolinas; or Father's all-male fishing sprees to Canada's Gaspé Peninsula on the Gulf of St. Lawrence.

Father and Mother were, by nature, friendly and sympathetic. To their many friends and acquaintances they ever brought warmth, gaiety and an enthusiasm for the things of the intellect. And they were public-spirited in the best sense of that phrase. I do not mean to imply that they were models of perfection or that there was never any friction in our household. Naturally, they had their shortcomings and inconsistencies. But in the large their lives built up into an outstanding achievement that affected all who came in contact with them, and extended far beyond.

As one of their sons, I can say that their children were truly blessed in possessing such affectionate, considerate, and intelligent

---

* Most of my father's correspondence and records are in the Baker Library of the Harvard Business School. (See page 196.) My mother's letters to her children are in the Florence C. Lamont Collection of the Sophia Smith Collection, a special section of the Smith College Library.

parents. All four of us settled down with our own families along the Eastern seaboard and visited back and forth with Father and Mother as long as they lived. It was always a joy to be with them and to have their companionship. Looking back now at sixty-nine on my past, if I could choose one day to live over again, it would be a day in the country, in Maine or at Palisades, with my parents and others of our immediate family.

I shall close this memoir by quoting the lines that John Masefield wrote about Father and Mother in 1954. They are inscribed on a tablet within the Great Cloister of Canterbury Cathedral, which my parents' generosity helped to restore after its bombing by the German Air Force in the Second World War. The full inscription follows:

In the Memory of Two Friends of all great Causes

THOMAS WILLIAM LAMONT

&

His Wife

FLORENCE CORLISS LAMONT

O Passer-by, remember these two Friends,
Who loved this Church of Christ, and greatly gave
To build anew the wreck the bombings drave.

All lovely giving is a Heavenly seed
Dropped to the chosen heart as glittering corn,
That everlasting gladness may be born,
Bread never spent, Beauty that never ends.

Though darkness dim and dying take away,
The gladnesses of given kindness stay.
O Passer-by, think gently of these Friends;
The Light within them made God's Kingdom speed.

9

BUSINESS AND PLEASURE IN TRIPS ABROAD

*by Thomas W. Lamont**

Every year with one exception, from 1920 to 1940, I made visits to Europe, and while many of them were designed for recreation, they frequently turned out to be filled with more serious affairs, especially during the early years of the 1920's, when the firm of which I was a member was endeavoring to do so much in the way of European economic reconstruction, with the approval of our own Department of State. During those years I was very active on both sides of the water in the series of stabilization loans made by American bankers and investors successively to Britain, Belgium, France, Austria, Germany, Italy. On those many trips I came in contact with most of the leading statesmen of Europe, prime ministers and presidents alike. In France, Clemenceau, Poincaré and Briand, all now dead, were statesmen of a high order. As for the other leaders of France not so much could be said.

More than once in the course of my visits to Italy I talked at considerable length with Mussolini, the first of these conversations being in May, 1923, after his illusive conquest of Abyssinia. He was always cordial, he was not always at ease. In the early years he wanted to rely upon America as his chief foreign financial connection. He was not eager for intimate contacts with either France or Britain. Both of these I urged. The French banking world, I told him, and as many of them had assured me, was keen for collaboration. "Well, perhaps," said Mussolini, "but France is like a very rich old lady who looks down upon her poor relatives living on the peninsula!" But he said it with a smile. As for Britain, I urged strongly that he should ask the Governor of the Bank of

---

* From the Fiftieth Anniversary Report (1942) of the Harvard Class of 1892.

Italy to visit London and make friends with Montagu Norman, the Bank of England's Governor. "Stringher is too old," said Mussolini, "name some one else." I suggested one Beneduce. "But he is not a Fascist," I added. "That makes no difference," said Mussolini, "he shall go!" And he went and the connection was established.

At my last visit, in 1937, just before King George's coronation, Mussolini showed little patience with the British who had tried to invoke feeble and wishy-washy sanctions against the prosecution of his Ethiopian campaign. "The English will never understand me," the Duce declared impatiently. "Perhaps, Excellency," I said, "you too fail to understand the English." He took no offense. "Perhaps," he nodded. "I want to have Americans know I am a man of peace," said the Duce, starting on another line. "Abyssinia is finished. Now we must have peace. I shall give my efforts over to stabilising my economy." "Admirable!" I rejoined, "we Americans shall be glad to know that, for we all feel that you are a man of war. We are frankly uneasy about you, Duce." He seemed to try to put on a puzzled look, as if my remark were inexplicable to him.

Going back again in years and to the other side of the globe, I cannot but recall my trip to China and Japan in the Winter and Spring of 1920 as a thrilling experience. I was asked by the Department of State and by the British and French Foreign Offices to visit the Far East and see if I could compose certain important differences that had arisen in connection with the composition of the Chinese Consortium of Bankers for the Assistance of China. This group had been first formed under President Taft in 1909, had lain dormant under the first Wilson Administration, and then had been set going again in 1918, just after the Armistice. On the trip to the Far East I again took with me as counsel our friend and classmate, Jeremiah Smith, Jr. My chief Japanese point of contact was Junoske Inouye, Governor of the Bank of Japan, highly enlightened, a generous and straightforward Japanese, years afterwards assassinated by the gangsters who began to work themselves into the government. I was also in constant consultation with the American Ambassador, Roland S. Morris, of Philadelphia. Our party were lavishly entertained by Japanese bankers and by the heads of the great Mitsui and Mitsubishi houses. Many noblemen came to call and extended private hospitality both in town and in the country, private theatrical entertainments were given for us and especial performances of the celebrated Noh dancers. We also traveled about the country a good bit, spent a few especially lovely days at Kyoto and visited other points of great interest in Japan. These, mind you, were the days of so-called Liberal governments in Japan, prior to the era of the ilk that wanted to make themselves masters of all East Asia.

From Japan we journeyed west by the Inland Sea, then by steamer south to Shanghai. The idea of the Chinese Consortium had been for political purposes badly distorted and the Chinese public had been led to believe that it was designed for the financial enslavement of the Chinese rather than for their help. One mid-afternoon in Shanghai I was told that a group of a couple of hundred of the Chinese student body were waiting in front of my hotel in order to show their disapproval of the Consortium by stoning me. I sent out word suggesting that the leaders come in for a cup of tea, and talk it all over. A dozen of them turned up at first in rather an ugly mood. But the tea was soothing and as soon as I was able to explain the facts about the Consortium, that it was designed to free China from the worst of her financial difficulties and help put some of her state enterprises on their feet, they readily understood, and agreed to co-operate. They kept their pledge. When I reached Peking, I found that word had gone along the underground and that my reception by the student groups was cordial and helpful. I mention this because at that time, the student body was a political force to be reckoned with. In fact its youthful leaders have many of them since become the leaders of the new China of today.

While I was at Shanghai Dr. Sun Yat Sen, the father of the Chinese Republic, sent me word that he would greatly like to talk with me but that he was reluctant to call at my hotel, as many of his friends had done, "for fear of being bombed," because his enemies were very active. Whereupon, although my wife did not seem particularly happy about the plan, I said I would go out to see him—he lived in the suburbs of the swarming city.

I spent a morning with Dr. Sun, but we were both disappointed. I asked him, as President Wilson had suggested I should, what, if anything, America could do to help heal the breach—almost war at times—between North and South China. Dr. Sun had a ready answer. "Lend me $25,000,000," he said, "and I'll equip a couple of army corps and march on Peking. We'll have peace in China, all right!"—or whatever the Chinese vernacular for such an assurance is.

While in Peking, the President of the Republic, Hsu-Shih-

Ch'ang, a delightful old mandarin, was kind enough to give a luncheon for me. Just then there was a good deal of talk of Bolshevism gaining a foothold in China. So I inquired from President Hsu what he thought about this. His answer, given quite simply, was: "Oh, no. China tried that in the eighth and again in the eleventh centuries, and it didn't work. We won't try it again."

Again in 1927 I visited the Far East, and Jeremiah Smith, Jr., '92 was once more my companion. I went out at the invitation of the Japanese Government authorities and business men to check the financial and economic conditions following Japan's recovery from the terrible earthquake and fire which, in the autumn of 1923, had brought death to hundreds of thousands of Japanese and destruction to the cities and countryside. A few months following that disaster I had been active in helping to arrange an international loan of $150,000,000 and $25,000,000 to the Japanese Government for purposes of reconstruction and restoration of normal life on the islands. It was for this reason that my party received an overwhelming welcome. On my arrival the school children had been lined up on the streets to shout "Banzi, Lamontosan," (Welcome Mr. Lamont!); I had a long audience with the Emperor; further trips to many historic spots in Japan, while at the numerous banquets arranged in our honor, scores of geisha girls were produced for the sedate approval of Jerry Smith and myself. Alas! the tragedy that the intelligent and liberal element of Japan has in the last ten years been so completely overwhelmed, and that now that country has crowned its infamy by making war against our own country!

In the Autumn of 1921, at the invitation of the Mexican Government, I visited Mexico to discuss with the Finance Minister, Adolfo de la Huerta, some plan of resuming interest payments on the Government's foreign debt. Our faithful Jerry Smith, '92, was again my counselor. I spoke in behalf of the International Committee of Bankers on Mexico, made up of representatives of the United States, Great Britain, France, Germany, Holland, Belgium, and Switzerland, in which countries the bonds had been originally issued. We had about a fortnight of negotiation which at the time seemed futile, but after later discussions in New York, we reached an agreement under which 30 or 40 million dollars have been distributed to the long-suffering bondholders in the countries mentioned.

My departure from Mexico City for home had been set in

advance for a certain date and train. But I finished my conversations earlier than expected and without making my plans public, I arranged to have my car attached to the train two days before my schedule. We went through all right, though I noticed that they kept a couple of guards, *rurales,* armed with rifles on our rear platform. When, however, two days later we reached San Antonio, Texas, we were told that the train on which I had been publicly scheduled to leave had been wrecked out on the desert by bandits who, captured later, declared their intent to kidnap me and hold me for 500,000 gold pesos ransom. "They never could have gotten away with it," said the genial San Antonio newspaper, "trying to conceal the Lamont party would have been like trying to hide Charlie Chaplin in a custard pie!"

In 1921 political conditions in Mexico were far from stabilized. The sweeping revolutions that began in 1911 with the fall of President Porfirio Diaz and his departure for France, had lost some of their force, but from my contacts with President Obregon, I could readily feel that of all the heads that ever wore a crown his was one of the uneasiest. On the first occasion that he received us his desk and chair had been placed in the very middle of a huge room with a resounding hardwood floor for the purpose, as he pleasantly explained to us, of enabling him to hear anyone who was approaching him from any quarter. (He was assassinated a few years later.) The moment we had seated ourselves, the President clapped his hands for an attendant, and shouted: "Bring whisky, wine, liqueurs," and added with a beaming smile to me: "At last, Mr. Lamont, you see you are in a free country," knowing that in the United States we were struggling in the throes of prohibition.

My friendship with General Jan Christiaan Smuts—scholar, soldier, Prime Minister of the Union of South Africa, started at the Peace Conference in 1919. Casual correspondence with him grew into a real friendship when in 1926 he and Philip Kerr (later Lord Lothian) came to stop with us in New York while he was giving some lectures on the League of Nations. He made a deep impression on us all and began to urge my wife and me to come out to South Africa to visit him and his family. In June, 1933, at the Economic Conference in London, for which he had flown up at the request of the British Prime Minister, we saw him again, and once more he begged us to make the trip. So in June, 1936, after a fortnight spent in England, we embarked at Southampton on one of the big Castle liners for the lovely, slow, seventeen-day trip to Cape Town with a day's stop-off at the Island of Madeira.

We stayed for a few nights with General Smuts and his family in their corrugated-iron farmhouse near Pretoria, away up in the Transvaal, and then went on a camping trip with the General and guides into the heart of the Kruger National Preserve, a region as big as all New England. Motoring slowly on sandy trails through the forest and open tawny-grass country, we came across all the wild animals of Noah's Ark, wandering about in search of game or taking their noonday siestas. The nights around the roaring camp-fire were perhaps the best part of it all, the General telling us tales of his adventures in the Boer War, of his visits to England, following the War, to try to establish loyal dominion status for a new unit of the British Commonwealth, to be styled (as now) the Union of South Africa; of his great World War campaign in 1916 in driving the Germans from East Africa; the guides regaling us with vivid tales of elephant hunts and other wild game adventures.

I chartered a big Junker airplane to take my party and the General and his family up to the magnificent Victoria Falls of the Zambesi. When I was first considering chartering the plane, I asked the Anglo-American Corporation to make a separate check on the efficiency of the service, etc. So their manager called up the chief engineer of African Airways and said: "Now, about the safety of all this—you are absolutely sure of your—of your landing places and everything else? Because, you know, you have a rather precious cargo, General Smuts, and Mr. Lamont and his party." "Safe? Safe?" exclaimed the rather irate engineer, "do you suppose we'd risk a £20,000 plane if it wasn't perfectly safe?"

Finally, there is neither space nor time to describe journeys that were after all more of a personal, family nature than official and for the record. But even so, perhaps I might mention my audience with King Alfonso of Spain in 1926, when he begged me to give to the French Minister of Finance, then struggling under a falling franc, his assurances that if he were to establish a "state lottery," all his financial troubles would be over! Two years later in Cairo, just before a long trip up the Nile, I had at his request an audience with King Fuad. He was the only man that I ever met that could speak as bad French as I could and still make himself intelligible. He was rather amusing. He began by saying to me, "Mr. Lamont, I will wager I am the only head of a foreign state who has ever received you without asking for a loan for his government." And he was just about right! Then he told me some of his ambitions for Egypt. He was anxious to establish an all-rail route from Marseilles in France around the Mediterranean, down through Asia Minor and the Near East to Alexandria. Three years later, 1931, found me in Athens where I renewed friendship with the Prime Minister Venizelos, that real Greek statesman, whose acquaintance I had formed at the Peace Conference in Paris in 1919. He and his English wife gave us a dinner. "Do you like Athens?" she asked. Whereupon I rhapsodized upon the glory that was Greece. "Ah, but you should see our new waterworks!" she said.

Shall the day ever come when we shall again be visiting these wonderful spots of beauty and delight across the Atlantic and Pacific Oceans? My answer is unhesitatingly—Yes!

A group present at the formal dedication of Columbia University's Lamont Geological Observatory on May 28, 1951, at Palisades, New York. Standing at the entrance to the former Lamont house are, left to right: Austin Lamont, Corliss Lamont, Mrs. Charles C. Cunningham, Dr. Grayson Kirk, then acting head of Columbia and later President, Mrs. Thomas W. Lamont, Thomas S. Lamont, Professor W. Maurice Ewing, Director of the Observatory, and Professor Walter H. Bucher of Columbia's Department of Geology.
Courtesy Manny Warman

10

A MEMOIR OF PALISADES
by Margaret Lamont Heap*

The bowl of dried rose petals stood on one of the tables near the backgammon table in the living room of the big house at Palisades. After luncheon a sunbeam, slanting through the window, struck directly on these rose petals, making them warm and vaguely scented. I remember standing there, sifting the petals through my fingers, watching my aunts and uncles and older cousins wander about the room while the coffee was brought out from the pantry. I remember wondering why on earth anyone would want dried rose petals in their living room, rose petals with no resemblance to their lovely originals in the gardens, rose petals now so dust-filled that I used to cough a little as I sifted them. And yet it was pleasant to stand there in the sun, waiting to be offered a tiny cup of coffee.

One night I stood by the rose petals looking at a bracelet in my hand. It was a beautiful bracelet, green stones set in twos, glamorous, and yet very much me. It was Christmas night, 1947, and Grandpa [Lamont] was lying upstairs under his oxygen tent, having been taken suddenly ill during dinner. He had given me the bracelet, and in a moment I was told he wanted to see me. Up in the plain bedroom Grandpa smiled gently at me through the plastic oxygen tent, and I showed him the bracelet on my wrist. He said, "I wish it could have been real emeralds, Margot, but I hope this will please you as the first step. It looks lovely on you." It was the last time I ever saw him, because shortly afterward he went down to Boca Grande, Florida, where he died, most unwillingly.

Christmas at Palisades was a beautiful, wonderful holiday for

---

* Mrs. J. David Heap, the eldest daughter of Corliss Lamont.

all of the children in the family. Grandma and Grandpa had sixteen grandchildren. Often the Christmas gathering saw one or
another of the families not represented, but nevertheless there
always seemed to be a crowd. We Corliss Lamonts arrived Christmas afternoon from our apartment on Riverside Drive. Our Baltimore cousins would have had their presents and stockings at the
Palisades house that morning, and we had a fine time examining
their treasures. At supper these same cousins ate the butterballs
whole, popping them one by one into their mouths. To see this
was a unique and marvelous Christmas experience.

Santa Claus arrived before suppertime. We all gathered in the
front hall dressed in our very best party clothes. Metcalfe stood
attentively at the front door as we heard the sound of approaching
sleigh bells. Santa Claus knocked and Metcalfe threw open the
door (a magnificent door to throw open, incidentally, because it
had a top half and a bottom half). The cold air and jolly St. Nick
rushed into the hall; we children were thrilled to pieces, all-knowing
about Christmas spirits as we might be. Each child had a present
out of Santa's bag, and, as he or she went up to get it, Santa
requested a poem or a song. Needless to say, we had rehearsed
for this moment, and though it was undoubtedly our elders who
really felt sentimental over the sight and sound of their little ones
performing, I look back on this particular part of Christmas with
sentiment too. I enjoyed the songs and the glamour of the sparkling
scene, and meanwhile I munched on "forbidden fruit," candies
from the cornucopias which hung from the tree.

As I approach the moment when I shall tell or not tell our little
son about Santa Claus, I want to make a full confession to all
the members of my family who hoodwinked us so well all those
years. I was hoodwinked until the very end. I never knew who
was playing Santa, or where the costume was stored, or why the
bells sounded as though they were on a sleigh pulled by reindeer;
and I never rushed to the window at the end to see Santa disappear
into the kitchen quarters. He always climbed back into the sleigh,
spoke softly to all those well-mannered, patient reindeer, and
simply took off in the sky. There are Santas in present-day exurbia
who ride around in red convertibles, tossing out presents to the
starry-eyed children on their block. If Santa Claus is a mythical
figure, more in our imaginations than anywhere else, he should stay
there, and not go traipsing around in a convertible, risking his
life on icy roads.

Early supper for the smaller children was every bit as festive and exciting as one could wish for. The food was so delicious that we used to look forward to that alone. The prospect of pureed spinach, which we were never given at home, decorated with lemon and hard-boiled egg, was enough to send any six-year-old into a trance. Late dinner for the grown-ups and older children was, of course, even more wonderful. For one thing, it was a milestone in a child's life when he or she finally achieved a place at the Christmas dinner. I was admittedly a bit too excitable over such matters, but at my first late dinner, I lasted, picking unhappily at my food, until the pudding was brought in *flaming*. At this point, to my mother's consternation, I arose from my seat with all haste and rushed from the room feeling very strange in the tummy. I crept into the bed next to my sister's, willing to forgo all the glitter and sophistication of the grown-up dinner for the safe, secure nursery world again.

After that inauspicious beginning, however, there were many more happy late dinners, with two turkeys being passed around, tiny table presents sitting in the Santa's sleigh centerpiece, and the poems and toasts coming between the second course and dessert (flaming). I got up one year and recited, "O Captain, My Captain," but much more stirring was the time Aunt Ellie* with a son in the Pacific and her husband in England, sang with her children, "Coming in on a Wing and a Prayer." Uncle Tommy was still giving us "Just before Christmas." The toasts followed the recitations, and more Christmas gifts followed the toasts, and by this time the scene had shifted back to that bowl of rose petals. I remember late one night when finally I had reluctantly gone to bed, I was out of bed again almost immediately, buttonholing Aunt Nancy† on the landing to complain that Florence was breathing and therefore I couldn't get to sleep. Aunt Nancy wisely pointed out that there wasn't much she could do about persuading Florence to stop breathing, and she advised me to turn her over. I was rather incensed that I had not been reinvited to join the party, and with lagging steps I climbed again to the third floor to face that beautiful blonde sister who was breathing. Christmas was over once again.

Other holidays had their unique qualities too. Thanksgiving had great meaning for all of us because of the solemnity of the

---

* Mrs. Thomas S. Lamont.
† Mrs. Nancy Lamont.

occasion brought about by the real prayers of thanksgiving. At Easter there was perhaps a slight element of forcing a custom because of the Easter-egg hunt. This was fine for the little ones, but some of us, as we got older, felt a bit ridiculous racing around filling our baskets with jelly beans found in plain sight under a rose bush. The Easter-egg hunt was conducted in the Walled Garden in the middle of which was the pool with goldfish and the false bottom. This was put in after Lansing,* as a wee toddler, had the audacity to scare everyone to death by falling in. (Now of course many communities require fences around pools by law.) A statue of Tommy† as a child stood in the Walled Garden pool.

Before Easter dinner we joined Grandma and Grandpa at their church in Englewood where Easter service seemed awe-inspiring and I was swept into rapturous singing by "Jesus Christ Has Risen Today." We wore new Easter outfits and felt chilly in the often wintry wind. If we had spent the night at Palisades, we usually found that various beautiful, stuffed animals had joined us under the canopies during the night.

There were many other more sporting events, however, than hunting Easter eggs. One of these was chasing Uncle Tommy from one end of the grounds to the other, as he cock-a-doodle-dooed in the underbrush; we were never able to see him, never able to catch him. Another was playing croquet with Uncle Coco (my father) on a day when he might throw his mallet away, if he missed an easy shot, and then hearing Grandma tax him on a hasty temper as the mallet fell to the ground, shattered. Or going for a walk through the woods, past the Lookout point off which young Tommy fell and broke his arm, past the playhouse where we often acted out Hansel and Gretel, and on through the forest. Or getting up at six in the morning to watch the cows come in to be milked, and then arriving back at the house in a nonchalant manner to face the nurse or mother whose only thought in life seemed to be that activity on an empty stomach was one of the naughtiest things ever dreamed up. "You must be feeling faint," was the cry. Or wonderful snow-filled winter days of sleigh-riding down the hill at the side of the house. And the fairy stage of dancing through the gardens, when my twelve-year-old friends and I would wind flowers in our hair and trip about the lawns, imitating the ballet stars of the moment.

---

* Lansing Lamont.
† Thomas W. Lamont II.

Storms came up very suddenly at Palisades, and the frantic line of baby carriages, nurses, and toddlers hurtling down the hill from the sandbox looked as though it were propelled by one of the lightning bolts. Once inside the house, we put on plays or charades, played Hide the Thimble, read in the library, or looked at the views of statues and scenes in Europe through the stereoscope. It was during rainy-day lulls that I read *The Little Lame Prince,* and then devoured whole all the Elsie Dinsmore books. The buckets of my tears, brought on by the trials and tribulations of the brave Elsie, which fell on the chaise longue in the Pink Room, did not fall in vain. I finally came to the startled realization that I was reading pure sentimental drivel. Tea was served in true English fashion, that is, cookies, cakes, bread and butter, and soon it was time to wend my way upstairs for a bath in either a rose, blue, or lavender tub with a rose, blue, or lavender soap ball, impossible to hold, impossible to equal for scent and luxury.

One of us might put a toilet out of order, resulting in vast quantities of water flowing out all over, and requiring the administrations of John. Or one of us, probably I, might have a cold, requiring a tray in front of the fire. I can see myself, basked cozily by the flames, waiting for my supper in my bedroom. A gentle knock would come at the door, followed by Metcalfe or Mary with the tray. This would be laid on a special table, and I would look down on a lovely array of china, the hot dish covered by a round, hat-shaped bowl with a hole in the center. Happily I would down coddled egg, pureed spinach, hot cocoa, and apple-sauce. It was the nearest thing to being a princess in a fairy tale. *The Blue Fairy Book* and *The Red Fairy Book,* which I found in the bedroom bookcase, told me all I needed to know about such a life. When I was bedded down later, the menacing shadows began to appear, and if I summoned up the courage to look under the bed, I might fall asleep reassured that only I inhabited the room. But often I lacked the courage, and in the high canopied bed I lay perfectly still, moving only my eyes, on the theory that the intruder would do me no harm if I appeared asleep. It is a fact that once when I was sleeping in Tommy's room up on the third floor, the door opened very slowly with all the proper accompanying creaks, and forever after I hated that room, and refused to sleep in it. Tommy adored it with a passion and kept his museum there for years, and wrote nostalgically about it long afterward.

It is strange that in the Palisades environment of security and warmth, an element of fear existed on the odd occasion. A couple of cousins agree with me in this matter, though I have no doubt that my imagination ran rampant, given such a setting. After reading *Wuthering Heights,* for instance, I really did think Cathy was trying to get in my window one night. There is a possible explanation, however, for the slight menacing atmosphere which hung over us children at Palisades. From the time of the Lindbergh kidnapping, Grandma and Grandpa had taken a few precautions, one of which was a man, armed, sitting on the second-floor landing. I can remember this inside guard, but I don't recall the guard who watched us as we played outside. I suppose the usual children's games of cops-and-robbers and bogeymen got taken more seriously by some of us than by others, when coupled with real guards around.

This was only a tiny drop in the bucket, however, and soon our daughter will be playing contentedly with the dollhouse I had as a child at Palisades. It sat serenely at one end of Grandma's morning room. No shadows hovered around this house. It was always sunny and warm in those tiny rooms, and behind me in the chaise longue Grandma read Blake's "Little Lamb, Who Made Thee?" to a cluster of rosy-cheeked children. The tinkle of a special music box filled the room with tentative music, and the romantic pictures of Grandma through the years smiled down on us. Grandma usually had her breakfast in bed and we children trooped in afterward.

On good days the nursery set cavorted up at the babies' sandbox, and we could swing right up into the sky, over our sisters and brothers, higher than any tree, almost out over the vegetable garden. Here a "mysterious" band of children once threw rotten tomatoes at Hayes,* who was not amused. Beyond, past the weeping willow tree, the tennis court and swimming pool and extra rooms for overflow guests stood virtually unused during the last years of Grandpa's life. The swimming pool was enclosed and unheated, and was a white elephant. We were in it enough to allow Tommy to get stabbed in the foot with some sort of door prop, and to play with the longest matches I ever remember, and occasionally to swim in the cold water. The woods stretched just outside, and here we built lean-tos of pine branches and made dams in the brook; we observed the birds, the shy deer, and the chatty chipmunks. It was also possible to work up a healthy respect for snakes.

---

* Hayes Corliss Lamont, brother of Margaret Lamont Heap.

Copperheads were found on infrequent occasions, and once I was running along a path and noticed a great big black snake running alongside me. I was not amused.

In the evenings, back in the living room, when the younger children were in bed, we waited for supper to be announced. We sat in front of a crackling fire, the red damask curtains drawn across the night-filled windows, with cocktails or tomato juice, and bacon-and-peanut-butter hors-d'oeuvres. At supper, perhaps consisting of creamed lobster and salad, the dressing for which was made on the spot by an aunt using a most complicated collection of bottles, the conversation usually became most animated. While Metcalfe was mixing the dressing into the salad, I was suddenly aware that Grandpa had just asked me what I was studying in history. I answered that I wasn't having history at my school, but social studies instead, whereupon the great debate was on. "Do you really think progressive education is educating your daughter?" Down the table Lansing was passing up ice cream and chocolate sauce, to my amazement, and the Chinese wallpaper of birds, bird cages, and delicate fields was weaving its spell of outer space, otherworldliness, escapism. I used to hear the arguments wax eloquent over the merits of Willkie and Roosevelt, but I was often drifting off into the wallpaper, imagining all sorts of lovely things.

Several times during the war I rode the Fifth Avenue bus up to 168th Street and Broadway to the bus depot. Here I caught a bus which crossed the George Washington Bridge and went up Route 9W, to the Sneden's Landing road. I was often the youngest person on the bus to be traveling alone, and though it was no high adventure to step down from the bus into the chauffeur-driven car sent down to meet me by Grandma, it intrigues me all the same that I should have felt drawn to go out to Palisades by myself. One evening while I was having supper alone with Grandma and Grandpa, I inquired why so many other places were set at the table. Grandma answered that she liked the table to look symmetrical, and three at an oval table simply wasn't symmetrical. At that same supper, later on, she was moaning slightly to Grandpa over her lost figure, but she said she thought she could still be proud of her ankles. He said he thought she could. Perhaps this is why I went out to Palisades those times during the war: I had Grandma and Grandpa to myself!

In spite of the shadows, the bedroom to which I was assigned seemed beautiful and luxurious, the bathtub curiously like velvet, the closet vast and aching for clothes. When I arrived I carefully hung my coat on a huge hanger and draped my hat on a hat peg, and then dashed down to supper. Upon my return I found my bag unpacked, my pajamas laid out on the bed, each separate garment in a separate drawer, and like all silly young things, I regretted that my clothes were so plain and some of them in need of mending. Luxurious as such surroundings might be for a young girl, or for anyone, Grandma had some good ideas which I have remembered. I think it is a splendid idea to have one's bedroom furnished with a comfortable reading chair or couch, and a good reading lamp. In this way, one can retire from the hurly-burly associated with a living room. My bedroom at Palisades was certainly a retiring place for me and gave me a chance to read for long, undisturbed hours. In the morning I had a lovely breakfast, just for me, served at the oval table in the dining room. As I ate the crisp bacon and buttered the newly-baked corn muffin, I gazed out the window to the Hudson River, misty in the distance.

Once in a while I ask little Jonathan and Andrea,* "Who will take care of me when I am sick?" And as we all laugh a little hysterically at the thought of Andrea staggering upstairs with a coddled egg on a tray, I am greatly refreshed to think of all those butterballs, Santa Clauses, copperheads, Elsie Dinsmores, symmetrical tables, scented soap balls, creaking doors, voices, voices, voices, and dusty rose petals, misty in the distance, at Palisades.

---

* Mrs. Heap's children.

11

A RESOLUTION ON THOMAS W. LAMONT

Adopted by The Phillips Exeter Academy Board of Trustees
(May 29, 1948)

Thomas William Lamont was what we like to think this school means.

He came here from a country parsonage, with resources slender in material things but strong in high purpose. He sought eagerly what this school had to offer. His mind toughened with the rugged teaching and the uncompromising insistence on excellence, and quickened with the stimulus of being made to think for himself. In the freedom of this school he learned self-reliance, and in its equality of opportunity he learned leadership.

He knew here all sorts and conditions of boys. Some of them widened his horizons; some of them became friends for whom he had a deep and warm and life-long friendship; from all of them he distilled an abiding understanding of the human mind and the human heart.

From this school he went forth, out and on and up until he walked in the high places of the earth. He became the first private citizen of his country, private only in the sense that his service to the public had its wellsprings, not in official position, but in his own unhesitating assumption that public problems should be the private concern of all of us. And so he made public problems his own, facing them firmly, investigating them in the clear light of his reason, dealing with them calmly and patiently, and pressing through to the solution called for by informed intelligence.

Few lives have been as broad in sweep or rich in content as his. The alert, searching quality of his mind, awakened we like to think in this school, led him not only into prominence in his

131

own calling, but into an enlightened and enlightening interest in journalism, poetry, government, literary criticism, economics, the arts, education, indeed all the facets of human activity which shone back at him the light of his own interest in them.

Few men have achieved what he achieved and been the kind of man that he was. The warmth of his personality, nurtured we like to think by the varied friendships he first formed in this school, could be measured by the light in the eyes of those who knew him.

He walked in the high places of the earth, but never did he forget this school. Indeed, we like to think that here was one of his deepest loyalties. He was generous to the Academy with a princely generosity; he presided over this Board of Trustees with felicity of phrase and crisp, good judgment; he gave to the school unstintingly of his time and interest and wisdom and devotion.

His school, which meant so much to him, here records its deep gratitude for all that he has meant to it.

12

A STATEMENT ON THE DEATH OF FLORENCE C. LAMONT

(Printed in *The Times,* London)

John and Constance Masefield   December 30, 1952

A cable brings the sad news that Mrs. Florence Corliss Lamont, the Widow of the late Thomas W. Lamont, of the Pierpont Morgan Firm, died peacefully at her New York home this morning.

The news, though for some days dreaded, will bring great grief. Few spirits more brave, daring, gay and delightful have ever gladdened friends.

To this country she was ever the staunchest of allies. Few English visitors to New York during the last forty years have failed to find in her a welcoming clever hostess, thoughtful, helpful and fore-seeing, whose friendship, later, endured and grew.

There was in her look and bearing such a spirit of gaiety, life and wisdom that none who knew her will ever think of her as dead. This living gaiety was of her very nature. It gives a matchless charm to those Letters from China and Japan published by her early this year.*

England has had no finer friend. Those who knew her will ever remember her as a most rare spirit, active, even to the last, in all great human causes.

---

* See pp. 91–92.

PART IV

Recollections and Poems

by John Masefield

John Masefield with "Mickey" (about 1949)

13

SOME MEMORIES OF THOMAS WILLIAM LAMONT AND FLORENCE CORLISS LAMONT

I am glad to be allowed the privilege of writing in the memory of the late Tom Lamont and his wife, Florence Corliss Lamont.

They stand out in memory as examples of what America possesses beyond any nation now in the world, what Whitman calls "an average stock" that is able on occasion to occupy any post and deal with any situation that the chances of life may bring.

I well remember being once asked by them how (in my opinion) American youth compared with European youth. I answered that as far as I could see, and know, European youth had always a tradition of a past perhaps two thousand years old, and, that owing to this, in certain feelings, knowledge and custom, European youth had an advantage.

I felt that certainly, the average youth of Europe knew more history; he was more deeply rooted in the past, and had nearly always also some of the prejudices of old quarrels. He belonged, moreover, to a Continent no longer living in the imagination, but in societies of critics, collectors and curators. His contribution to thought was mainly the criticism of what the past had thought. In such societies the European youth had some advantage, or (if it were not direct advantage) at least this difference.

The American youth (as far as I could see) was a very different being. He had a national past, stirring indeed, but comparatively recent. His immediate ancestors had often been pioneers or rebels, and in either case had had to face death on more than one frontier within each generation.

Danger, freedom and immensity of opportunity had brought together and made one the natives of all Europe. When one con-

137

siders that only a hundred years ago most of the Far West was
the Wild (or very Wild) West, the achievements of American
youth cannot but stagger the considerer. Three generations of
American youth took to heart John Soule's advice,

"Go West, young man, and grow up with the country." They
had, as their descendants still have, a vast continent to subdue,
to plan, to bridge, to people, and to make splendid. In action, in
achievement, in hope, as in every inventive and mechanical faculty,
they were and are far ahead of any European youth.

Tom and Florence Lamont were of the settled European stocks
that did not go west. They were of the Scotch and Dutch strains
of the New York and New Jersey settlements. I would say that
no human beings could have a finer, more sterling parentage. Both
were robust and lively children of the very best of parents, who
gave to them their own high character and purpose, and the best
of schoolings and trainings in lovely country.

These are advantages of birth that outweigh the advantages
that fortunate youth in Europe so often has (or had) of an assured
position in society and the influence of family wealth and position.

They knew from childhood that they would have to make their
own ways by what light and instinct their natures gave. Both had
(I would say) in a high degree the high American eagerness to
make their own ways. From the very first, the light was clear and
the instinct bent on excellence.

From early youth, both were eager readers, with unusual aptitude for writing. Those years of the eighteen-seventies and eighties
were great years for readers; the thoughtful youth had not then
the counter-attractions of today: even the safety-bicycle had hardly
begun among us. Reading was the main recreation. Books were
plentiful at prices undreamed of today: in England an immense
range of fiction at sixpence the volume, later at fourpence half-
penny a volume. In America a still greater range of fiction could
be had at five cents, then two-pence half-penny, a volume. Then
there were in America Sunday newspapers of some of which it
was said that a single issue contained more reading than the Bible.
Many reprints of masterpieces could be had for five or ten cents.
Even the poorest youth could buy at least a hundred good books
in a year without feeling the pinch. Among the many books then
appearing were many cheerful and welcome books of light verse,
such as Little Breeches, Hans Breitmann, and the gayer pages in
Bret Harte.

Long since, I was allowed to see some light verse by Tom Lamont written, I believe, at Harvard. I felt from what I saw of this,
that he had a talent for that way of writing. He kept throughout
life a fondness for poetry.

I shall never forget how he once thrilled me by telling me how,
while at Harvard, he sometimes saw William Cullen Bryant walking across the campus.

"And did you, once, see Shelley plain?"

At an early age, when the exacting life can be most delightful,
he had some varied experience as a journalist. From what I saw of
his work, many years ago, I should say that his Editor must always
have blessed him for his grasp of the essential and the perfection
of his statement. I would say, too, that his compositors blessed him
for the well-formed, swift, neat clearness of his hand-writing.

Florence Lamont had a similar interest in writing, and a com-
parable talent for it. Her reading was probably always mainly in
religion and philosophy but she read widely in all that shed light,
or tackled human problem. At all times, she excelled as a letter-
writer.

Each of the two, towards the end of life, wrote a book of memories. Both books are quite unusually good reading, full of the bright
sense and happy gaiety that enchanted all who knew them.

In their persons, both showed what William Blake called the
greatest beauty, a presence that changed little with the years, that
depended on the quality of the nature within, not at all upon the
colours and liveliness of youth. I never saw them in youth, but
neither of the two seemed to age at all; both looked young, and
kept the active youthful mind throughout life. Both had also, to
the full, the happy American distinction of a sprightly carriage.

I remember that Florence was staying with us in England, when
the news was cabled to her that she had become a grandmother.
The late W. B. Yeats, the poet, who was with us that afternoon,
on hearing the news, looked at her in some amazement. He then
said to her:

"Do I hear that you are a grandmother?"

"Yes."

He paused an instant, then slowly said: "Not thus did grand-
mothers appear when I was young."

Like most Americans, both Tom and Florence Lamont had at
all times, a natural aptitude and readiness for speech. Their minds
were ever clear, and both would speak in conversation or in public

with natural delightful point and purpose. As both had seen much of the world, its wonders, its rulers and its chosen, their conversation was unusual in range and interest. Their political views, national and international, were ever generous and liberal. They always seemed to me to be in touch with the generous and the liberal of every country known to me.

Much rubbish is written (and more talked) of the evils of great wealth. Wealth is a form of power, and frequently an abused power, or a power wilfully and selfishly withheld from use. But much of what good there is in the world comes from a generous and liberal use of wealth. Few people in modern times, even among the generous Americans, can have made more generous and enlightened use of their great wealth.

Surely the evils of the world come not from wealth but from a poverty of soul, of mind, of nature, which every generous act helps to lessen.

All who knew them must have talked with them in many delightful discussions of great matters; but after these came always the delight of multiform amusement, ranging through Bridge, Backgammon, many noisy and merry children's games, from hide and seek to the game called "Murder," to charades and serial story-telling till it was time for Bridge again. All these were episodes in the art of friendship that they knew so well how to practice. As friends, they were famous among America's many famous.

Few Europeans (of the many whom they guested), ever knew, at first, what thought their hosts gave to the comfort of foreign friends as they travelled about America. In time, they learned, to their wondering gratitude, that while they travelled in the United States their New York hosts had frequently intervened in secret for their greater comfort, and that the lucky seat in the overcrowded train, or the unexpected berth in the crammed ship, had been due to one of these forethoughtful marvel-workers in distant New York City.

In all the years of my friendship with them, they were eminent in world affairs of much importance to the nations. They travelled much among these nations and knew many people then governing. Of these matters and people of course we could not talk; but from most of their journeys they brought back clear views of the scenes and admirable descriptions of the life lived. They also brought back from some of their rovings a fund of songs, which they sang delightfully.

They had long delighted me with their singing of Negro hymns, such as "Swing Low, Sweet Chariot" and "Give Me that Old-Time Religion." On their return from their visit to General Smuts, in South Africa, they brought some enchanting Dutch songs (with English words).

It was a rule of Tom's that in affairs of importance the friendly way was always the best, and that every friendly way should be tried, with every well-meaning hopeful suggestion, with an unfailing patience and forbearance, and that usually this way would win even the stoniest opponent.

I remember that while they were with General Smuts in South Africa, a herd of wandering antelopes kept them penned within the house for a day or two. They told of this most marvellously. Old W. H. Hudson could not have told it better.

There was an English lady who once asked Mrs. Lamont where her husband did his "calculations," thinking, seemingly, that there was a kind of bookmaker's stand somewhere, in which the operators booked the bets and took the frenzied signals from their partners outside.

"The calculations" became a frequent phrase between us, though, of course, their nature and their details were never mentioned.

Once, long since, I happened to hear that a most unusual man, slightly known to me, had formed some scheme, like himself, out of the common, that seemed to need help into the world, yet might not be richly rewarding.

As it came from a most unusual man, it was a matter that deserved study: the bare outlines of it were moving.

Some people nearer home had treated the suggestions as crazy, and had been rude to the begetter, who had deserved, at least, the courtesy due to genius.

Tom Lamont, who must have heard many appeals in his time, gave to the case his instant attention. With patience and thoroughness he saw the genius, recognized his quality, encouraged him, and put him into touch with fitting help.

In conversation, Tom especially delighted me with his knowledge of American history and of the main characters of its critical years. He knew much of the War of Independence and of the Civil War, had visited many of the sites, and grasped the movements in the panorama in a masterly way. He had a clearness found in few minds, and must have made a great name had he given his gifts to history.

In conversation, Florence delighted all hearers by the gaieties of her stories, and the eagerness of her enquiries into the truth or value of statements and methods found in books new and old. She mixed much with people wherever she went: she heard many stories: she read much, met many writers, and never failed to question their pronouncements with the cleverness of a most shrewd enquiring counsel.

Throughout life, they played a good deal of golf together. In the summers they went away with the family to the great event in their year, the rapturous weeks at Sky Farm on the coast of Maine. This was the place of bliss and peace, of endless sailings, races, picnics on lonely islets, fishings and cruisings, looked forward-to from year to year, and ever ended with regret.

Both of them had seen many of the places most famed for beauty in three Continents.

To both of them the Maine Coast seemed the most beautiful of all. If they ever hesitated, before some unusually lovely scene, they often spoke some word of apology to Maine for seeming to hesitate, and then said that Maine was better. I suppose that Maine is a great austere scene having nothing in it that is not a power abiding from of old, and that it could not fail to haunt the feeling heart.

I remember well, how, when I first talked with Florence Lamont, she eagerly sought for some such undying power in minds and systems.

She had read widely in philosophy in a search for some system that explained or illumined the chaos into which life had fallen. In the eagerness of her search, the keenness of her sense of value questioned everything that system or friend tried to offer. She searched the bases of every position held or proposed. The traditions, the old mines of human joy, may disappear when shrewdly questioned from every angle, but they exist, and reappear.

Galileo, when shrewdly questioned (on a rack, by experts) agreed that the earth stood still, but on the slackening of the tension is said to have murmured, "And yet it DOES move."

We, here, in the nineteen-twenties, felt that Maine had given to her both the explanation and the joy for which she sought. Those rocks and waters abiding from of old held a peace for all from a power undying, however changing.

It is said that the Indian seeker wanders India till he finds the one Guru, or Teacher, who can teach him what his being needs.

In life, if no teacher appear, there is still the universe, speaking with many voices, to which some souls are tuned.

During the years of our friendship, there was, both here and in America, a great city-population hungry for Nature. This population eagerly read books about open-air life, on the plains, in the forests and at sea. The clever writers of these books added to them tales of animals and birds. There sprang up (in both countries) a new interest in the lives of wild creatures, especially in the little known lives of birds. All of that time will remember the eagerness with which we followed the books of John Burroughs, Bliss Carman, C. G. D. Roberts, W. H. Hudson, Thompson Seton and the many gifted others, down to the wonderful Major Jim Corbett.

Mrs. Lamont, like other active readers, delighted in these books. When in England, she was keen to learn what she could of the British birds, the nesting migrants and the natives. She wished to be able to identify them by sight and by their songs.

In this house of bird-watchers, she made much progress in the study. Often when walking and talking in the garden here, she would seek to see some singing bird, or ask what bird it was that sang. In a leafy garden the bird was seldom seen clearly, but she came to know about twenty British birds by their call, cry or song, and nearly all of the following by sight: rook, crow, jackdaw, woodpecker (all three sorts), heron, moorhen, wild duck, pheasant, partridge, starling, pigeon, dove, brown owl, tawny owl, blackbird, thrush, chaffinch, bulfinch, grasshopper-warbler, peewit and robin.

Few observers can resist the charm of the English robin. Mrs. Lamont was delighted with him. At that time we had with us, following us about the garden wherever we went, a very tame robin with only one leg.

This bird was accustomed to eat from the human hand the dried currants always carried for him. He gave Florence Lamont one new little bird-experience that she often recalled with pleasure.

She held out her hand with three currants upon it to try to tempt the bird to her hand for them. He was, at first, too shy, but by keeping very still and closing her eyes she gave him confidence; he came to hand and took the currants.

The next trial was to lure him to take currants from her lips. This was a sterner trial to his courage; but showing the currants between her lips, closing her eyes and keeping motionless, she at last persuaded him; he fluttered in, took a currant, and then returned for the others.

This is always a strange experience to one who does it for the first time. The eyes are closed so that one cannot see the bird, only feel a tiny fluttering eagerness very close and exquisitely delicate, with terror and swift certainty. There is also a thrill, as though the bird brings its gladness as thanks. There is also a joy at being so trusted by a thing so tiny, so lovely, and so wild.

Most of our best friends in England and France knew the Lamonts; the knowledge was a bond the more in friendship.

Death has since then sadly thinned the company, but the survivors will ever voice the feeling of all of them, that Tom and Florence Lamont were a wonderful couple who gave to friendship a thought and sympathy uncommon in the world.

Burcote Brook, Abingdon
June 1961

14

THE WESTERN HUDSON SHORE

by John Masefield

Verses in the noble memory of Thomas W. Lamont and his Wife,
Florence Corliss Lamont.

In a long life's first independent day,
As a Septembral mistiness grew bright,
I saw the Hudson River where it lay*
Westward, all silver in the windless light.
There, like a giant guard,
Ranked as a rampart, proud yet battle-scarred,
Were precipices silent in array.
Endurance in eternity grown gray,
Sentinel in implacable regard,
Watching the ending of another night.

"What is the cliff?" I asked. "The Palisades."
Thereafter, daily, I would look across
And watch the silences of their brigades,
Enduring their eternity of loss,
The sun, the wind, the cold.
Often I watched the setting sun glow gold
Down to their summit at a day's decline.
I saw no dwelling in the rocky line,
No lighted window starred the dusking shades,
Sombre the fort, from rampart-top to fosse.

Often I wondered what the rampart hid.
What was it that the cruising eagle saw
Below the forest tree-tops as he glid
Searching the rock for quarry for his claw?

* In his early manhood Masefield came to the United States and worked for two
years in a carpet mill at Yonkers, New York, on the east bank of the Hudson and
opposite the Palisades.

Was it the West, untamed?
Manless, as yet, with creatures yet un-named,
With ashes of the Indian camp-fires strown,
The earth as yet unploughed, the grass unmown,
Where nothing of adventure was forbid,
And knife and bullet gave the only law?

Whatever wonder or alarm might be
Beyond those clouds aflame as the sun sank,
I felt that something great awaited me,
Awaited all who sought beyond their rank.
There, in that haunted ground
By present search the future might be found . . .
The hardly-hoped, new, unexpected thing,
That must be sought-for, seeing naught would bring
The pearl within its nacre from the sea,
Or nuggets from the mountain torrent's bank.

Daily that solitude of frontier lured.
Before the winter struck I rowed to find
What people, by such rampart reassured,
Beyond such wall, were wonders of mankind.
I neared the rocks; I saw
The eagle and the cranny-nesting daw;
No sign of human life but screes and crags,
With scanty sumach showing scarlet flags,
An ebb that passed, an iron that endured,
In stony silence daunting to the mind.

But in a gully, as I came to land,
A couple, lad and lady, stared at me,
Seemed, for an instant, prone to lend a hand,
Then, doubting, changed their minds and let me be.
They seemed about to speak . . .
I made the boat secure within the creek,
I wished to speak to them, but did not dare,
(Myself a boy) and, wondering what they were,
I left them to the river and the strand,
And picked my way through boulders up the scree.

Above the cliff the timber scattered sparse
In land no coulter yet had made to yield.
All was untended waste, of unfenced grass,
An untamed naught, not forest and not field.
No sight of house, no farm,
No church-bell struck, no dog barked an alarm,
Save for the flies, no moving life at all.
Naught but the splendid silence of the Fall.

Whatever dangers lurked to see me pass,
None gave a symptom, nothing was revealed.

But, pushing on awhile, I found a track,
I followed as the latest hoof-marks led
(Hoofs going westward, that had not come back)
Into a grassy woodland just ahead.
I paused: I heard no sound.
I seemed alone upon a no-man's ground;
Saw nothing but October-coloured trees
From which, at times, a leaf, by slow degrees
Came rustling to the seepage rotted black
From branches still in blueness overhead.

But, the sun southing, it was time to go.
I meant to ask those friends, as I returned
What farms were westward; surely they would know.
But both had vanished thence I soon discerned.
All desolate the scene,
Rock to the sky in majesty of mien,
Rock above water, water below rock,
Waiting the dawn when destiny should knock.
I pulled into the trouble of the flow
Eyeing the patches where the sumach burned.

I travelled to that rocky coast no more,
But often thought about that vanished pair.
Seemingly sole possessors of the shore,
Often I wondered who and what they were.
Three ships about to speak
The strings of rolled-up signals at the peak,
But then, by impulse, never broken-out,
Their nation and their nature left in doubt,
For memory (regretting) to restore,
And fantasy (regretting) to make fair.

What could that couple, man and girl, have been?
Had they come fishing? Was their boat at hand?
Were they two lovers, being King and Queen
In two young hearts, supreme o'er sea and land,
Where, in that Jersey side,
(Seemingly peopleless) did they abide?
Had they but spoken, what would they have said?
If questioned, what reply would they have made?
Why should their apparition come to mean
Something too great for me to understand?

Long afterwards, I trod New York again,
Earth's loveliest, liveliest City, shining new:
And new friends asked, who never asked in vain:
"Come up the Hudson and enjoy the view . . .
Old Yonkers from the West."
They took me, straightway, to the very crest
Just where I once had climbed, but, oh, what change,
All the old waste was utterly made strange,
With traffic hooting onwards in a chain
And all the Sunday merry with ado.

There, underneath, the Hudson sought the sea,
Beyond, a miracle of city shone,
City, where only forest used to be,
The lovely New York City thrusting on . . .
All shining city now,
There Yonkers lay . . . I well remembered how.
I said, "I worked there, many years ago,
I rowed once, to the gully here below . . .
Two strangers saw, and almost spoke to me,
Later, I looked for them, but they were gone.

"Strange that that man and girl should haunt me so.
Say, could it possibly have been that you
Came, one October Sunday, just below,
And saw me pass . . . were you the very Two?"
They answered: "No . . . not we . . .
Though we were living near, it could not be.
Then we were still in Puritanic days,
Our Sunday mornings passed in holier ways.
Forget the couple that you didn't know,
Take us instead and try to make us do."

Friendship is sunlight scattering man's cloud,
Making a life a sunbeam's spangled dust,
Soon they were showing me, when time allowed,
How far the energies of Man had thrust
Bringing that shore to use,
Giving, and promising to give, no truce
To that unknown alluring Jersey shore.
The distance I had hungered to explore,
Was now inhabited, adorned, endowed,
Its Might-Be, brought to Being by Man's Must.

All, changed or not, those friends together showed.
Westward and northward, seeing all, we went,
Through forests where autumnal maples glowed,

Up golden miles of turbulent ascent;
Past West Point, flagged and fair;
By clearings that old pioneers laid bare,
And gave, or kept, the Dutch or Indian name,
Each having still its little touch of fame,
Its storied ferry, or remembered road,
Or, on the green, its laurelled monument.

After long years, those glad companions built
A woodland mansion near the rocky crest
That in my youth the setting suns had gilt.
I lived for days in that enchanted West,
Walked there, and came to know
The unknown country that had lured me so.
There, as the destinies decreed, I learned
The change that follows when a soul has earned
Leave to proceed . . . as earthly flowers wilt
So mortals change and enter into rest.

They died, but, dying, left that house of theirs
To be a seat of knowledge, home and shrine
To those who track the Hidden to its lairs
Down in the depth of cosmical design.
To probe beneath the crust
For ancient rocks that made the modern dust;
To bore beneath the bottom of the sea;
To learn the doings of eternity,
The frosts and fires of immense affairs,
Incalculable, splendid and divine.*

Still, therefore, now, my thought turns every eve
To that great wall of rock, with fancies fond,
Of what the Sun, in sinking, must perceive,
By me, unseen, undreamed of and unconned.
Thus far the search has gone:
Over the River, into Jersey, on,
By bridge, by ferry and by multitude
Into the secrecies where none intrude,
Into realities where none can grieve
Feeling the certainty of Truth beyond.

Such are the links between the rocks and me,
The lure that seemed to promise, and the thrill
That what the promise seemed might come to be

---

* This stanza refers to the fact that the Lamont estate at Palisades, New York, was willed by my mother to Columbia University, which established the Lamont Geological Observatory there.

Spite of all punishments that thwart us still,
Chains of old time, old lacks,
The stones in wallet on the pilgrims' backs;
Then, spite of all, the unexpected friends,
The widening of the scope that never ends,
The Sun forever sinking in the Sea
Lighting a path to consecrated will.

15

TO THE GREAT FRIENDS
IN LIFETIME

by John Masefield

This, I believe, that we remain in Time
Holding the purpose of a quest incurred
Outlasting Death, to struggle and to climb
Mountainous Life with living deed or word,
Achieving light (if lucky) out of grime.
So, when Life's breath has gone,
Aspiring spirit smiles, and ventures on.

Newly arrayed, the spirit re-assails
Despairs unconquered in the past, and longs
For fellow treaders on the ancient trails
Loved in the past's forgotten toils and songs,
Old friends, linked by old chain
Re-met, are welcomed and are friends again
Exultingly the old ship spreads her sails.

Naught that is living can the soul forget.
Companions now were helpers in the past
Erasing blottings, nullifying debt.
Lovely, all lacks secured,
Attended, recreated, reassured,
Manful, in life more hopeful than the last,
Onward the great soul goes to greater yet.

* * *

Never has such assumption seemed more true
Than now, when lovely spirits, lost to sight,
In memory return
Nearer than ever to the hearts that yearn,
Giving again the happiness they knew,

151

Reviving occupations of delight
And winning, all too late, the praises due.

That we are linked in long-established schemes
Is, still, my thought; and so
That we shall meet again I dearly know,
Under the tidal moon, swayed by the sun.
Darkness besets man's living with its dreams,
Eternity from mortal conquest streams,
Joy, Order, Peace and Wisdom's Justice done.

PART V
Thomas Stilwell Lamont

Thomas Stilwell Lamont

16

OF THE FAMILY PAST

by Thomas Stilwell Lamont

Most Lamonts of today, like most Americans, pay too little heed to their own worthy past. More's the pity, since the reading of history and biography enlarges our understanding of life by creating a more perceptive awareness of the contrasts between present and past, of the interplay of old repetitions and new surprises. I do not think it vainglorious to examine the lives of one's own ancestors. I have found it a pleasant pursuit. Though my grandsires did not write the Declaration of Independence or hold high command in the Revolutionary armies, they played their part in making the United States of America what it was in its beginnings and what it is today.

I like to think that this account of who my ancestors were and what they did will give the Lamonts of our branch of the family a renewed appreciation and knowledge of their heritage, of the character and purposefulness, not just of our Lamont grandsires alone, but of all our forebears, and of their honorable and active participation in the life and progress of the English and Dutch colonies in America and of the growing young nation. I hope it may stimulate us to learn more of our ancestors, their history and how they lived. The means by which to pursue such learning are near at hand.

For example, there is the Sherwood-Jayne House on Long Island. Only a few of us have motored forty-five miles out of New York City to Setauket to visit this beautiful saltbox home, built about 1730 by one of the sons of my great-great-great-great-great-grandfather, William Jayne. This lovely old house, with the white plaster walls of its formal rooms so gaily decorated with painted designs of the mid-eighteenth century, was faithfully restored fifty years ago by Mr. Howard Sherwood, an Exeter classmate of my father's. It is now owned by the Society for the Preservation of Long Island Antiquities.

Any Lamont with an interest in genealogy would be fascinated by the cemeteries in which so many of our forebears found a resting place. They are at North Hillsdale, New York, on the western edge of the Berkshires, and in Charlotteville, across the Hudson in the Catskills.

The Hereditary Mixture

Only a very small part of me is Lamont. I am a Jayne and a Ferguson and a Corliss and a Parmelee and a Fitch. I am a Bradford and a Paine and an Allen and a Stilwell and a Lansing. So what I write of our forebears for three centuries past involves hundreds of men and women who, though they never heard of the Lamonts, had, nevertheless, some hereditary share in making the Lamonts what they are today. From such data as is now available to me I find that all my ancestors, going back for over three and a half centuries, were of Scottish, Irish or English blood, with but a single exception. My great-great-grandfather, David Allen, married Hester Lansing of Lansingburgh, New York, and the Lansings were among the earliest of the Dutch families who settled along the upper reaches of the Hudson River.

Some of my own children as well as nieces and nephews have introduced other new strains into our predominantly Anglo-Saxon blood. One niece married a husband of Scandinavian ancestry, another has married a Rosenthal of Jewish parentage, and a third, a young man whose mother was Mexican. A nephew has married a Silkovskis, born a Latvian. One son of mine has married a Jung, whose great-grandparents were German, and another has married a young lady half French in her ancestry. All hail to the Lamonts of the future through whose veins will flow an enriched potpourri of all good bloods!

"Evangelizing the Sons of Ham"

I referred above to the Jayne House at Setauket, built in 1730. The Jaynes, beginning with the earliest Jayne in America in 1670, were a clan always characterized by energy. Yet few of their Lamont descendants know how lively they were. My Great-grandfather Jayne, whose adventure I now recount, typified the Jayne vigor.

Two years ago my zealous and purposeful niece, Nancy Lamont Bowles,* was preparing to depart with her husband for Northern Nigeria where they were both to teach school. She was naturally quite excited by the challenge and opportunity; quite pleased and proud that she was the first of our family, as she thought, to venture a life of service in a new African country just emerging from colonial status. On the other hand, I was proud that Nancy was the *second* of our family to serve in Africa, the first having been her great-great-grandfather, Walter P. Jayne. He was my Grandmother Lamont's father. In 1838, in response to an appeal by the Missionary Society of the Methodist Church, he volunteered to go to that part of Africa then known as Liberia. It was not yet a nation, only the beginning of one—an experiment in resettling, among the primitive tribes of that area, American slaves who had been freed.

So far as I can discover, Walter Jayne was the first of our kinsmen to write anything longer than a letter or a will, the first, therefore, of nine or ten Lamonts and near relatives who were writers: authors of books, editors and journalists. After he reached Monrovia in Liberia, Walter Jayne was placed in charge of printing a missionary periodical, *Africa's Luminary*. It has been said that this was the first English-language journal ever printed in Africa. Walter Jayne also kept a diary of his adventure.† It began on December 12, 1838, with the following entry:

> This morning about ten o'clock I took leave on the Battery [New York City] of my dear wife and family to embark on board the ship *Emperor* for a distant clime, the shores of benighted Africa, to assist, in the fear of God, in evangelizing the sons of Ham. . . . Nothing but a sense of duty to God, whom I desire to love and serve, could tempt me to bid adieu to my happy country, my family, my friends, my all, and go to a distant and sickly clime, even for the noble object of assisting my brethren in spreading the knowledge of Salvation to the heathen tribes of Africa.

Walter Jayne was not quite twenty-nine when he set sail for Africa; and he left behind him a young wife of twenty-four and two children, aged five and two. He had an extremely hard time in Liberia, and he became very ill of what he called "the fever";

---

* Mrs. Samuel S. Bowles.

† The diary has been given to the Library of Drew University, Madison, New Jersey. Drew is a Methodist-related University, and its theological school, founded in 1866, has always had a particular concern for missionary work.

probably it was yellow fever or malaria or both. They were endemic in that tropical land. Life was on a primitive level. The heathen tribes were not too friendly to the white missionaries, and the tribes themselves constantly warred upon each other. A score or more of Walter Jayne's fellow missionaries in Liberia died of "the fever" while he was there. He was lucky to return alive, on June 30, 1841, when his diary recorded his ship's American landfall: "This afternoon we had the great satisfaction of being overhauled by the pilot. All hearts were made happy. . . . All of us are in joyful hope of embracing our friends soon again." Walter Jayne's return in late June 1841 was very lucky for us because his daughter Caroline, my Grandmother Lamont, was born a little over nine months later on April 15, 1842!

The reader will know that in writing of Walter Jayne's African experience I have not meant to belittle the devoted service in Africa of my lovely niece, Nancy, whose adventure bears witness to her courage and spirit. I hope that she too will soon return in safety, as happy to reach our shores as was her great-great-grandfather. I have mentioned the trials of our grandsire, Walter Jayne, to remind all of our family that we are from a breed of men and women who ventured boldly. The knowledge of such a heritage should inspirit us.

The Name Lamont

Before writing in detail of our Lamont forebears I would present some explanation of the varied spellings and pronunciations of the Lamont name. Its spelling and, I believe, its pronunciation also, were changed in the 1850's. My father wrote an account of this change in which he stated that at that time "the then young women in our branch of the family, who had been studying French, got an idea that the name was French and suggested the [new] spelling. . . . It was adopted," my father continued, "by a good many members of the family. . . . About thirty years later, however, we began to look up all the records very carefully and found that the name was indubitably Scotch where the spelling has always been as I spell it. So," concluded Father, "we went back to the old spelling."

I have a family Bible which I believe was the property of one of my great-aunts, most likely Aunt Lucy Lape. Between the Old and New Testaments of this volume there are the customary blank pages reserved for recording births, baptisms, marriages and deaths. These are well filled with the written record of these events in the lives of my grandfather's brothers, sisters, parents and grandparents. All the writing is in the same Spencerian hand, and I judge it to be a lady's hand. Every name listed—and there are dozens, including that of my great-grandfather, Thomas W. Lamont—is spelled "La Monte."

I believe that two or three years before his death in 1853 Great-grandfather Lamont had succumbed, in part at least, to the blandishments of his daughters, since I have one of his books on the flyleaf of which he has written "Thomas W. La Mont, 1852"— La Mont without the "e"! Yet I have a letter of his, written shortly before his death, in which he signs his name "Lamont," just as had his parents and his other American forefathers. References to his death in the local press all used the original spelling. So it was probably a year or two after his death that Great-aunt Lucy and other "young women in our branch" succeeded, after assiduous efforts, in persuading many Lamonts to change the spelling of their name to La Monte.

My La Monte Bible, a very fine edition published in New York City, bears on its title page the year of its publication, 1860. I suspect Great-aunt Lucy of buying the new Bible for the definite purpose of writing within it the records of all her family, spelled in the new—and perhaps to her more glamorous—fashion. Actually, it was not till the late 1880's that my grandparents and their children, including Father, reverted to the correct spelling of the name.

However, some of my father's first cousins, in particular the children of his Uncle George, continued to spell their name "La Monte," and their descendants still do today. Incidentally, Great-uncle George was the only one of Grandfather Lamont's brothers who went into business. He became a most successful paper manufacturer, making his home in Bound Brook, New Jersey. I well remember a visit in my boyhood to his home to meet some of my numerous second cousins. In the earliest years of this century we Englewood, New Jersey, Lamonts regarded the Bound Brook La Montes as the affluent, worldly—and worthy—branch of the family. They were fine people and still are.*

---

* Another well-known La Monte and cousin of my father was Robert Rives La Monte of New Canaan, Conn. He was an author, a radical, and a member of the Socialist Party for many years. His debate with H. L. Mencken on the respective merits of socialism and capitalism appeared in book form under the title of *Men versus The Man: A Correspondence,* Henry Holt and Company, 1910.

It is probable that when my more recent progenitors adopted the French spelling they also changed the pronunciation, accenting the second syllable. The evidence indicates that our earlier ancestors in the country pronounced the name as it was and still is pronounced in Scotland and Ireland, Lam'-ont, with the accent on the first syllable. Should any American Lamonts wish to reassume the correct pronunciation of their name, I give them my blessing. And I would gladly present ties, or even kilts, of the Clan Lamont tartan to those of the Bound Brook La Montes who should decide to spell their name correctly!

The Lamonts in America—The Earlier Generations

The first Lamonts of our branch to come to America were Robert, from whom we are descended, his two brothers and their mother, Mrs. John Lamont. They settled about 1750 in the Hudson Valley at North Hillsdale, Columbia County, New York, about fifteen miles east of the river. For the next century and a quarter, most of the Lamonts remained in or near the Hudson Valley. One of Robert Lamont's three sons was William, a Revolutionary soldier and my great-great-great-grandfather. He moved to the west of the river in 1801, and cleared a farm in the forest near Middleburg, Schoharie County. That area in the Catskill Mountains west of the upper Hudson River was, as my Grandfather Lamont wrote, "a beautiful country of high hills, lovely valleys, heavy forests and rushing brooks."

The first four generations of Lamonts in America were pioneers. They built their cabins in the wilderness, cleared the land and farmed it. Into the fifth generation of American Lamonts, that of my great-grandfather, husbandry was their second nature. Yet by the second quarter of the nineteenth century Great-grandfather Lamont, and his brothers and numerous cousins as well, began to supplement their agricultural activities by shopkeeping and trading and school teaching. As the land was cleared, as forests changed to fields, so the Lamont dwellings changed from cabins, located in scattered and isolated clearings, to neat frame houses clustered near the crossroads. And thus the village was created. It was not until my grandfather's generation, the sixth in America, that the transition of the Lamonts from lives centered upon the farm to lives of varied occupations became complete.

Perhaps it was a bit easier for the Lamonts of central New York

State in the eighteenth century to protect and secure their freedom than it was for our other and earlier American ancestors of the seventeenth century who, like the Lamonts, lived for the most part away from the coastal towns. But, whatever the relative hardships, Nature itself was the stern taskmaster, and its tough demands exacted unusual efforts from those who would carve a good life out of the American wilderness. Thus our forefathers were bred in independence and self-reliance. On into the last quarter of the nineteenth century, our ancestors, men and women alike, had to be adept in every homemaking talent and in all agricultural skills. The constant struggle to improve life in a frontier community steeled the character of its people and sharpened ambition to better their lot in life.

The Prolific Progenitors

One of the best ways to improve living standards in the agricultural economy of Colonial and post-Revolutionary times in America was to produce children. Put to work at an early age and for long hours on the family farm, sons and daughters were assets of very considerable economic value. The farm came first; schooling came only after the crops were harvested. The long summer vacation of three months or more, a unique feature of the nation's schools and colleges today, is a survival of the pattern of farming and education established in America's early days. So large families were the rule, especially among those who tilled the land. That was certainly the case with my own farmer forebears. The men were virile, the women sturdy and prolific, the children numerous.

A good example of procreative persistence was my grandmother's first maternal ancestor in America, William Jayne. He came from London, a widower, in about 1670. He was then fifty-two years old, having been born January 25, 1618. He left behind him three adult sons in England. In 1675 he married Annie Biggs of New Haven, his first American wife. By her he had four children, from one of whom, William Jayne II, we are descended. Annie Biggs died in 1692, but seventy-four-year-old William Jayne married soon again, taking for a wife Mehitabel Jenners. By her he had four or five more children, the last being Stephen Jayne, born in 1700 when old William was eighty-two years old. I must assume he stopped trying after that! He lived on to the ripe age of ninety-six without any further additions to his brood.

My Grandmother Lamont's grandparents, James and Jane Ferguson, reared a family of twelve children. They were farmers in Delaware County, New York.

Corliss, Parmelee and Allied Family Histories* is the title of the volume containing detailed genealogical records of my maternal forebears. I have counted my great-grandfathers listed therein who had ten or more issue—some with the help of a second wife. The impressive result shows that five grandfathers of various degrees of "great" achieved each a family of ten children; seven had eleven children; one had twelve; three, thirteen; and one, fourteen.

Teachers and Founders of Schools

As the harsh wilderness changed gradually into pleasant rural country, our ancestors turned from self-education and guidance of their children at home to the organization of good schools. They aspired highly for their many children, and they realized that good education was necessary if their children were to live full and useful lives.

Beginning in 1850, the Lamonts gave their pedagogic all to the establishment and support of Charlotteville Seminary, in the village of Charlotteville, Schoharie County, New York. Charlotteville was located on Charlotte Creek, a tributary of the Susquehanna. It was here, forty-four years earlier, that my great-great-grandfather, William Lamont, Jr., had settled—five years after his father had also moved to Schoharie County from the Lamonts' first home in North Hillsdale, east of the Hudson. The Lamonts remained in Charlotteville for three generations.

By the middle of the nineteenth century it had become apparent to the Lamonts that better educational facilities were needed in Schoharie County. As a matter of fact, schools with standards which could qualify their students for college were few and far between in the rural areas of New York State. It was the objective of its founders that Charlotteville Seminary should prepare boys for higher education—and girls for useful lives!—and many of its graduates attended Wesleyan or Yale or Union. Great-grandfather Thomas W. Lamont played a leading part in bringing about the establishment of the Seminary in 1850. He was the first President of its Board of Trustees. His children, his cousins, his nieces and

---

* See p. 16.

nephews—the whole family—pitched in, playing their brief parts as administrators, teachers or students in the Seminary. The main building of Charlotteville Seminary was built in 1850; but unfortunately it burned to the ground in 1854 at what was probably the high water mark of the school's prosperity. Yet the Lamonts, undaunted by adversity, continued to run their Seminary for another sixteen years.

Grandfather Lamont, both before he matriculated at Union College and at periods during his somewhat interrupted college course, had taught at three different schools in Schoharie and Otsego Counties. After he graduated from Union in 1856—sporting a Phi Beta Kappa key—he taught at Charlotteville for three years as an ordinary member of the Faculty. But then he was honored by appointment as the school's Principal in the fall of 1859 at the age of twenty-seven. Let's hope that it was his experience and ability as a teacher which earned him the job—not just nepotism! He continued to be the school's leader for two and a half years before resigning to give full time to a pastorate in the Methodist Church.

Charlotteville Seminary Closes

Later, in 1865, the rest of the buildings of the Seminary were destroyed in yet another conflagration. The school carried on for five more years in an abandoned hotel in the village before it finally expired. My grandfather writes that the school to which "the Lamont family gave much in efforts and contributions, may be said to have had a history lasting about twenty years." Yet it had served its useful purposes. For ten years or more its enrollment had totaled from 250 to 300 students, and two or three times in its earlier years attendance had approached 400. It was a challenging example to other communities: within six years after its founding in 1850 similar academies had been founded in eight different towns within fifty miles of Charlotteville. Certainly in the rural areas of New York State at this time the good people seemed eager in their pursuit of better education.

The pattern of interest in education continued into the later generations of Lamonts. My uncle, Hammond Lamont, was an Instructor in English at Harvard and later Professor of English at Brown University. My father was long a Trustee of Phillips Exeter Academy and President of its Board. He served two terms as an Overseer of Harvard. He was a Trustee of the Carnegie Foundation for the Advancement of Teaching and of the American School of Classical Studies in Athens. My brother Corliss was for many years Lecturer on the Philosophy of Humanism at Columbia University. My brother Austin has taught and practiced anesthesia as a member of the medical faculty at the Johns Hopkins University and at the University of Pennsylvania. I have aspired to emulate my father in service to Exeter, Harvard and other educational foundations.

The next generation of our family circle has given evidence of a similar attraction to the teaching profession. I have already mentioned my niece, Nancy Lamont Bowles, who with her husband has taught in Nigeria. Her sister Lavinia is married to Alan Rosenthal, member of the faculty of Hunter College in New York City. My nephew, Hayes Lamont, plans to follow the teaching profession after spending several years at Harvard in advanced scientific studies. Prior to her marriage my own daughter, Elinor,* taught at Shady Hill School, Cambridge, and at Grace Church School, New York City, for a year each.

The Warriors

A characteristic of our ancestors was their readiness to fight for good causes. They fought to hold their lands and preserve the safety of their families on a dangerous frontier, and they fought for their personal freedom. First there were the Indian fighters. My great-great-great-great-great-great-great-great-grandfather, Nicholas Stilwell, was an Englishman who, for religious reasons in which he felt his individual liberty involved, chose to live with the Dutch of New Amsterdam. His bowery, or plantation, was well outside the walls of New Amsterdam at Deutil Bay, now the area in Manhattan called Turtle Bay. Unfriendly and thieving Indians made life in his country retreat almost too rough for Nicholas and his wife Ann and their nine children; so now and then they had to return to town—below the Wall—for a period.

But Nicholas Stilwell's adversities raised his dander and he achieved renown as an Indian fighter. It was said of him that he was bold and skillful in defense, vigorous and resourceful in battle. He was chosen by the burghers of New Amsterdam to be leader of their military company, and he was given the rank of

---

* Mrs. Andrew Anderson-Bell.

lieutenant by the Dutch Government. His military ardor carried him far afield. In 1644 Nicholas Stilwell left New Amsterdam to serve a year as leader of the forces organized by the English colonists in Virginia to prosecute their recently renewed hostilities against the Indians. Incidentally, it is of interest to note that in the seventeenth and eighteenth centuries the ranks of lieutenant, captain and major, whether of Colonial soldiers of the King or in Washington's armies, carried with them command responsibilities over bodies of troops considerably larger in number than such ranks commanded in our recent wars.

My great-great-great-great-great-great-grandfather, Major William Bradford, was also a doughty Indian fighter. He led the Colonial troops in the Narragansett Fort Battle of King Philip's War, December 19, 1676; and he was wounded in that action. Major William was the son of an even more distinguished father, William Bradford, who sailed to America aboard the good ship *Mayflower* in 1620, and served from 1621 onwards for forty-two years as Governor of Plymouth Colony. The Governor, my grandfather prefixed by seven "greats," was the first of our ancestors in direct line to set foot upon the American continent.

It would be an endless effort in genealogical research were I to attempt to learn all that my many ancestors of the late eighteenth century were doing during the Revolutionary period. I imagine that some were Tories, unswerving in loyalty to King and Crown; if so, they too were brave. The readily available family records tell only of my patriot ancestors. From them I have extracted the information that at least six of my sixteen great-great-great-grandfathers—and there may well have been more—served in George Washington's armies: an Allen, a Corliss, a Fitch, a Parmelee, a Lansing and a Lamont.

A Corliss Fights at Bunker Hill

The Allen was David Allen. He was lieutenant in the Fourth Regiment of Connecticut Militia. His home and barns and shop at Fairfield, Connecticut, were destroyed in the raid of the British forces on Fairfield, July 7-8, 1779. Elihu Corliss, of the New Hampshire Militia, fought at the Battle of Bunker Hill, and in 1777 he served for a time in the garrison at Fort Ticonderoga. Jabez Fitch seems to have had a record of continuous service with a Connecticut regiment from 1775 through 1780. He held the rank of captain. Hezekiah Parmelee, Jr., was a member of the Connecticut Militia. Cornelius Lansing was a captain commanding the Sixth Regiment of the Albany County Militia which was engaged at the Battle of Saratoga, October 1777, when the English under General Burgoyne were defeated. He would not have known young Private William Lamont of the Ninth Regiment of the Albany County Militia which also fought at Saratoga.

Private William, my great-great-great-grandfather, served the patriot forces with honor; so did both his brothers. William began his service in 1775 at the age of nineteen. He was in uniform off and on for six different periods through June 1780; and, as indicated above, he served in the Battle of Saratoga and throughout the prior campaign of which it was the successful culmination. His army record was typical of many: active service for a period of months, release to work on the farm, return to military duty again. William's brother John, while fighting on the frontier, was captured by Indians under the command of Brant, the famous Indian leader. John Lamont remained in captivity for two or three years. His Indian captors forced him to run the gauntlet, and in this test of courage he performed with such sang-froid that he was presented with a squaw. However, the red lady did not so attract his affections as to deter him from an eventual escape back to his own people. His son, Captain John Lamont, Jr., fought and died by a British bullet in the War of 1812. William Lamont, Jr., my great-great-grandfather, was captain of the local military company in Fulton, New York, during the War of 1812, but perhaps due to his age, he did not see active service.

The family once again served with credit in World Wars I and II. My first cousin, Gordon Lamont, Uncle Hammond's son, has written me a gay letter describing his military service in World War I:

I succeeded in getting in the first Officers' Training Camp at Madison Barracks, N. Y., in the spring of 1917. As you may have heard, at Exeter and Harvard I was known as "Skinny" Lamont, and with good reason. I weighed 125 pounds and was six feet tall. I didn't fit the picture of a good soldier. But I drank about two quarts of water, crouched an inch off my height, and the kind-hearted examiner passed me. But at Madison Barracks my sin found me out. What with the drill and the marching, and the really terrible food, I even lost a pound or two, and the medical examinations were made without giving me a chance to get to the water spigot. They carried me up to the end, but refused me a commission on medical grounds. Even the draft would not have me.

After that slap in the face I went to the Royal Canadian Flying Corps recruiting fellow on Fifth Ave.; and they would take you if you had a pulse. They bought me a ticket to Toronto, and after the usual ground school I was posted to flight training. (This was still in 1917.) I got my wings and commission as second lieutenant, but instead of being sent overseas, I was assigned to the job of pilot instructor. The armistice found me at the School for Special Flying, Armour Heights, where I and other dizzy pilots were engaged in what was then known as "precision flying." In this group we convinced ourselves that we were the very hottest pilots who ever touched the joy stick of that flying orange crate known as the Curtiss Jenny! But we had never fired a machine gun in anger.

Thomas W. Lamont in World War II

Even my father, aged seventy-one at the time of Pearl Harbor, found a military activity in World War II—an activity which for a time heavily engaged his mind and energy. He headed a civilian committee appointed by Henry L. Stimson, Secretary of War, to cooperate with the Army Air Forces in collecting all manner of maps, photographs and other information which could be guides to the location and to the relative importance of manufacturing plants on the European continent. His own familiarity with European industry, and his acquaintance with other American businessmen having specialized knowledge in this field, made him an ideal leader for this particular project. And of equal importance, his stature in the American business community made it easier to attract the interest and cooperation of all American industries that were in a position to contribute information to our Air Forces. From the material gathered under my father's direction the staff of our Air Force received the greatest help in selecting important targets for our bomber commands in Europe.

My own service in World War I was insignificant. I was a member of the Harvard Reserve Officers' Training Corps during my freshman year, 1917–18. I attended the summer encampment of the Harvard ROTC in 1918 and then enlisted in the United States Army. I was admitted to the Field Artillery Officers' Training Corps and ordered to report at Camp Zachary Taylor, Louisville, Kentucky, early in November. I was there only a week before the armistice was signed on November 11th. I remained there in training till mid-December. However, when we officer candidates were given an opportunity to obtain an immediate honorable discharge I applied and received it. I arrived home by Christmas, proudly strutting about in the uniform of a private.

In World War II, I again enlisted and flew overseas to England in July 1942 as a major in the Services of Supply. I was stationed in London. Soon after reaching there, I obtained orders assigning me to continued service in London but with the Eighth Air Force. My job was the procurement from British sources of supplies, equipment and services under Reverse Lend Lease. Our procurement unit spent the equivalent of hundreds of millions of dollars in obtaining for our air forces, through the Royal Air Force and the Ministry of Aircraft Production, huge quantities of general supplies and aircraft equipment, much of the latter being highly technical and specialized. Without this important help from the British, our bombers and other aircraft of America's strategic air forces based in the United Kingdom would have been much longer delayed in becoming operational and much less effective in action.

German Air Raids on London

During my service in London in the years 1942–44 raids by German aircraft dropping high explosive bombs were not infrequent. Anyone who lived in that embattled city in those days will vividly recall the mournful wail of the sirens announcing that enemy bombers were about to pay a visit. After the sirens had given their warning there would be an uneasy quiet for a minute or two, and then one would begin to hear the distant booming of the antiaircraft guns, as London's outer defenses tried to impede the progress of the Germans in their flight to the center of the city. The sounds of an air raid always reminded me of an approaching summer storm, though the action was, of course, in much faster tempo. There were the first claps of thunder in the remote distance, and then the rising crescendo of noise as the storm's center came nearer. It was only a few minutes after the first warning before the Germans were overhead and the night skies crisscrossed by a hundred searchlights attempting to pinpoint the bombers for the antiaircraft gunners. The storm center was upon us and the thunder of London's ack-ack guns—supplemented in late 1943 by the roar of Hyde Park's massive rocket barrage—made, together with the bomb detonations themselves, a deafening cacophony. Two or three times in the so-called Little Blitz of March 1944 there was a downpour of incendiary bombs with resultant conflagrations. I remember one such raid where the number of separate fires in the neighborhood of my apartment house was considerably more than the fire brigades could attend to.

A week after D-Day, that is, on June 13, 1944, the Germans started the bombardment of London with their V-1, jet-powered, flying bombs, commonly called buzz bombs. This attack was much more unpleasant and more devastating than the air raids which I had experienced. For some weeks the buzz bombs, flying noisily only a few hundred feet overhead, came almost continuously day and night. But by the end of July gradually improving defense techniques had changed the steady rain of explosives to an occasional drizzle. Altogether 7,840 of these flying bombs and another 500 rocket missiles (V-2's) came to England. There was no defense against the latter, and almost all of them found their London target. Of the flying bombs (V-1's) about 2,500 got through the defenses on the South Coast and hit London. Buzz bombs were not blockbusters, but one of them could completely destroy two ordinary-sized city homes or a church or a theater. The flying bombs and, to a much smaller extent, the rockets caused heavy destruction and casualties, with 8,908 killed and 24,448 injured, mostly in London.

The officers of the American military contingents based in London had to get on with their jobs. We were the supporting services for thousands of our troops and men of our tactical air forces already on the Normandy beachhead. We could not seek protection every time we heard or saw a buzz bomb coming in our direction. Nor could the people of London run away either. In point of time a minute, and in distance 300 yards, I missed the fall and explosion of buzz bombs several times. So did a million others.

I remained in London until early July 1944 when, having previously transferred to the Ninth Air Force, the tactical force in direct support of our troops, I crossed the Channel to Normandy. In Normandy, particularly before July 25th when the American forces finally made their break-out through the German defenses at St. Lo—and put the Heinies on the run—I experienced the excitement which comes with nearness to the front line and with hearing and seeing guns fired in anger. A tent pitched on a pasture in the Normandy beachhead was not replete with all the comforts of a London flat or office, and enemy aircraft made the nights unpleasantly noisy. However, on balance, life for me in Normandy, minus buzz bombs, was much less tense than in London, plus buzz bombs. I remained in France for the rest of the summer. For various reasons I sought a discharge from the Air Force prior to the war's end, and I retired from active service in October 1944 with the rank of lieutenant colonel.

The war record of my own son, Thomas William Lamont II, has been set down in another volume.* He volunteered as a sub-mariner, and upon his third patrol in Far Eastern waters his ship was lost and he never returned. Tommy's brother, Edward, two years his junior, served in the Navy toward the end of the war and was in the V-12 Naval Officers' course at Princeton when the peace came.

Pioneers Don't Stay Put

As stated earlier, great-great-grandfather William Lamont, Jr., the first Lamont to settle at the crossroads which later became Charlotteville, had twelve children; and each of them, including especially my great-grandfather Thomas William Lamont, reared very large families. By the middle of the century Charlotteville was mostly Lamonts or their relatives, as the old village graveyard still bears witness. Yet there was also a certain amount of leakage out of Charlotteville. The Lamonts of Scotland, and for that matter the Scottish people as a whole, have always tended to leave home and settle in regions far away. So, in due course, did the Lamonts of Charlotteville.

It is apparent that many Lamonts went west year by year, and in increasing numbers, throughout the nineteenth century and on into the first quarter of this century. I would be reasonably sure that some of these Lamonts—cousins and second cousins of my father, grandfather and great-grandfather—were responsible for the fact that there are eight communities in our country and one in Canada named Lamont. The family metropolis is the town of Lamont, California, with a population of 3,600 people; in fact, of all places bearing our name, except a village in Alberta, it is the only Lamont that boasts a population in excess of 600! The good people who made these communities in Idaho, Oklahoma,

---

* *Things To Be Remembered: The Record of a Young Life,* edited by Corliss Lamont and privately published, 1946.

Wyoming and other states did not give them names like Lamont-ville or Lamontown. With proud and admirable forthrightness they named their villages Lamont. Indeed, there is only one town named Smith in the United States, only six named Jones, only one Kelly. But mark you, eight Lamonts!

Father used to boast about having forty-two first cousins, but as a boy I saw hardly any of them. That was because they had ended up in every part of our country except the East. That was why Father could write of his final visit to Charlotteville some thirty-five years ago: "The byways and the whole village were filled with ghosts. Lamonts had come, had seen and had conquered, and then had all gone, leaving only memories behind them."

The Writers

The Lamonts of the present and of recent generations have written a great deal. It has been in the family tradition. After college Father started his career as reporter for the New York *Tribune*; and prior to that he was President of the *Harvard Crimson*, as I myself later became. My library shelves contain many bound volumes of old school papers and college literary magazines to which my father or my sons contributed. My son Tommy was editor of the *Phillips Exeter Review*, and the volume *Things To Be Remembered* attests his skill as a writer of prose and poetry, diaries and letters. My son Lansing started his career as a newspaperman and became a reporter on the staff of *Time* in its Washington Bureau. Then also, of course, I have the books by both my parents to which reference is made in my brother's memoir; and my collection includes Corliss's own numerous volumes.

Father's older brother, Uncle Hammond, took his first job after college as a reporter on the *Post Intelligencer* of Seattle. Later, as I have already mentioned, he became a member of the faculties, successively, at Harvard and Brown. During his academic years he wrote a book on rhetoric and one or two other textbooks on English composition; at the turn of the century these were widely used in the schools of this country. Uncle Hammond became managing editor of the *New York Evening Post* in 1901, and in 1907 editor of *The Nation*, which was a weekly magazine well regarded in the literary world and known for its vigorous expression of liberal opinion. Uncle Hammond's son Gordon was a reporter on the *New York Evening Post* and for three years its city editor.

My uncle, John P. Gavit, who married my father's sister Lucy, had a long career as a newspaperman with the *Hartford Courant,* the *Albany Journal* and other publications. For some years he headed the Washington Bureau of the Associated Press, and he later became managing editor of the *New York Evening Post.* The three best books he wrote are on my shelves.

We Share Our Pride of Past

Having identified some of our ancestors individually by word and deed, I would question the prideful implications of my story. Why should an American heritage which goes back to the seventeenth century warrant more pride of past than the heritage of parents or grandparents who may have come to this country only fifty years ago or less? The latter were usually classified as "immigrants," but they too were pioneers. By what right or reason can one evaluate less highly the quality of an immigrant's courage than that of an earlier settler on our continent? It will be argued that the life of the earlier pioneers was a much harder one and their risks greater. That is true, but it is also true that life in the British Isles and throughout Europe was much more difficult in the seventeenth and eighteenth centuries than in the nineteenth. Thus the strength of will required of one who was setting forth to a new life in a new world may have been of like measure at all times. I make this point so that, as we think of our own forefathers' bravery and initiative, we remember also that those qualities are not exclusively inherent in an ancestry like ours which is readily traced back to the earliest Colonial days.

Nor should we Lamonts forget that many thousands, perhaps millions, of other Americans can boast as easily as we—and some more impressively!—that they were of Colonial stock. I doubt not that many thousands of our countrymen could, if they wished, write as I have of ancestors whose lives were equally deserving of their descendants' pride.

Some readers may feel that I have given an impression that I assumed our forebears to be the exclusive possession of our small branch of Lamonts. A look at the past generations of Lamonts clearly reveals that we can have no monopoly of pride even in as recent ancestors as Great-grandfather Thomas William Lamont and his good wife, Elizabeth. Their descendants are now numbered in the hundreds. Therefore, as we think proudly of our fine heritage, let us not forget that we share the same ancestors equally with thousands of other living Americans.

There must be, for example, several score thousands of Americans who can claim, as I have, direct descent from William Bradford. The Governor was of the seventh generation of my great-grandfathers, which makes him only one of 512 grandparents of mine in his generation. Thus the blood of this Puritan, to the extent that we Lamonts possess it, can be no more than a few drops in each of us. Should any of us happen to have characteristics akin to Bradford's, it would be coincidental rather than hereditary. It could be argued, therefore, that this paper of mine implies too intimate a relationship with our earliest forebears in New England and New York—the Bradfords and Stilwells, the Jaynes and the Lansings. But interesting, lively and courageous people are worth writing about; and they were our grandsires from whom we are directly descended. I claim no more than that.

Actually, beginning with William Bradford's generation of my ancestors, I have had a total of 1,020 grandparents! Today's Lamonts may perchance through heredity have acquired a few of the traits of our earlier ancestors. It is likely, however, that a much larger hereditary influence upon the Lamonts in my generation would be the talents and temperaments of the recent generations—our parents, our grandparents and our eight great-grandparents: a Lamont, a Paine, a Jayne, a Ferguson, a Corliss, a Hoyt, a Parmelee and an Allen.

And heredity, of course, includes the bad with the good. My parents, grandparents and great-grandparents were all good people. Yet among my forebears it would be normal to expect that some few had been men and women whose aspirations were not high and whose manners and mores were second-rate. Surely in such a numerous company of grandparents there must have been ne'er-do-wells and rolling stones. Yet neither in my grandfather's book nor from family memorabilia have I been able to find any reference to our black sheep. They remain hidden in the past.

Lamonts Past and Present—The Contrasting Lives

As indicated in an earlier section, our forebears in America up to the middle of the nineteenth century were, in the making of their families, greatly influenced by the necessity to provide both physical and economic security. The agricultural economy of the new continent encouraged a binding union of husband and wife and a unity of the whole family. There was in fact no great over-supply of wives ready to leave the seaboard towns and live in log cabins; and being scarce, their value to pioneer husbands was high and their position as homemakers and mothers quite secure. Economic necessity, therefore, was a great influence in preserving the family unity; but marriage vows, the sexual urge and love played their part then as now. In those tough old days the love of a husband and wife grew more tender as mutual respect developed from the sharing of hardships.

How utterly different were the lives of our ancestors from those lived by the Lamonts of the mid-twentieth century! None of us has had to join with our parents and brothers and sisters—after family prayers each morning—in sharing the hundred and one chores which were part of the everyday life of most of my American ancestors. None of us living Lamonts collects the ashes and the skillet drippings to make the soap. We do not drive the cattle, milk the cows and churn the butter. We do not clear the stones, hold the plough which the oxen pull, cradle the grain and thresh with the flail. We do not dig potatoes or slop the hogs. We do not even get a chance to indulge our sweet tooth by tending a "sap-bush." No daughters are needed to help mothers bake the bread and sew the quilts. Where we happen to have a vegetable garden or a fruit orchard, I haven't noticed any Lamont mothers of today preserving their produce in order to keep their families well fed and healthy during the long winter. Instead we swallow little red capsules in order to get our winter's quota of vitamins. Further back, in the generations before my great-grandparents, there were the added chores of a pioneer life: clearing the forests, building the cabins, preparing defense against the Indians, fighting to create a new nation.

A little over a century ago social evolution in rural New England and New York began to accelerate. Economic pressures changed. Itinerant labor became available. Textile mills started to produce cloth better in quality and cheaper in cost than that produced by my great-grandmothers on their spinning wheels and looms. Both the need for large families to run the farm and the economic importance of wives began to decline. Life eased up a bit and hardships, which bred mutual respect and love, were ameliorated. The growing cities of the nation attracted ambitious youth, and the old homestead lost its importance as the center of a unified family.

Of course, the average American family today has no easy time establishing itself upon a secure economic base. It is a real struggle for millions, and the struggle still strengthens character and nurtures mutual respect within the family. But with our small branch of Lamonts things are different. Thanks to America's freedom of opportunity open to my father, his children and his grandchildren inherited a good measure of material security. Our marriages and our families have to stand or fall—and they do both—without the same old-time economic compulsions to prop them up. The evidence indicates that our ancestors were for the most part a happy breed of men and women. I like to think that today's Lamont families are equally so, but circumstances make the achievement of happiness harder for us and for our children. This isn't a complaint. It is an inescapable fact.

So many of our forebears were highly motivated toward achieving a better life for their families. As a natural result many became leaders in their communities. Their spirits seemed indomitable. Today's easier conditions of life can discourage initiative. The high aspirations, the drive, the sense of purpose of the earlier Lamonts will be difficult to pass on to future generations. However, most members of the next generation—sons, daughters, nephews, nieces —are already hard at work and appear serious in purpose. Is that good luck or a good upbringing or a good heritage? What of our grandchildren's generation? I don't know the answers.

Destiny and Duty

We have been brought up in an atmosphere pervaded by the high standards of performance of parents and grandparents for generations back. It is up to us to maintain that tradition of high performance, and to instill it in the generations which follow. We owe it to our Past, to ourselves and to our world. We must continuously and always explore our talents fully, seeking every challenge, and never leveling off our full efforts before we bump against the ceilings of our capacities. I hope the Lamonts will enjoy the benefits of abundance without becoming ensnared in its disadvantages. I hope they will find some equivalents of the frontier's hardships to strengthen their characters.

It is possible that those equivalents lie just ahead, still unseen by us whose sights are dim. Perhaps they are already here. Our country and our world may be nearer to the edge of a greater change than has been witnessed for centuries of history. I do not refer to a nuclear catastrophe (which I do not anticipate) or to a visit through space to the rest of the universe. I am speaking of our own world's future. It seems probable to me that the new forces of science, and the renewed aspirations for liberty and economic progress, which have found their power in the pervasive spread of modern communications—these may soon bring changes to our nation and the world, changes as basic as were the beginnings of a system of agriculture and the invention of the wheel so many millennia ago. All our institutions, our relationships between peoples and their governments and between nations, our societies and the nature and form of our economies—all these may well be changed by the new forces and influences which are stirring the minds of men.

Thus I'm inclined to feel that Lamonts now living, as well as their descendants, may be faced with greater challenges and greater opportunities than their pioneer ancestors ever met. To prepare themselves for this future, Lamonts would be wise to tend the cultivation of the inner spirit, to reaffirm by their lives and thoughts their basic faith in a Divine Power, a Power which shapes our great world and even each of our own small worlds, a Power whom they would seek to please by their will to goodness. Beyond this fundamental way of life are all its outward manifestations including courage, energy, imagination and generosity.

The Lamonts must ever defend the cause of individual freedom within this society of ours which so frequently tends to curtail it. They must have the ability to discriminate between a happy dream and a practical solution—yet with tolerance of the dreamer and no easy acceptance of the opinions and acts of those who would oppose every change and of those who would abandon each worthy concept of our past. All these qualities may be required of Lamonts of the future much more than they were required of Lamonts of the past.

Grandson and Grandmother—The Captured Hearts

Several pages back I wrote of Love. I almost implied that it was something only to be found in log cabins. Yet every day of our lives its beauty blossoms about us, and love will find expression in all our families till the end of time. With all Lamonts of the future, as with Lamonts of the past, every hoped-for strength will be stronger when love is in their hearts. So this last section, written by others than I, will be of love.

I shall quote briefly from a letter written by a young man, and at greater length from a young lady's diary. Their expressions are alike in intensity of spirit, in the earnestness and reality of their emotion—of love newly come into their lives. Here are the inmost secrets of their hearts. Doubtless it never occurred to them that years later their thoughts would appear in print to warm the hearts of others, of those who would keep fresh every happy memory of them both. Yet, under all the circumstances, I doubt that the writers would object to this revelation of their thoughts.

In a city in the northwest part of our country there lives a lady, a happy wife and mother with a long and tender memory. A year or so ago she gave me a final message which she had received from my sailor son Tommy, aged twenty, who loved her as she also loved him. He had written it early in June 1944, only a few days before he left on assignment to submarine duty in the Pacific, never again to return. He wrote:

> My dearest: I feel I should set down on paper a few thoughts while I have the time. . . . Most boys my age have had their lives before them, but for us there remains only the temporizing heaven of a week or so. . . . a week or so which will be shadowed and haunted by the terrible certainty of separation. . . . I love you, darling, and believe me these weeks, snatched with a smile and tear from the great, cruel, befuddled rush of war, have been the happiest in my life. . . . But why should I be sad when the very thought of you is a treasure few men find? I love you, darling, on and on into the stars which have no end.

The letter which I have quoted was written by my son fifty-two years *after* the diary I am about to quote. He was the first grandchild of Florence Corliss, my mother, the diarist. And this is from her diary which she started writing at Smith College when she was eighteen years old. The first passage is for November 17, 1890:

> I went to . . . [Harvard's] Commencement [last June], and of course had a glorious time. The fellow I liked best was Thomas W. Lamont, Esq., now a junior. . . . He liked me quite a good deal too. Though I don't think he would pine away if he never saw me again. But I had *very* good fun with him. . . . We sat on the stairs and had fun. He announced some quite

startling things about his head and heart. In spite of what that boy says, *I* think he is the worst flirt I ever met. Sunday afternoon we went to Mt. Auburn Cemetery. He walked with me. Monday we went on the Wellesley Drive. I sat with him. . . . That's the last time I've seen him. . . .

February 26, 1891—Well, the great 22nd has come and gone, and what a good time I did have! I asked Mr. Lamont up and he came. I like him very much, more than I ever liked anyone before. . . . I wore my old rose dress. I was very much rattled when I first saw him for I did not know what to say or how to act. . . . In the afternoon was the Glee Club concert. He had sent me two dozen lovely roses and I carried some of them—the yellow ones. He stood by the platform and I talked to him between times. . . . And then the evening—how shall I tell about that! I don't think I ever had such a nice time in my life. T.W.L. told me a lot of interesting things about myself and himself. I think he really likes me very much, and is not fooling with me as I thought. . . . We walked home via Hubbard House and my rubbers kept tumbling off. He said he would see me in the spring. Oh dear, I wish it would hurry and be spring.

May 5, 1891—Last Saturday . . . I drove over to the Harvard-Amherst ball game. T.W.L. was there. . . . He said he would come up to the Hatfield House as soon as he got to Northampton. . . . So I was all ready and waiting real early. At last we heard a heavy tread coming upstairs. I thought it might be the maid and held my breath in expectation and it was T.W.L.! Needless to say I was extremely happy. The next morning it poured. We went to church and after church took a walk in the pouring rain, which I enjoyed immensely. . . . After supper we took another walk, the nicest of all. . . . He left early the next morning. I wish I knew how well I liked him. I am so afraid to say I really like anyone very much after all that has happened to prove how fickle I am. So I guess I won't say it.

Sunday, July 3, 1892—I was twenty years old last Friday. . . . [Tom] told me last night how dearly he loved me, and I told him I loved him too. . . .

September 27, 1892— . . . I am so glad I love Tom so much and so glad he loves me. I ought to be the thankfullest girl in the world. I do so long to be more and more to him—to be everything to him, to love him, to help him, to inspire him with every beautiful and fine thing. For he said I was an inspiration to him though I do not understand how. Dear Tom—I wish I could begin to be the fine girl he deserves to have and to love. But I shall try hard anyway.

And finally an undated letter written on a Sunday evening sometime that same year:

Tom dear, it does all seem so wonderful—that you should love me so very much, and that I should love you so very much. It all seems too good to be true. But it is true and I am very, very happy. I shall try so hard, dear, to be strong and true and unselfish and I shall love you so much, and I shall try to help you all I can about everything. I have thought of you a great deal today. . . . Good night, dear. . . . With love, Florence.

North Haven, Maine
August 1962

17

T. S. L.: A HAPPY MAN, A USEFUL LIFE

by Edward M. Lamont
(1968)

Thomas Stilwell Lamont was born on January 30, 1899, in Engle-wood, New Jersey. He died on April 10, 1967, at the age of sixty-eight in New York City.

My father, known to his friends as "Tommy," led a happy, full, and useful life. The keystone for such a life is usually home and family, and my father was no exception. He loved his family and his devotion embraced all the members of the large Lamont-Miner family circle. He took a keen interest in the progress and achievements of each family member, as children—sons and daughter, nephews and nieces—grew up and matured into men and women, a new generation with distinctly individual personalities and goals. And then the process began again. He loved to chat with the younger generation about their hopes and plans, or gossip about the latest news in each family over a breakfast cup of coffee on the porch at North Haven in the summer. These were happy moments, and we welcomed and appreciated his concern and wise counsel.

My father's own moving words in his will express his love for his family:

> I would remind those who may have to read this Will that however formal, legalistic and complicated it may sound, it is primarily a family document whose provisions are intended to reflect the love I bear for all in our large family circle: infinite gratitude to my fine wife, high satisfaction in the integrity, modesty and sense of humor of my three good children, happy affection for their wives and husband, and joy in my nine merry grandchildren.

My father was happiest when he was with his family, but business, of course, often kept him apart from them. One summer when most of the family were in North Haven he wrote to me as follows (and I did not forget his advice):

The summer life of a New York businessman, living alone in the Big City, is not too exciting. You and Lansing take a tip from me: whatever you do in life, arrange it so you spend all your life with your wife and family. Eight weeks or even four weeks are too many to be alone if you are married and love your wife and children. There are a few other bachelors around town, some very nice, but the wisest fellows are home in the suburbs with their families most every night.

And during World War II, when my father served in England for over two years with the Eighth and Ninth Air Force, he wrote Lansing from London:

Just about my chief pleasure over here is to sit down at my own desk quietly in the evening and write letters to those whom I love—especially you and mother and Tommy and Ted and Elinor. It is the next best thing to talking with you. Crowding duties and obligations to be nice to people prevent me from doing as much letter writing as I should like. But my roommate, Mr. Smith, says I am forever sitting up too late at night writing letters. I wish I were. Sometimes I fear my letters may be so long as to bore you and mother. I hope not, but if they are, just tell me to make them shorter. When I sit down to write a letter I am inclined to spout all my thoughts.

I missed you all very much at Christmas and thought of you constantly. I couldn't get to church Christmas Day, but I went the next day, Sunday. I inquired as to what services I should go to. Everyone said I should go to the carol services at Westminster, or hear the choir sing at St. Paul's. Well, I fooled them all. I looked up the church notices in the paper and found that the nearby neighborhood church was having a children's service at 3 p.m. I wanted to go to something that was more like a family church—like St. James or St. Paul's in Rochester. I didn't want to sit in a great crowd at a huge cathedral. So I went alone and sang "Away in a Manger" and "Once in Royal David's City" and "Oh Little Town" and "Good King Wenceslaus" and lots of others. There was a Christmas tree and all the children from about three years old up to about thirteen left their seats and paraded up to the Christmas tree behind the old verger and left their presents beneath it. A little boy Elinor's age walked up to the pulpit and read the first lesson and a big girl about your age read the second lesson. I guess you know how the first lesson began: "Now it came to pass in those days there went out a decree from Caesar Augustus"—and the next several hundred words are among the most beautiful in the English language.

So I had a good sing, and I enjoyed the children and the spirit of the little neighborhood church—and I went home thinking of what a nice family I had and how much I wanted to see them.

As the children grew older they were away from home more and more—first school and college—then the Navy for Tommy and myself, and later the Army for Lansing. Lansing and I later settled with our families in Washington, D.C., and Elinor in Cambridge, Massachusetts. My father enjoyed letter writing and maintained a steady and prolific correspondence with his children as well as with numerous friends here and abroad. He felt it was important to keep alive a spirit of family unity and loyalty among the children when they had left home. To this end he wrote us long letters filled with news of his and mother's life in New York, of the latest events in various branches of the family. These letters also dealt with the practical side of our lives. At least in my case during school and college years, he was often called upon to handle my latest request to "send more money!" He also sent us clippings of articles he had found especially worthwhile and circulated copies of letters we had written home. In later years, when his health forced him to give up golf and tennis, his literary output increased. Often he would return to the office from Laurel Hollow on Mondays carrying lengthy tapes of letters and memoranda he had dictated into his machine over the weekend.

He took seriously the responsibility of being a father, and some of his letters reflected his concern that his children should be mentally and morally tough, that they early acquire the habit of hard work, that their ideals be high. When my brother Tommy's submarine was lost in the Pacific in April 1945, he wrote me:

> Well, so far as you are concerned, the future will have to take care of itself—and it will—and happily and successfully, I am sure. You are coming to an age where you will mature even more rapidly, and when you will realize all the more fully the responsibilities which are on your shoulders as my oldest son and as the oldest Lamont of your generation. I know that you will accept those responsibilities gladly and ably. Don't ever worry about them—enjoy life all the time, but all the time also, keep your ambitions and objectives for yourself high—and set the best example you can for Lansing and Elinor to follow.

At this time he also wrote:

Tommy had grown into a fine man during the war, while he was in the Navy, and had written us some wonderful letters, some of which you have seen. He would have contributed greatly to the life of our country had he lived, because he thought hard and had an independent mind.

You must think of the meaning of Tommy's death. We have many friends whose children have died, but none of them can have quite the same pride that we have and that you can have, for Tommy gave his life in the greatest cause. In this Great War and in the previous World War, it has been only the boys with highest spirit and deepest understanding who have volunteered for the dangerous kind of job. Tommy had strong convictions about his responsibility in this war. He knew why he was fighting and what he was fighting for. His letters showed that he was determined, unafraid of danger, and fully prepared in his own mind for whatever personal sacrifice was required. It is hard not to be sad, of course, because we shall miss Tommy so much, but most of all at this time you should be filled with greatest pride that you had Tommy as a brother; and after a while pride and the happy memories of him will gradually efface the sorrow which we all feel now.

My father's business correspondence was prodigious also. He was one of a dwindling band who prefer to communicate their ideas precisely and for the record by letter rather than telephone. Gordon Wasson, a long time colleague and friend of my father at the bank [Morgan Guaranty Trust Company], wrote about some of his business correspondence:

He was sometimes impatient of what seemed to him (and was) stupidity, either on the part of others or more especially in the operations of large organizations that have become impersonal and mechanical, whether governmental or corporate or charitable. He would write devastating letters, all the more effective because restrained in his words, to the people in charge after having seen, or perhaps himself been a victim of, an exhibition of the folly of such organizations. His letters were not sputters of indignation: they were factual. He wasted no words, he would not over-emphasize his points, but he would take extraordinary pains to set forth his observations and views lucidly, if necessary at considerable length.

Charles Dickey states in a memoir about T.S.L.: "He loved life and after family friends ranked at the top of his list." He

Aerial photograph, with a northward view of Pulpit Harbor, on the island of North Haven, Maine, summer home of Mr. and Mrs. Thomas W. Lamont, their children, and grandchildren. The Lamont houses are set back from the further shore, but are for the most part hidden by the trees. To the left and in the background is a view of West Penobscot Bay.

Courtesy Peter Gilchrist

was beloved by many friends for his loyalty, his warmth, and wit, which was normally of a gentle and unbarbed nature. He was a kind and generous man; many friends and others he knew less well sought and received his advice and help. My father's reminiscences about his close friend, Thomas H. Gammack, described his wide circle of friends in words that apply to their author: "He preferred for friends those whose shirts were not stuffed, who had a sense of humor, and ideas in their heads. These qualifications were common to his intimate friends, but otherwise there were wide differences between them in character and background."

He had a special fondness for celebrating in verse the birthdays and wedding anniversaries of old friends. He took particular delight in giving lengthy toasts at the bridal dinners or wedding receptions of his children and those of his friends and relatives based on humorous episodes in the past of the bridal participants. Who can forget the special twinkle in his eye, the droll delivery, dramatic pauses, and the subtle humor of his remarks on those occasions?

North Haven, a lovely island in Penobscot Bay, Maine, is mentioned many times in this book. My father's family started spending summer vacations in North Haven more than fifty years ago and succeeding generations of Lamonts have continued to come to the island with their families. Beginning in 1953, my parents lived in the big house called Sky Farm, where my grandparents had lived before them. It is a large rambling yellow house with a magnificent sweeping view of the bay, a chain of spruce-covered rockbound islands in the foreground and the majestic Camden Hills as a backdrop. On a northwest day the sparkling bay is alive with whitecaps, as sailboats of varying size and rig, including the stately old coastal schooners now on tourist cruises, enter and cross the mammoth stage. In the evening when the sun sets behind the hills a truly glorious scene unfolds: the golden western sky, against which low-lying darkening clouds are silhouetted, and the warm orange glow of the setting sun itself, give way to deepening shades of blue and finally starry night and the twinkling lights of Camden across the bay. All is still, except perhaps for the chug-chug of a fisherman's boat returning from mackereling and the wash of the waves on the rocky beach below the house.

A new day dawns and there is a strengthening smoky southwest breeze. In earlier years, my father might play golf or tennis in the morning and then sail the dinghy with an offspring as crew in one of the regular afternoon races in the Thoroughfare. These races can be very exciting. On a Saturday in August, twenty-five to thirty boats will start; in a good blow, a skillful skipper and a hefty crewman leaning over the windward rail (when he isn't pumping) are both necessary to avoid a dunking in waters famed for their chilling shock effect.

My father especially enjoyed family picnics on one of the islands to the east or in Hurricane Sound to the south. The motorboat and perhaps a sailboat would be loaded with parents and children, uncles and aunts, baby-sitters and house guests, and picnic paraphernalia. Exploring the island and swimming before lunch in the icy bay water are standard procedure, at least for the children. My father, usually wearing his long-visored swordfisherman's cap, was often slung with cameras, and his slides and movies of picnics in Maine have enlivened many an evening.

Of course, life in North Haven was not without domestic trials and incidents. As the families multiplied so did the dog population. An aunt's Norwegian elk hound nipped my father; others took to chasing sheep or raiding a local farmer's chicken coop. And one summer, to cope with the canine problem that was most annoying to my father and damaging to the lawns, he equipped us all with children's sandbox shovels with stern instructions to use them! There were other wildlife problems and one summer he wrote:

> I am glad to hear that Ted is handy around the house. His mother would not say that he inherits that from me. However, I consider myself a good handyman in certain respects. For example, in the last ten days at North Haven I have killed two mice with a broom, one squirrel with a broom, and then I drowned it, and I caught one mouse with a trap after an abortive first effort when I caught my finger. Our house in North Haven suddenly became this summer a refuge for lots of wild life.

When my brother, Tommy, was in the Navy he wrote home: "North Haven is my Tivoli, my Mandalay, my favorite place on earth." My father was in complete agreement.

In later years my parents looked forward each winter to visiting Peg and Lew Douglas at their farm outside Tucson, Arizona, to relaxing with old friends in the sunny, dry climate and enjoying the wild beauty of the Southwest. But earlier, and lasting for a period of about twenty years when we were growing up, my father's favorite winter recreation was skiing.

I started skiing with my father in the late thirties, and the first ski resort I remember was Woodstock with its rope tows, Bunny's and Suicide Six. When the rope was wet or icy, it took all the strength a young boy possessed to keep a firm grip on it. Skiers bought clamps and other gadgets to grip the rope, and my father bought me a pair of rubber mittens which actually froze to the rope. At the top of the tow as I was being literally lifted into the air, I finally wrenched my hand free; mitten and ski pole were carried into the big wheel which clattered to a stop. Father and son quickly agreed that rubber mittens were not the answer!

We also spent many weekends at North Conway, where we stayed at Eastern Slopes Inn and skied Mt. Cranmore with its multicolored ski mobile tramway to the summit and Hans Schneider himself in command of the ski school. In those days one took the Pullman from New York on Friday night, returning Sunday night. The small band from the Swiss pavilion at the New York World's Fair played at the Inn, and North Conway was a very lively place indeed for a young boy. My father loved the life and once wrote: "It would be good to recapture the spirit of those ski weekends— the meeting at the train, the excitement and anticipation, the two or three days of crowded glorious hours, the return, exhausted and content."

Over the years Lansing, Elinor, and I spent many weekends and school vacations skiing with my father in the Green and White mountain ranges of Vermont and New Hampshire, and a few times in the Laurentians. I was with my father when he broke his ankle on the old S-53 trail at Stowe one March when the warm spring sun made skiing tricky on the melting stop-and-go surfaces of the slopes and trails. In those prewar days of baggy pants and black caps with little bows over the visor, a serious ski injury was still an event to be commemorated. Accident victims, including my father, received a "Purple Heart," a small silver badge in the form of a human bone, properly fractured, to pin on their caps. I also was with my father on several ski parties organized by Lowell Thomas, the news broadcaster. A favorite photograph in our family shows T. S. L. assisting Lowell in his evening news program which was being broadcast from the base lodge at Cannon Mountain. We continued to share many happy times skiing with my father for another ten years or so after the war.

My father was, I believe, a very broad-gauged, tolerant, and open-minded person; his intellectual vitality was extraordinary. Many, many aspects of life interested him as an observer or a participant. However, his central interests were his bank, for which he worked throughout his entire business career, starting in 1922, and the field of education, especially two institutions, Phillips Exeter Academy and Harvard University.

His business career and his special contribution to the bank are well summarized in the Resolution of the Board of Directors of Morgan Guaranty Trust Company.* He often spoke of his pride in being a businessman and a banker. His views on the vital im-

---
* See chapter 18 below.

portance to our country of free and competitive markets and an internationalist outlook in foreign affairs are contained in several speeches. Again his own words describing his father are equally descriptive of the son:

> First of all, he was devoted to his own country. But his was no narrow nationalistic patriotism. He loved his fellow man, whether he might be from New York, Kansas, China or France. He saw clearly that, for the peace and well-being of America, Americans must understand and appreciate their neighbors across the seas as well as their neighbors on Main Street, that only a peaceful world could insure a happy home anywhere. Between every line of this story of Father's, implicit in his every activity, one can see his hope and prayer for the future: the wish for his children's children that no frontiers would ever bind their minds or set limits upon their achievements.

In the following passage from his will, my father expresses his deeply felt conviction as to the vital role of education in our democratic society:

> Representative and democratic government needs an electorate which has knowledge of the nation's history and a pride in its traditions of liberty. Only through higher standards of education can our citizens develop a sure determination to preserve our cherished heritage of Freedom: freedom of the individual to express himself as he will and to engage in enterprise and to own property subject only to the fair restraints necessary in a democratic society. The nation's security and the health of the nation's economy, in which private initiative must play so large a part, depend upon free markets including especially a free market for ideas.

I think that perhaps the trait that many will remember best in my father was his sense of humor. Gordon Wasson has written the following:

> In the heyday of the firm the Morgan partners were a gay band of men: They had little occasion to remind each other of "Rule No. 7"—this was a private short-hand way of suggesting that one should not take oneself too seriously. But I believe that no partner in my time could rival Tom's sense of humor. He would come hurrying into the morning meeting, a slight quiver of the lip hovering over his expression. We knew at once that a story would be forthcoming, something that had happened

to him and that he was eager to share with us. His stories would be revealing of the character of someone we knew, enfilading so to speak the personality of the victim. There was no malice in those stories, simply accurate observation. None of us who knew Tom will ever forget his capacity for seizing a humorous situation and retelling it.

I remember especially the stories he would tell at family lunch on Sundays—for example, about a humorously stuffy Britisher he had sat next to at a black-tie business dinner the week before—which would convulse us as they did him in the telling. He had a gift for superb understatement; and, à la Jack Benny, was adept at deflating someone else's silly exaggeration with a significant pause and a highly audible and meaningful "Mmm!"

T. S. L. loved to kid the ladies, including his dear wife, especially when they professed a degree of innocence about youth or sex incompatible with the facts of life. When my brother, Tommy, grew a beard on submarine duty in World War II, Father wrote me:

> Mother has relented on her first idea of hiding the snapshots of your brother, Blue Beard, and apparently is willing to show them to a few of her intimates who come in from time to time. Apparently she takes a sort of morbid pleasure in doing so. Mrs. Tuckerman was greatly surprised that so young a man could succeed in growing so full a beard, so I had to explain to her the facts of life, which included the observation that if her daughter could produce a baby, as she had, there was no reason why a son of exactly the same age couldn't produce a beard.

And he enjoyed that All-American pastime of joking about his wife's family. In 1953 he wrote us:

> Lansing finished his job in Chicago and came home and, with Ellie and me, we all went to Rochester for the announcement of Anne's engagement to Bradley Richardson who, as you know, is one of Lansing's oldest friends. Aunt Leight was also there from Boston, and you can imagine how I loved visiting my mother-in-law when I had to share a bathroom with eight other people and live in a house where every window is closed air-tight, with the temperature at eighty, and the air still smelling of the cigars that Grandpa smoked in 1905. The weekend was a succession of luncheons, cocktail parties and dinners, all with the same people. I had to make a spectacle of myself by jumping to my feet and proposing a toast and telling long-winded stories

on every occasion. Lansing played the piano occasionally and it was all very jolly. We wished you and Ted had been there.

One letter written a year or so later describes a few typical weeks in my father's life:

I wish I could sit down and write a letter to each one of you, but the lively life which your mother and I lead consumes almost every instant of my waking day. I had planned to give up last weekend to writing each of you letters, then Uncle Ranny* turned up and came to spend the weekend with us in Laurel Hollow. When I wasn't playing golf, in order to get a little exercise which I badly need, I was engaged in a hard tussle at scrabble with Mother and Uncle Ranny—afternoon and evening and far into the night. Mother is a brilliant scrabble player and it is very difficult to beat her. Only occasionally am I able to do so.

Both Saturday and Sunday mornings I drove Mother in the new bright red Ford station wagon over to a nearby nursery and loaded it up each time with pansies, geraniums and whatnot to go into the little flower garden at the side of the house. I liked that job because it meant doing a lot of lifting and carrying of heavy pots and very heavy lilac bushes too. It is good for an old man's back to have a little pressure put on it. So we had a nice quiet weekend and my golf is a little better than normal for this early season period of the year.

A week ago I was in Chicago for two days, flying out one morning and coming back on the "Twentieth Century" the following night, and last Monday I was in Cambridge for a Harvard Corporation meeting. I stayed over and went to dinner at High Table at Lowell House. After dinner half a dozen undergraduates got me in a corner and plied me with questions about Harvard. They were very bright, articulate boys and they really gave me a brainwashing. So it continues.

This weekend Rufus Smith, my English friend and partner, is coming down to stay with us. He is taking Mother over to the Belmont Park races on Saturday, which will be quite a new experience for Mother. They are having a big steeplechase race and the idea is to revive steeplechase racing at Belmont Park. Mr. Smith's sister is bringing her Irish hunter over. It is all very exciting. I shall play golf.

The letter goes on to describe the events of the week, first, opening night at the opera:

I always enjoy getting the white tie, top hat and tails out of

_____
* Ranlet Miner, brother-in-law of Thomas S. Lamont.

mothballs (Remember Fred Astaire's song about that?). And to think that at half the dinners and most theater parties in the Twenties and early Thirties that was routine. I always wore an opera hat to the theater—folds up nice and flat to go under your seat. All kinds of notorious characters were present and at each intermission we went up to the Opera Club and sipped champagne as we sat at Rudolph Bing's table. News photographers' flashes were going off all around us, but we were not wearing our white mink (nor the diamond tiara on the head) so we were not photographed.

And he met a fascinating new friend:

At dinner at the Knickerbocker Club I turned to the pretty lady on my left and asked where she was born and brought up. "Fiji," she said, "I am a Fiji Islander." "Well," I said, "you seem to be clothed above the waist, your skirt isn't made of grass, and you have a Scotch-English accent. How come?" I suppose her father was a Scotch missionary or merchant at Suva —the chief town of Fiji which is some sixteen hundred miles north of New Zealand. She went to New Zealand to school at the age of ten, stayed there for her education, and married a man who is now the New Zealand Minister to the United States, and a very nice man, too. They were both so interested to meet me. Auckland and the whole country is just full of Lamonts, they said. Their best friend in New Zealand is Tom Lamont!

The letter includes this social note: "Mother's activities with Women for the United Nations and English-Speaking Union continue to bring an unwonted—but not unwanted—potpourri of Lords and Ladies into our circle. It is only occasionally that I can contribute a lion." And the letter goes on to describe a trip to Washington, another dinner, and a U.N. reception where the New Zealanders were still saying: "My goodness, to think we've met another Tom Lamont. You must come to Auckland and meet your namesake—a great chap he is!"

The future schedule seemed no less hectic with an Exeter Trustees meeting at the Academy, a flight home Saturday evening, and an 8 A.M. plane from La Guardia the next morning to join the Santa Fe Directors' inspection trip in Colorado Springs. The letter concludes: "What a life! Are we sane? What do you think? I'd like your advice. Should I retire and take it easy or keep in touch with the world as now?"

Of course, the question was completely rhetorical. My father would never have lived any other way. He looked forward to the stimulation of meeting new and interesting people; he relished life every day, a life of involvement, commitment, and hard work. His intellectual vigor remained keen to the end, his spirits high. A friend he lunched with in March of 1967 wrote: "His remarks, his questions, were quick with life and probing interest in every question that came up, without a shadow of apprehension over his own future; his serenity was breathtaking."

My father once said that happy men are those who try to make their lives useful and keep their hearts generous. He was a happy man. More than twenty years ago he voiced the expectation that ". . . in the years to come I shall continue to find everlasting joy in my fine family, occasional moments of high gaiety, zest for work and pleasure in a completed job, and happiness in the companionship of friends." His hopes were fully realized.

As he once wrote about a friend: "If there are degrees of immortality, surely the immortality of one whose influence for good was so penetrating and pervasive will be the more real."

18

RESOLUTION OF BOARD OF DIRECTORS OF MORGAN GUARANTY TRUST COMPANY

(May 3, 1967)

Our beloved friend, Thomas S. Lamont, died on April 10, 1967, in his sixty-ninth year, marking the end of an association with this Bank which extended over forty-five years.

Following in the footsteps of his father, who was a partner, Tommy Lamont began his business career with the banking firm of J. P. Morgan & Company in 1922 and became a partner seven years later. When the firm became an incorporated bank and trust company in 1940, he was elected a Vice President and a Director. He served successively thereafter as Senior Vice President, Vice Chairman of the Board, and Chairman of the Executive Committee.

When J. P. Morgan & Company Incorporated joined with Guaranty Trust Company of New York in 1959, he was elected Vice Chairman of the Board of Directors of Morgan Guaranty Trust Company of New York. In that office he played a principal part in the development of the merged institution. He retired as an officer in 1964, at the age of sixty-five, but continued thereafter until his death to be active in the affairs of the Bank as a Director and member of a number of Committees.

He was also a leading director in some of the Nation's most important mining, oil and railroad companies. He devoted lifelong attention to the field of education, most importantly to Harvard, and still found time to foster his interests in cultural, medical, and humanitarian causes.

The institution Tommy Lamont cherished most throughout his

business life, however, was this Bank. In his thirty-eight years as a partner, senior officer and director he made a unique contribution to its management and to the formation of its policies. His concern with the Bank was both deep and wide-ranging. He was especially interested in maintaining the highest standards of quality in the services the Bank offered. While both his name and his service linked the Bank's present to some of the most notable chapters in its past, his active mind and restless energy were incessantly occupied with its future. His passing leaves this institution poorer in many ways, but the influence of his generous spirit upon the conduct of its affairs will abide.

For those of us on this Board, the personal loss is hardest. Gentle and kindly by nature, completely sincere in his response to all human relationships, he was beloved by a great band of friends. We are sad at the passing of this dear associate, but we can rejoice in all that he was and all that he gave us while he lived.

19

MY BROTHER TOMMY
by Corliss Lamont

My memories of my brother Tommy of course go back to childhood and the many years, up till 1929, when our family lived in Englewood, New Jersey. Still standing is the big house on Beech Road, with its ample grounds, that Father bought from Henry P. Davison, his partner in J. P. Morgan & Company. Tommy and I shared the same bedroom in that house. I can remember his organizing games for friends who came to play with us, especially the lively game of run and hide called "kick the stick."

Before Tommy went away to school at Phillips Exeter in 1913, he attended a private institution, the Morse School in Englewood. While there he founded and edited a small newspaper called *The Cricket* that came out every other week. Thus Tommy's journalistic career started when he was about eleven or twelve years old. Later he became Editor-in-Chief of the *Exonian* at Exeter and President of *The Harvard Crimson* at Harvard. It was always my opinion that he could have been very successful as an editor or publisher. He was a good writer and had all the executive ability needed to run a big newspaper.

However, my father was hopeful that one of his three sons would follow in his banking footsteps. Tommy fulfilled that hope and, in other ways as well, ably carried on the Thomas Lamont tradition. This was especially true in the field of education, in which my brother was even more active than our father. Like Father, Tommy served as a Trustee of the Phillips Exeter Academy for many years and became President of the Board, a position he held with distinction for a decade. As for Harvard, he first served on the Board of Overseers and then for fifteen years as a Fellow of Harvard

195

College (member of the small executive board known as the Corporation).

Tommy also made a substantial contribution to Harvard affairs as Secretary of the Class of 1921 from the year of his graduation through 1950. He spent considerable time and effort on this job, and was in charge of seven Class Reports, for each of which he wrote a brisk and buoyant Foreword. His successor, James A. Lowell, pays tribute to him in 1921's Thirtieth Anniversary Report: "I want to recommend for your particular praise our former Secretary, Tommy Lamont. . . . In his twenty-nine years as Secretary he gave us the utmost of his vast capacity for service, loyalty and friendship."

In 1963 Tommy further solidified Lamont-Harvard ties by establishing the Thomas W. Lamont Collection at the Baker Library of the Harvard Business School. This Collection contains virtually all of Father's correspondence and papers on his banking affairs and on his many business trips abroad—to China, Japan, Mexico, and other countries. Tommy also continued to expand the John Masefield Collection which Father had set up in 1942 at Harvard's Houghton Library. In 1966 Tommy added to the Collection more than forty letters that Masefield had written him.

Tommy was also a Trustee (1941-51) of Smith College, which has obviously been the favorite women's college for the Lamonts. Mother was graduated from Smith in the Class of 1893 and received an honorary degree from the College in 1952. My sister, Eleanor Lamont Cunningham, obtained her A.B. from Smith in 1932; my daughter, Florence, later Mrs. Ralph Antonides, in 1955; and my niece, Priscilla Cunningham, in 1958. Shortly before he died, Tommy gave all his correspondence with Mother to the Florence Corliss Lamont Collection in the Sophia Smith Collection at Smith College.

What the Phillips Exeter Board of Trustees said about Tommy when he retired from the Board in 1961 well sums up the high quality of his work in *all* of his educational activities. The Board Minute reads:

> With the most profound regret this Board accepts the resignation of Thomas Stilwell Lamont, a Charter Trustee (or member of the Advisory Committee which preceded the present Term Trustees) since 1935, and President of the Board for the ten fruitful years from 1946 to 1956.
>
> No one in this School's long one hundred and eighty-year his-

Eleanor Lamont Cunningham

tory has served it more faithfully or devotedly than Thomas S. Lamont. Distinguished Exonian son of a distinguished Exonian father, he has enhanced the family tradition of public service to this, the family school.*

Never, in a crowded life of high achievement in finance, in business leadership and in good works, has he failed constantly to think of Exeter, to come to Exeter, to inquire diligently and perspicaciously into Exeter's present and to plan prudently for its future. For twenty-six good years the objectivity of his thinking, the forthrightness of his opinions, the realism of his common sense and the soundness of his judgment have invariably guided this Board toward wisdom and deterred it—usually—from error.

It is not only the recollection of his wisdom and his princely generosity and that of his family that will stay with us—his unfailing consideration of his fellow Trustees and tolerance of their occasional waywardness, his outgoing companionship and his warm friendliness will always be present in the memories and hearts of this Board.

After Father's death in 1948 and Mother's in 1952, Tommy assumed without hesitation the responsibilities of being head of the family. He took a deep and affectionate interest in all the Lamonts, down to the latest grandnephew or grandniece. Of course, on the financial side he guided us with great acumen. He was a bulwark of strength for every relative, always ready to spend time and thought in advising us. The visible and invisible support he gave to us was enormous.

Tommy and his immediate family usually went to North Haven for the summer, and it was there, in the expanding Lamont colony at Pulpit Harbor, that he was most easily able to visit with his relatives in the various branches of the clan. He was always available to us at the Big House at Sky Farm and always most welcome when he dropped in at one Lamont cottage or another for an informal chat. He rarely missed our big picnics on the beautiful White Island, owned by the Lamonts, off Vinalhaven. And I recall so well his reading aloud a favorite poem when the picnic lunch was over. Tommy's pleasant baritone voice lent itself well to the art of reciting poetry.

With his many lovable qualities, Tommy was popular in the

---

* Tommy's son, Edward M. Lamont, ably carries on that tradition today by serving on the Phillips Exeter Board of Trustees, of which he has been a member since 1963. His son, Edward M. Lamont, Jr., is a student at Exeter in the Class of 1972 and represents the fourth generation of Lamonts to attend the Academy. He is head of *The Exonian,* the school newspaper, as were his grandfather and I when we were Exeter students.

family circle, as in all the other circles where he was well known. He was amiable, affable, modest, interesting in conversation, and blessed with a fine sense of humor. He had a host of Exeter and Harvard friends, as well as the many friends he made in his business life, in his educational work, and in his trips to England. I might add that he was popular not only with men, but also with the ladies. And I can never forget the Boston newspaper story, when Tommy was at Harvard, which reported that Elinor Glyn, author of the sexy novel *Three Weeks,* was rapturous over his "beautiful brown eyes" after she met him on a visit to the College.

Tommy's will brings out very clearly his warmth and affection for his family and friends. In making bequests to various individuals, he includes a special word of praise for each one. Thus, in his bequest to his cousins, Katharine Lamont O'Donoghue and Gordon Lamont, Tommy says: "I have happy recollections of our childhood days together in Englewood, and I take pleasure in their continued friendship." About his niece Anne Miner Richardson and her husband, he writes, "in recognition of their high ideals and their gay spirits and of the meaning of their friendship to all my family." In reference to his niece Nancy Lamont Bowles and her husband, he states, "in admiration of their teaching services in Nigeria and of his high ambitions in academic life." About Mrs. Betty Thompson Tuckerman, Tommy notes: "In time of sorrow for my wife and me she gave us without stint the understanding help which we needed."

While Tommy and I disagreed on a number of basic economic and political issues, every so often we found ourselves casting our ballots for the same candidate for President of the United States. Thus it was that we both voted for Al Smith in 1928, for John F. Kennedy in 1960, and for Lyndon B. Johnson in 1964. Tommy of course participated frequently in the lively family discussions at our parents' dinner table and good-naturedly tolerated a wide variety of opinions that differed from his. He and I also carried on debates by letter about such controversial topics as Soviet Russia, Socialism, and American foreign policy.

Though most persons are supposed to become more conservative as they grow older, I think that Tommy became more liberal. I am sure that Senator Joseph McCarthy gave him a push in that direction when in the early Fifties he tried to do a smear job on Harvard by repeatedly attacking the University as a hideaway for "Fifth Amendment Communists." Tommy had no use for McCarthy or

McCarthyism. And he supported me in my successful battle (1953-56) to have the U.S. Courts rule that the McCarthy Committee's questioning of me was invalid and unconstitutional. He was not unmindful of the fact that back in 1933 a Senate Subcommittee on Banking and Currency had far exceeded its legal powers in asking him and Father loaded questions concerning their activities as bankers and as officers of J. P. Morgan & Co. Tommy approved of the U.S. Supreme Court's decision in 1965 that declared unconstitutional a Congressional censorship statute that I had challenged in a suit against the U.S. Postmaster General.

When my wife and I were at North Haven during the summer of 1966, we went up one day to the Big House to have lunch with Tommy. We were not sure what he thought about America's war in Vietnam and wanted to tell him why we so opposed President Johnson's reckless military venture. But T.S.L. seized the initiative to give us *his* reasons for disapproving the Administration's Vietnam policy. In the first place, he said, he could see no great, fundamental issue at stake such as confronted the United States in World War II. And, he said, in the last place, even if the U.S. Army should somehow win a "military victory" in Vietnam, it would face the impossible task of staying there permanently to keep the victory won.

Some of Tommy's little known public speeches in his later years are indicative of the liberalism about which I have spoken. Thus at a dinner of members of the Harvard Class of 1921 in 1950 he said: "The winds of freedom blow through the Harvard Yard, and so long as the right to free inquiry remains the first care of Harvard's administration, the University will continue a bulwark against those ideas which would stifle freedom. . . ." Later, at a bankers' convention in 1959, Tommy stated: "It is the competition between ideas which makes for more complete understanding of our nation's problems and creates an informed public opinion. The maturing mind of youth is made the keener, his critical faculties the stronger, if in his educational experience he has been forced to discriminate and choose between competing ideas."

I like, too, the idealism Tommy expressed in remarks at a dinner in 1960 given by the Harvard Corporation to the members of the Yale Corporation:

It is little enough time out of our lives which we give to Yale and Harvard. Yet who can say that that little time has not been of some measurable influence in the forward march of Man, perhaps easier to measure than all that we may have honorably achieved in our several callings? Of course, the businessman, the lawyer, the merchant, if he be a man of imagination and social conscience, gives impetus to human progress. He also searches for the truth, but his best efforts, if confined to his own calling, will have influence within an area far narrower than that encompassed by his work for a university.

Early on an April day in 1967 came the crushing news of Tommy's death. His loss was a heavy blow to the Lamonts. He had been for so long a beloved presence and sustaining factor in the familiar framework of our lives. For many years he had been the most vital link I had with my parents and my youth. I had lost a precious brother and a wise friend whose counsel was ever at my disposal. And many beyond the family circle have missed his genial companionship and his helpful cooperation in enterprises important for the welfare of the community. It was sad for Tommy to die at what must be considered these days the premature age of sixty-eight. But death, the great built-in tragedy of life, strikes when it will and no man can escape it.

20

THOMAS S. LAMONT AND HARVARD

*by Nathan M. Pusey**

One of the unwritten rules of the Harvard Corporation is that no member of that body can receive an honorary degree from the University, at least until after his retirement from active service. It is a source of deep regret to me that Thomas Lamont did not live long enough to stand before the huge throng at Commencement where other distinguished sons of Harvard have stood, his own father among them, to hear first his name called out, and then a brief and simple phrase which would have sought to distill the essence of his life of service. I should have found a very special pleasure in awarding him a degree.

If anyone ever had earned the plaudits of a grateful University, it was Thomas Stilwell Lamont. Yet it would have been a poignant and difficult task to try to encapsulate in a few words all that Tom Lamont did for Harvard. His citation would surely have had to include words like thoughtfulness, kindness, generosity, abiding and profound affection, questioning, dissatisfaction, sympathy, conviction and fidelity. But even these words could not have told the whole story.

There was a deep sense of duty embodied in Tom Lamont. Perhaps it was an inheritance from his clergyman grandfather passed to him through his wise, charming, and generous father whose "boyhood in a parsonage" engendered a sense of high principle that could not but have helped permeate young Tom's being very early in life. It was Harvard's great good fortune that the two Thomas Lamonts, father and son, reserved so large a part of

---

* Dr. Pusey was President of Harvard University from 1953 to 1971.

their lives for the well-being of education and allotted so much time and thought to the University.

Harvard was for both of them an avocation. For both, but particularly for the son who early caught the infection of his father's interest and enthusiasm and almost from his student days seemed to sense the opportunity and obligation which so many Harvard men feel toward their alma mater. Prepared by inheritance, he built on that inheritance through experience as *Crimson* editor, as Secretary of his College Class for twenty-nine years, as helper for the Harvard Fund, and finally as member of both of Harvard's Governing Boards.

My own path did not cross with Tommy's until 1953 at the time my name was suggested as a presidential prospect. But from the first moment of our acquaintanceship it was unmistakably clear to me that here was an extraordinarily concerned, helpful, and well-informed son of Harvard, and I never once had cause to reverse that initial judgment. He was even then showing his profound regard for Harvard in the lengths to which he went in helping to identify and to evaluate the presidential candidates under consideration. Particularly impressive to me was the fact that once he and his colleagues had reached their decision, he came all the way to Wisconsin to visit the Lawrence community and to bring the new President back to Cambridge. It was during this period that I began to come to know him, and from such beginning, as the years passed, the feeling of comradeship in a common cause ripened into a close friendship. We worked together for Harvard for fourteen years, and my admiration of and gratitude to him know no limit.

Initially there were two personal qualities in Tommy Lamont which particularly struck me. First was his innate courtesy and thoughtfulness toward others. The Puseys were very frequently the beneficiaries of Tommy's and also of Ellie's* kindness as they tried properly to set us on our course at Harvard. There were countless people to meet in those early days, new paths to tread, at first gingerly and then more boldly. In so many ways Tommy became a wise advisor and guide. He had an innate sense of what was right for Harvard, and he wanted to be sure that the new President set off in the proper direction and found those people among the alumni and the general public who had the interest and the capacity to be most helpful. There were frequent opportunities for friendly talk and consultation, in and away from Cam-

---

* Mrs. Thomas S. Lamont

bridge, but I looked forward most especially to those fortnightly Mondays when Tommy and his colleagues, so prudent, perceptive, and wise, gathered for the Corporation meetings which I learned to cherish, not least for the moments of friendship they afforded and for the sense of support they gave to an all-too-busy and frequently troubled president.

It was on occasions such as these that I began to appreciate the second of Tommy's specially memorable characteristics, the role of the questioner. Those were tense days. The University had been much in the limelight because four individuals, then or previously members of the teaching staff, had been identified in Congressional hearings as having once been associated with the Communist Party. A kind of anti-communist hysteria, aimed particularly at education, was sweeping the country under the influence of Senator Joseph McCarthy. To stand fast under unjustified abuse directed at the University was of the first importance, and it was inspiriting to have the understanding support of such as Tommy, who, while standing fast, looked constantly for fresh opportunities to tell the story of what Harvard was really like and what its contribution to the nation had been. Tommy was always asking what more we could do to turn the tide of adverse criticism.

A few years later when the temper of the times had vastly changed, the moment was at hand to consider what could be done within the College to catch up with the backlog of unfilled needs— necessarily postponed in depression and war time—to reinforce and take on new strength for the coming years. At the time of our discussions I remember arguing strongly that Harvard should expect to grow, slowly and steadily, but should not deliberately set out to increase by any substantial degree. Tom Lamont, impressed with the arguments of Charles Cole at Amherst and some other presidents of small colleges, argued, or at least questioned, whether it would not be more sensible for the University to declare a halt to growth and concentrate on quality. For some months, letters and memoranda on this subject passed frequently between us and among the other members of the Corporation. Eventually Tommy became convinced, by factual studies, that some growth for Harvard was inevitable. But equally convinced of the importance of enhancing the quality of the College, he bent every effort toward planning and promoting the ambitious effort which resulted in the eighty-two and one-half million dollar Program for Harvard College.

Tommy was singularly blessed with the gift of friendship. His personal popularity, the circles of acquaintances among whom he moved in New York and elsewhere in this country and in Britain, made him a particularly helpful agent in the matter of encouraging and obtaining support for large plans like this one. Not only did he know how to ask and obtain adherents to the cause, but he gave generously both from his own purse and his own time to push the Program forward. As a vice chairman of the campaign, and later as an inactive but much concerned behind-the-scenes advisor for the fifty-eight million dollar effort for Harvard medicine, his role was an indispensable one.

His solicitude for Harvard was never limited in its scope, although naturally certain subjects interested him more than others. Sitting as he did in a position of executive responsibility for the whole University, he was particularly convinced that the central administration should be well staffed, have funds at its disposal to make possible wise disposition of power throughout the institution and actual help whenever one part of the University particularly needed it. He himself showed special concern in very practical ways for the University Library, for the Divinity School, for the Business School, for the College, and for other divisions of the University when their needs seemed uppermost. Like others on the Corporation, he directed his personal gifts to the central administration on an unrestricted basis or to specific departments of current concern.

He had his special crochets too, and his colleagues never let him forget them, laughed with him about them, yet unconsciously deferred to his good sense of the appropriate. Were the promotional activities of the *Harvard Business Review* entirely in keeping with the usual practices of a supposedly scholarly publication? Just what are the qualifications of the new Assistant Professor of Economics? Are we sure that such and such an architect will give us a distinguished building rather than a boxlike eyesore? Does the proposed inscription for that memorial plaque speak directly, forcefully, and appreciatively of the donor's great gift? Why is such-and-such a Harvard professor always attending the same New York dinners that I am; isn't he ever in Cambridge? Despite the recommendation of the dean and the art experts, do we have to accept the contemporary art object in question? And so on. Although never a teller of humorous anecdotes, Tom Lamont had a wonderful wit and a sense of the absurd. He enjoyed his colleagues' jibes at his conservative taste in art and literature. In turn, his good-humored impatience with academic pretentiousness frequently cut to the root of issues and helped his colleagues to arrive at reasonable decisions in the University's interest.

His particular concern was that the University should always put its best foot forward. As one of the University's warmest friends and understanding supporters, Tommy saw no reason why Harvard as an institution, from the President on down to the least important teacher or administrative official, should not be willing to explain or even defend his work, to answer his mail courteously and promptly and with some sympathy for the views of his correspondent. Information requested should be quickly and politely supplied. Official communications should be simply, clearly, and carefully written. Publications should be attractive and well designed, in keeping with what he conceived to be Harvard standards. Evidence of the lengths to which he would sometimes go to assure this end was his quiet gift of the necessary funds to erect near Forbes Plaza at Holyoke Center a large and handsome slate tablet, designed and lettered by John Benson, honoring (in terms which he helped frame) the achievement of Edward Waldo Forbes.

Himself a fine writer and a voracious reader, he made great efforts to keep abreast of public issues and attitudes. His lively and questioning mind collected and tested ideas and impressions. His curiosity led him to remote corners of the University and over and over again to those parts of the University he loved best, like the Library. He gave countless hours to his trusteeship—far, far beyond the requirements of his office—and Harvard was constantly in his thoughts, as was clearly evident by the outpouring of notes, letters, and memoranda which came from his hand or his dictating machine on his free evenings or weekends or even vacations.

A man of the highest personal probity, he insisted on a superior measure of excellence for his University and set an example which was inspiring to all his friends and colleagues. A passage written more than twenty years ago* in the foreword to the Twenty-fifth Anniversary Report of his College Class is worth recalling for what it says of his love of Harvard and his faith in the future:

The disorder within our nation and throughout the world casts a long shadow. In two wars we have lost many whom we loved. We ourselves have fought for ideals which still appear

* The year 1946.

far from fulfillment. But let us not be discouraged. Let all of us continue, even more zealously in the future, to serve our professions, our communities, our country, and our world, as the record shows we have tried to serve them in the past. By so doing one can save one's own conscience; and that is the first step, the fundamental contribution, which one can make towards saving a sick world.

If we are only as wise as when we left Harvard, we should be regarding the future with hope, not fear. If we are wiser, then also our belief in the rights, and the duties, of the individual and in the concepts of Democracy is the deeper, while our tolerance of change is the broader. This is merely restating the simple Christian principles upon which our own beloved Alma Mater was founded, and to which she has cleaved for over three hundred years.

When retirement from business and then ill health contributed to reducing the amount of his outside activity, he still found time for Harvard affairs and for the many problems of the Harvard Corporation. He accepted his handicap with courage and obeyed his doctor, although his colleagues sometimes observed him sneaking half a cigarette or sampling a particularly rich and tasty gravy. When an operation for correcting his heart condition became inevitable, he knew well the risk involved, but he chose his surgeon with care, confidence, and quiet courage—and even felt it necessary to apologize for being hospitalized in New York, nearer his home, and attended by Columbia University specialists rather than by Harvard men in Boston!

He devoted the same care to his will as he did to all other important matters, almost as if it were not himself for whom he would be speaking but for all who intimately know and value privately supported education. Although his directions to his family and executors have been much quoted, they deserve repetition and remembrance, since they were written with Harvard and Exeter in mind, and they epitomize the conviction of which his whole life was an example.

Representative and democratic government needs an electorate which has knowledge of the nation's history and a pride in its traditions of liberty. . . . I am convinced of the prime importance to our society of good public schools and tax-supported universities. It has seemed to me, however, that those educational institutions whose leaders and governing boards may administer their affairs with maximum independence of all political considerations have, generally speaking, led in the setting of high standards and in initiating educational change and experiment.

His University will long remember in gratitude this concerned and loyal son. And I shall always count it a privilege to have shared his friendship, and to have worked with him in serving the multiform activity of Harvard which he knew with an intimacy to which few can aspire, and which knowing, he not only understood, but loved.

PART VI
Thomas William Lamont II

Thomas William Lamont II

21

SONNETS ON THOMAS W. LAMONT II

by Francis T. P. Plimpton*

I

He bore an honored name, another's name
That stood for high achievement, leadership—
Most boys who start with someone else's fame
Are quite content to let their lives just slip
Along prepared and easy grooves; not he—
He was himself, and no one else. He thought
His own way through until he reached the free
Convictions of a searching mind that's taught
But tests the teaching. His the sturdy kind
Of independent thinking that insists
That no idea has any right to bind
Men to it, but that each idea exists
For man, not man for it. And so began
What happens here—a boy becomes a man.

II

Whatever others did, he stood erect
And straight for what he thought was right, without
The unsecure and qualified effect
That's left by those whose faith is really doubt.
And then the war, that cut across the length
Of all our lives. His generation lost?
Not lost, but found in their awakened strength—
They faced their task although they knew the cost.
He chose the silent service, submarines,

---

* Francis T. P. Plimpton, of the Class of 1917 at the Phillips Exeter Academy, wrote these two sonnets about T. W. L. II when in 1953 the Lamont Art Gallery at the Academy was established and named after him. The dedication of the Gallery read: "To the enjoyment of beauty and to the happy memory of Thomas William Lamont II."

Where courage isn't flame, but means the test
Of taut and tightened nerves against machines.
And now—the restless sea, it gives him rest.
He bore an honored name, but what is more
He added honor to the name he bore.

22

MY NEPHEW TOMMY

by Corliss Lamont

Thomas W. Lamont II was born in New York City in 1924 and was the eldest child of Thomas Stilwell Lamont and Elinor Miner Lamont, as well as the first grandchild of Mr. and Mrs. Thomas W. Lamont and Mr. and Mrs. Edward G. Miner. From 1930 to 1937 Tommy attended the Buckley School in New York. During the winter of 1937-38 he went to a school in Switzerland, Ecole Nouvelle de la Chataigneraie, near Geneva. Then for four most fruitful years, from 1938 to 1942, he was a student at the Phillips Exeter Academy, where he was prominent in extracurricular activities of an intellectual nature.

T.W.L. II became one of the school's best debaters, as a member of the G. L. Soule Debating Society, the P.E.A. Senate, and the Academy Debating Team. At his graduation exercises in June 1942, he delivered the Class Oration,* making an address of singular depth and maturity. On the literary side Tommy was a member of the Lantern Club, Feature Editor of *The Exonian*, and President of the *Phillips Exeter Review*. He was also on the All-Club Soccer Team for two years.

In June of 1942 Tommy entered Harvard College and remained there for the full Freshman year. It was of course a Harvard on a war basis, with normal academic and extracurricular life drastically curtailed. None the less, Tommy very much enjoyed his months at Cambridge and felt that he got a great deal out of his brief experience of college. One thing that must have particularly pleased him was his election to the Delphic Club, to which his father belonged.

T.W.L. II was the first of that large family group centering

---

* In chapter 23 below.

around the Thomas W. Lamonts and the Edward G. Miners to lose his life while serving in the armed forces of the United States. When the Second World War began in the fall of 1939, Tommy was only fifteen years old. Yet he saw through to the fundamental issues involved far more clearly than most of his elders.

As one of his friends at Exeter wrote: "He understood this war, from the Spanish Civil War on, better than anyone else my age that I have ever known. He never for one moment mistook the Wave of the Past for the Wave of the Future." Tommy knew that he was taking part in a World War revolving around world issues. Essentially it was a battle between democracy and Fascism, with the whole earth as its arena and the future of humanity as its stake. And Tommy constantly insisted that victory would be in vain unless the war resulted in a better world in which, among other things, the United States fully cooperated with other nations to establish enduring peace. So he consciously fought and died not simply to defend America but also to further its highest ideals and to advance the liberty and well-being of all mankind.

Tommy's awareness of the deeper implications of the greatest war in history did not come as a sudden awakening. For many years, and even before he went to Exeter, he had been keenly alive to the big problems, national and international, of the day. In 1937, when Tommy was thirteen, he saw in London, during the family trip to Scotland and England, a news reel of Italian troops marching through Spain, and Japanese guns firing into Shanghai. This picture affected him strongly and he put in his diary this revealing observation: " 'What a world,' meekly murmur some. 'What a world! And something has to be done about it!' say I."

In his letters, English themes, and debates Tommy was forever discussing the fundamental social and political issues of our time. And in the broad, tolerant democracy of the Lamont family circle, at the dinner table at Palisades and North Haven, he took up the cudgels on many a burning question with aunts, uncles, parents, grandparents, cousins, or anyone else who might be present. He was not always consistent and he was sometimes impatient of views he thought wrong. But he was steadily working toward a sincere and intelligent appraisal of the confusing social currents in the world about him.

Tommy made a lasting impression upon those with whom he talked seriously, on both teachers and fellow-students at school and at college. Thus Mr. George D. Williams, an instructor at the

Buckley School, writes: "My memories of Tommy are very vivid. In current events classes, especially, he was a delight. He knew how to participate in discussions . . . and whenever he spoke he really said something. Really, I used to marvel at that 12-13-year-old boy." And Delmar Leighton, Dean of Freshmen at Harvard College, says: "No youngster who has gone off from Harvard to fight this war has given higher promise or had a more eager spirit to find out what was wrong with the world and to do something about it." John Crocker, Jr., a close friend of Tommy's at Harvard and North Haven, remarks: "Talking to him was real fun because he was always so quick. . . . I can honestly say that conversations with Tom prompted more thinking in me than those with any other guy and it was really stimulating and helpful."

It was primarily because Tommy understood so well the far-reaching import of the Second World War that he was so eager to get into the fight and strike a direct blow against the Axis enemy. Naturally there were other factors in his desire to be in the thick of things. Youthful love of excitement, the example of school and college friends, impatience with the routine of formal education in such a stirring time all played their part. But I think that Tommy's major decisions regarding his role in the armed forces were based on careful and serious reflection. He wanted to serve in a great cause to the best of his ability and to make that ability count as quickly as possible.

In enlisting first in Naval Air and later volunteering for the Submarine Service, Tommy well realized the dangers he was facing. He knew that he would be encountering fearful hazards again and again. And the final sacrifice of his life at the early age of twenty, with all the bright, long years of his manhood before him, was a fully conscious and meaningful act. With unassuming heroism Tommy went down to his death, in the great tradition of American sailors and fighters of the sea.

When a person so young and vigorous and beloved as Tommy suddenly dies, it is almost impossible to accept in one's heart the fact of his going. The news first came through on May 14, 1945, in a telegram to Tommy's father and mother from Washington, D. C. "The Navy Department deeply regrets," it began, "to inform you that your son Thomas William Lamont II Seaman First Class U.S.N.R. is missing following action while in the service of his country." At the time, I simply refused to admit to myself that Tommy was dead. Indeed, for months I held out private hopes that somehow, somewhere, he would turn up alive and well; that he would call long distance from a remote Pacific island and make a merry wisecrack over the phone about the situation. Most of us, I am sure, cherished some such secret dream.

No one will ever know, probably, exactly what happened to Tommy's submarine, the U.S.S. *Snook*. There can be no doubt about the important and gallant part this submarine played in the Pacific war, a fact recognized by the Navy Department in awarding the Submarine Combat Insignia to all members of the *Snook*'s crew. Nor can there be any question as to the invaluable role of U. S. submarines in general in the defeat of Japan. A total of fifty-two of them were lost, almost all in the Pacific theatre, of which the *Snook* was one of the last to go down. Secretary of the Navy Forrestal gave the American underwater fleet primary credit for the destruction of Japan's merchant marine. And it shared the honors in the annihilation of the Japanese navy.

Tommy was a great letter writer. I myself carried on a running correspondence with him for years. And we covered most of the prime issues of the day, with special attention to Soviet Russia and Spain. I was constantly impressed by Tommy's intellectual awareness, his maturity of thought, and his ability in argument. But even I was surprised, in reading through the vast amount of material from which I made the selections for this book, at Tommy's far-ranging mind and his genuine literary promise. In some of his later letters Tommy expressed the hope of becoming a reporter. He would have made a first-rate one, in my opinion.

I am convinced that Tommy would have gone on to outstanding achievements in the field of writing. And it is fitting that an Exeter classmate, Bill Sharon, has established in his memory an annual prize for literary excellence at the Phillips Exeter Academy. It was during his four years at Exeter that Tommy, to a major extent under the stimulus of his work on the *Exonian* and the *Review*, especially blossomed forth as a writer. "No one in our class," states Sharon, "wrote more forcefully or with more vision than did Tommy."

Tommy's venture into the sphere of poetry was characteristic of his many-sidedness. As his mother has told me, you could buy almost any sort of a present for Tommy, because his interests were so diversified. This is apparent all through his letters. He was a great lover of music and spent long hours playing records from his considerable collection. As his diaries in particular show,

Mr. and Mrs. Thomas W. Lamont, with their children and grandchildren, sitting on the steps of their house at North Haven, Maine, in the summer of 1938. Front row, left to right: Charles C. Cunningham, Jr., Lavinia L. Lamont, Priscilla Cunningham. Second row, left to right: Austin Lamont, Austin F. Lamont, Edward M. Lamont, Thomas W. Lamont II, Mrs. Nancy S. Lamont (holding baby Nicholas S. Lamont), Hayes C. Lamont. Third row, left to right: Margaret H. Lamont, Lansing Lamont, Mrs. Thomas S. (Elinor Miner) Lamont, Thomas S. Lamont, Elinor B. Lamont, Corliss Lamont. Fourth row, left to right: Thomas W. Lamont, Mrs. Charles C. (Eleanor Lamont) Cunningham, Florence Lamont, Mrs. Thomas W. Lamont. Fifth row, left to right: Mrs. Corliss (Margaret Irish) Lamont, Charles C. Cunningham.

Tommy early developed an interest in birds as part of his general enthusiasm for the outdoor life. He was an ardent skier and a keen sailor. And after he entered the Navy he would grow nostalgic for those marvelous summers in Maine that are such an integral part of every Lamont's life. North Haven he considered the nearest thing to paradise.

A first-rate sailor, Tommy occasionally showed poor nautical judgment. I can remember a late August afternoon when, after an island picnic, a stiff sou'wester was blowing and Tommy started to tack home in our 17-foot knockabout. His brother Lansing and a friend were with him. Older people in the party urged Tommy to take a reef, but he didn't want to bother. As the afternoon wore on, the wind grew stronger and skipper Tommy had increasing difficulty in keeping the sailboat under control. Waves kept splashing into the cockpit and overflowed into the forward compartment below. Finally, when Tommy realized that the craft was in danger of sinking, he made for shore. There were some 100 yards to go when the boat began to founder. Tommy and the two younger boys, who fortunately had put on life jackets, jumped overboard and swam for the beach. They all reached it safely. When they turned around to look for the boat, it had disappeared. We were able to haul it up from the bottom of the bay the next day.

Though Tommy passed through moods of youthful irritation and despondency, he was essentially a healthy, happy individual and full of the zest of life. Sensitive and discriminating in temperament, he yet had a fine, invigorating gusto for experience. And he possessed a wealth of friends among both boys and girls. I like this passage in his diary in 1942 while he was at Harvard: "Went up to Dublin for a girl's coming out party. Everybody was there. Got to know a bunch of new guys. Swell party. Champagne, women, wow! Mighty glad I went." In personal relationships Tommy was always frank and sometimes intolerant. His Exeter friend Norman James put it just right: "He was a rare person— intelligent, attractive, with an entertaining scorn for those he disliked and genuine affection for those whom he liked. He was occasionally irritating, in the way in which all fascinating people are, but he was usually immense fun."

That August day in 1945, at the Island Church in North Haven, showed how people felt about T.W.L. II. The Memorial Service was crowded, by both summer and native residents. It was a great outpouring of love and affection for Tommy, of admiration for his courage and devotion in giving up his life that all of us might live in peace and happiness. It seemed to me that everyone there must have been thinking in his heart what Corning Benton, a member of the Exeter faculty, expressed in a letter to Tommy's father: "It is unbearable to think of boys so young and tender and full of promise crushed in this mad world struggle; but they rise to heroic stature by the nobility and maturity of their sacrifice."

23

LETTERS, ADDRESS, AND POEMS

by Thomas William Lamont II

1937

La Chataigneraie, Switzerland, Oct. 17, 1937

Dear Daddy,

I have received many letters from the family during the week. A couple from Mother, a couple from you and one from Teddy. Teddy wrote me all about school. . . . He mentioned that Mr. Cameron read part of my letter to him to the class. Please ask Ted just what he read and why? Tell me sometime. I also got a letter from Mr. Roper. He has been travelling around Europe this summer.

Your long, type-written letter of Oct. 6 was exceedingly interesting. I want to make myself clear on Spain.

I believe the most important thing in the world today is the maintaining of peace. I sincerely think that Communism or Socialism typifying Russia and maybe France does more toward peace than Fascism typifying Italy, Germany and Japan. Fascism has already proved itself a symbol of war to me. Japan is now at war with China. Who started it? The Japs. What's the reason? Greed for territory and power. Italy has just finished conquering Ethiopia. The reason is the same: lust for land and power. Hitler has cruelly treated the Jews and broken numerous treaties. I admit some were unfair. And what has Russia done? As you said, innocent people have been shot. But the number is very small compared with the victims of Il Duce and Hitler. Think of all the people white and black who died in the conquest of Ethiopia. A few weeks after the fall of Addis Ababa a couple of Ethiopians threw a bomb at Marshal Graziani. Nobody was killed. That night squads of Italian soldiers prowled through the native quarter of the city and any native found owning any kind of firearm was immediately shot with his family. About 1000 were killed.

In 1934 Hitler purged his army because of a small revolt!

In the last month thousands of innocent Chinese civilians have been killed by Jap air-raids!

Italy and Germany have helped the Rebel cause in Spain tremendously, thereby prolonging the war. Have Russia and France done the same? No! At the beginning numerous Russian and French volunteers entered the ranks of the government. But soon Russia and France fell in with England and upheld strict non-intervention. While all the time Italian government troops poured into Spain. Italy and Germany are always the ones who don't cooperate. They're the ones who withdraw from the non-intervention patrol. They're the ones who won't attend conferences on non-intervention and peace. Why Mussolini's excuse for not attending the conference at Nyon was the most stupid, bigoted, small headed, little trouble-making note I've ever read. Can't that man see what he's doing? But the U.S.S.R. attends the parleys and cooperates pretty well.

I ask with Uncle Corliss why is Russia always referred to as a warlike, aggressor nation? Why is Stalin, though a dictator, put in a class with Hitler and Mussolini? What has Russia done to warrant these accusations? Why do people *always* take Russia as an example of dictatorship and despotism?

At the present I think it is a struggle between the right and left in Spain. I favor the left for those good reasons mentioned above. I favor a government duly elected by the people. The Madrid government was such before the revolution. Also it was not Communist. There were a tiny number of Communists in the Chamber of Deputies. It was a weak government because the Fascists wouldn't stop making trouble. At last the Fascists, who were beaten in the elections, knowing they could count on the support of Mussolini and Hitler, broke into open revolt. Now the Madrid government is Communistic I admit. It has changed hands a few times and is unstable. But anything is better than a Fascist Spain. If Franco wins, it will be one more feather in the Fascist hat. Franco is just a puppet in the hands of Mussolini. When Franco wins Spain will be an Italian colony. Mussolini will say, "Come on now, Francisco, if it wasn't for me you wouldn't have beat the reds. Now I'll put an air-base here, and a naval base here, and guns here so we can blow up Gibraltar in 5 minutes."

Now please don't get me wrong. I don't agree with the principles of Communism at all. If I had the choice of a government like that of Russia or a government like that which Franco intends to set up or they have in Italy or Germany, I would pick Russia. Communism and Fascism are both evils, I believe the lesser of which is Communism. Peace is all that matters now!

One of the two Spaniards in the school is Uruttia, who speaks good English. If he is typical of those supporting Fascism, heaven help the world if Mussolini gets more powerful. These things he said shocked me. He lauds Mussolini and Hitler. Everything they do is justified. What struck me most was his inconsistency. He likes complete dictatorship, with all that goes with it. "America is a bad country because there is no order. Presidents are useless things and Roosevelt is very stupid. Why does he allow people to criticize him and his government? The newspapers criticize him and anybody can say anything they want. And all the Communists march around with placards and banners. That's an awful government. First of all order and then peace, but order first." I tried to explain to him that that was "freedom of speech" and "freedom of press" which is the foundation of democracy. He said that democracy of that sort was very foolish. A government in power should preserve strictly order. Any government that can't preserve order oughtn't to govern. Now in Italy if you say anything Il Duce doesn't like, you go to jail. That's good government.

If you ask me Uruttia's type of order is nil. He went on to tell me how bad the Madrid Government is. He said "Why before Franco declared war anybody that said 'Viva Spain,' the Fascist battle-cry, was arrested. Isn't that unfair?"

I deplore that action of the Madrid Government, but look how inconsistent he is.

The boys of this school are very political minded. They are all real Fascists. Maybe that's why they like to fight so much. They talk about Spain and China all the time. They never think of the cause of the war or the results. "Japan won this battle!" or "I bet you Italy could lick the U. S. and England put together." They wear pins with pictures of Mussolini on them. Uruttia has one with all the flags of the Fascist nations entwined around the banner of Rebel Spain. In the room of Rieusset the other Spaniard there's a picture of Franco with underneath a picture of Christ. They never call it a revolution but always a "crusade." I don't think Christ admires a crusade like Franco's. I don't think Christ admires the way Hitler, Mussolini, and Franco hide everything under the mask "for the sake of peace."

The boys here are just a lot of suckers who fall for Mussolini and Hitler and all their show off and propaganda. One day I walked through the gym and gave the clenched fist salute. Immediately three boys jumped on me. They were really intent on destruction but a teacher came just in time. I shall not do that again.

I have read 6 books since I arrived, and I am now on "Quentin Durward." I have plenty of time to read and I have never liked it so much before. I am allowed English books after all because "I have to read a lot to get into Exeter." Whether that's true or not I don't care. . . . I wish I had brought more books along. There are very few English books here and those are old and falling apart. They have paper covers and the print is tiny. Many pages are missing in "Quentin Durward." Anyway I'll wait till I've read all the English books here and then maybe you can send some more over. Are you going to send me "Time"? I'd like it better than anything else. . . .

La Chataigneraie, Switzerland, le 24 Octobre, 1937

Dear Mother,

Yesterday I received those three magazines. Oh how wonderful it was to read them. For an hour or more I was in America with the wild. Everything told is fascinating. Then to my dismay I remembered I was still at "La Chataigneraie." It gave me a certain, different kind of homesickness. I have just finished a book about Audubon by Donald Culross Peattie. In that unique book the author relates that he once experienced the same feeling I have now. He was in Italy but he felt something was missing and he had to return to America. He left Italy, returned to the United States and in a cabin in the wilds he wrote this "Salute to J. J. Audubon." "Singing in the Wilderness" is not really a biography but a tribute to that man "who was America" by an admirer. Instead of telling every detail of Audubon's roving life he plays mostly on his remarkable character, what he stands for and how today what Audubon loved and learned is disappearing in the hands of Americans of the wrong kind.

In the Nature Magazine, Bird Lore, and Junior Natural History every page pleads for the vanishing wilderness. My hope rises when I read of the establishment of new sanctuarys, but my hope sinks when I read of increasing numbers of hunters. About 20 hunters for every poor duck. There's another open season this year. A million or more wild animals and birds all over the U.S.A. will be slaughtered to make an American holiday! Everything depends on the growing generation! . . .

1939

Exeter, N. H., Jan. 5, 1939

Dear Mother,

This is my first night back at Exeter. I had a very uneventful trip down and I spent my time well reading that beautiful book, "America Sails the Seas," which Daddy gave me for Christmas. Of course I am blue.

On coming into my room I immediately missed my school-bag with most of my text books in it. Tomorrow is time enough to search for it. I shall find it. . . .

It is one of those nights so few and far apart when the barriers of affected austerity and disinterest with which I too often surround myself at home are broken down. It is one of those nights when I ponder over thoughts like—What would my life be like if the airplane from Miami to Martinique crashed with you and Daddy on board?

I have just left the home, the room, I love. I said goodbye to Teddy and he said "goodbye" to me as he was walking out. I didn't want to show that I really hated to say goodbye and he was darned if he'd be sentimental. Maybe it is best that way.

As I sit here tonight I love and remember with a touch of sadness my school, my friends, my family, Palisades, and all of a thousand mental scenes of a life I loved, but will never lead again. . . .

Now I shall say something new. It ought to have been said long ago. *Thanks for everything! I have the best Mother and Father on earth!*

1944

U.S.S. *Snook* (SS 279), Nov. 15, 1944

Dear Father:

It is good to have you back, and, believe it or not, I, miserable wretch, have prayed to God for your safe return. If you don't consider 26 months under [censored] enough, and are tempted by that damn conscience of yours to try the Pacific, I can only say that you will find it a dull war compared to the European theatre. There is little of the pageantry and none of the civilization. Would you prefer to liberate Paris or Tacloban? One doesn't have the feeling of being part of momentous events. There are no nice uniforms or anti-fascists, or women, or liquor, or Oxford accents, or historic places or big battles on land—not that S 1/c Lamont would have anything to do with them if there were. But *you* would find it dull—especially in your line.

Well, we made a very successful patrol and now I can say I have heard "a shot fired in anger." A couple of days ago we put into an outlying base with battle flag flying. We tied up, and the band played the *Beer Barrel Polka* and *Anchors Aweigh,* and swarms of captains and commanders and plain sailors rushed aboard to congratulate the skipper and the crew, and I had the gangway watch and stood there saluting my arm off, with a .45 at my hip, feeling very proud. Then I heard them shouting "Mail-call" back aft and I was plenty eager for those letters, as the most studious cynic would be after a while out here. Pretty soon a guy came running up with a stack of mail for me, but I had to wait until the party died down before I could read them.

Pearl Harbor, Nov. 25, 1944

Dear Father,

. . . After leaving the states in June I went to Pearl Harbor where I was very soon transferred to the sub-tender U.S.S. Fulton, one hell of a tub—overmanned, overcrowded, and G.I. as hell. She pulled out for Midway almost immediately. I spent about two months in Midway, which is a pleasant, clean white sandy little island—definitely nice compared to some I've seen. Of course nobody in the States quite realizes just what goes on aboard these God-forsaken islands where Marines spend 22 months at a stretch and Seabees the same. The officers drink stateside whiskey in hotels while the coolies drink two beers a day and knife each other in $5000 gambling games—and that isn't half of it. Us sub sailors have it easy, but a lot of these people out here have a hellish time. . . .

I was transferred to the Snook Aug. 28. It is a good boat with an excellent record, 30 ships, but all the original officers have been transferred and even the captain is pretty green.

We ran down to Saipan. I went ashore at Saipan but you can read all about that in *Time*. Nothing much, but mud and ruins and heat and souvenirs. We were forced to return again to Saipan sooner than we expected, because the port screw developed a noise the Jap sound gear could pick up ten miles off. We were just on station at the time and that meant another week's run back to Saipan and a week there with divers over. Finally we shoved off somewhat depressed by consistent bad luck.

Our area was a strip of the China Sea between Luzon and Hongkong. At first things were pointless. Every night we fruitlessly chased down contact reports radioed by other subs. Guys were speaking of a "dummy run," not uncommon out here now.

A few days after the Philippines were invaded we got our break. We heard about a convoy of Jap reinforcements and ran it down. There were five cargo ships and two or three escorts. When we arrived on the scene three other subs of our wolf pack were already attacking, but they made submerged runs and were soon being depth-charged. We went in fast on the surface. The Jap radar is lousy and very scarce or we couldn't have done it. Our radar is wonderful. I stand battle stations on the APR, which is radar detection device. The Jap convoy had air support all night and their radar almost screamed the phones off my ears, but they didn't make out.

We attacked three times on the surface and fired 20 fish. We sank three ships and damaged one. Each time we caught the escorts at a disadvantage, because of our radar spotting, and each time we hauled ass at 19 knots, easily outrunning them. At 3 A.M. we submerged.

The wolf pack was depth charged all the next day. We got off easy though—very easy. One of the other boats didn't.

We sank one more Jap in the course of the patrol and picked up an American naval pilot off Luzon. These were the only other high spots. I am not kidding, I could have used a lot more excitement. Perhaps I'm just green.

We went straight to Midway and then Pearl. We were out 75 days—a very long patrol. Food and dispositions were damn poor when we got in.

I am now on two weeks rest cure at the Royal Hawaiian Hotel. Your buddy Quentin Reynolds is around. Should I stick him for a drink? I would just as soon be back at sea after four days here. No nothing except millions and millions of sailors and Doggies.*

Well, don't ever worry about me. I am mentally at ease now that I have a real job to do. But everything sours in time.

---

* Infantry.

U.S.S. *Snook,* Pearl Harbor, **Dec.** 29, 1944

Dear Uncle Corliss,

Some subversive person slipped a copy of *Soviet Russia Today* into a shipment of magazines which lately came aboard. It was the August issue and included an article by you, which reminded me I owe you a letter on various subjects.

Grandpa sent me a clipping of my old friend, Benjamin **De** Casseres', recent attack on you. Your letter to him was **awfully** clever. It obviously left him speechless with rage, because his comments in reply were incoherent, to say the least. What that old dud needs is a good punch in the nose, and I am tempted **to** write telling him to have his boss William Randolph Hearst assign a few bodyguards his way. If I ever get stateside, I'd like to hold field-day on him.

But what kind of talk is this? The main intent of this letter is to express my extreme misgivings and disappointment at the general drift of Soviet foreign policy. I see that you have written a tract entitled *Soviet Russia and the Post-War World*, of which I would greatly appreciate a copy, my entire fund of information on current events being the gleanings of pocket editions of such capitalist, right-wing publications as *Time, Newsweek,* and *Life.* Indeed for long periods I have no other news but the briefest of press releases via the ship's radio. Perhaps, therefore, you will excuse the factual sketchiness of my argument in some cases. As to your pamphlet, though, I expect you have some inside information on Russian purposes and policy. American and British correspondents in Moscow, hampered by the NKVD, censorship, and secrecy, and lack of freedom of movement, must rely upon the rather rare statements of Stalin and Molotov on foreign policy in writing their articles. Without adequate information, you can't blame them for sometimes drawing conclusions with which you disagree. I noticed that even *Soviet Russia Today* was unable to produce the text of a recent important Soviet decree on marriage and divorce—"unavailable."

The thing that bothers me most is Poland. It seems to me that in her dealing or lack of dealing with the Polish Government-in-Exile the Soviets have been unpardonably arrogant, intolerant, dictatorial, and blatantly unfair—a very bad example of diplomacy in our "bright new world" and an ill omen for the future. The technicalities of boundary disputes are not the important issue, to my mind, because nobody has the moral right or physical might to deny Russia what she wants in Eastern Europe. Nobody will deny that Russia has played an overwhelming part in the German defeat to date, and at a ghastly and stupendous cost to herself. Granted, however, that the Soviets cannot be expected to gush with the political purity of Wilson or the magnanimity of Lincoln, it could reasonably be hoped that the Soviet Union would at least make a gesture toward the new order of international fair-play, frankness, tolerance, and forbearance, which the American, and also the British, governments are fighting this war to establish. But the Soviets have not made much of a gesture even.

They used the patent pretense of insult over the alleged murder at Minsk of Polish officers to break relations with the London Poles. They then turned their native press and foreign mouthpieces to a campaign of vilification, crying "Fascist, traitor, reactionary" at the Sikorski and Mikolajczyk governments. . . .

I had hoped that the Soviets would abstain from political and physical reorganization of Eastern Europe, until after complete victory—then at a conference table, seated *with* her allies, for appearances' sake alone, if needs be. But the Soviets are playing power politics already, and the British, not to be outdone, follow suit. There is talk of "spheres of influence" for the British in Italy and Greece and, for the Russians, elsewhere to the East. I have read that in the Victorian and Edwardian eras Africa and Asia were split into "spheres of influence" by the great powers. This policy worked for a while, but inevitably spheres clashed. There were incidents between the British and French in the Soudan and between British and Russian in Afghanistan. I don't like the idea of civilized and independent European nations being apportioned off to the big winners in the present conflict—even in most circumspect fashion. A bloc of nations gathered together by mutual consent for defense or economy in common is another thing. A western European bloc under the aegis of Britain was suggested, but the Soviets saw anti-Russian designs in it, and squelched the idea with a barrage of stage whispers. This seems a bit dog-in-the-mangerish, for the Russians are protecting their western flank by somewhat similar methods, only the Red Army and the occupation commissars don't wear suede gloves, and Poles, Rumanians, and Bulgars being a diverse and unreliable lot, naturally the sunshine and mutual confidence angle doesn't bulk large.

Speaking of gloves, it appears the Limeys removed theirs in Greece. I suppose the Greenwich Village and Riverside Drive

Muscovites are still calling Gen. Scobie a dog. I suppose the British attitude toward the disarming of the Elas bears out your worst fears concerning Churchill's ingrained imperialism. The whole damn thing is very regrettable. But, like the Soviets, the Communist led Resistance groups in Europe seem to be utterly lacking in humility, in patience, and in tolerance in this day of near victory. Neither we, nor they, can afford to be too Wilsonian and ethereal, especially now. From the Anglo-American viewpoint *order* is a primary requisite, for the one mark in favor of a Pax Romana or a Pax Germanica is the guarantee of *order*. To sell democracy (and I mean *democracy,* not a dictatorship of the extreme left) to the tired people of Europe the Allies must firstly supply food and, secondly, the assurance that freedom from fear is a reality. If we were to let the numerous factions of the centre and left shoot it out on every street corner in Europe, we would soon have the great mass of politically disinterested, hungry, worn-out people feeling that liberation was an empty blessing indeed. . . .

I think my personal peace plan would be about midway between the Big Four concept and the Wilson, John Foster Dulles self-determination and every-nation-equal idea. We cannot afford the luxury of complete self-determination of peoples (to paraphrase my Grandfather Miner). The Big Four or Three must undertake morally and financially the responsibility for policing the world. You can't expect Paraguay or Switzerland to be particularly eager or decisive on the subject. An international police force to guard the pie after Russia has taken her slice seems to be the current Soviet attitude. The British outlook is somewhat too old-line and seems to be conditioned by their traditional fear, now proved by four years of fire, that they are weak without the safety of alliances, ententes, a balance of power, and European economic dependencies. An Anglo-American-Russian military alliance might get out of hand. It might look to many small nations like the beginning of another axis in benevolent form, but I would rather overstep the line in that direction than towards laissez-faire, loose organization, and too much reliance on the mere wording of those beautiful Four Freedoms.

I don't want you to infer from this letter that I am pouting in a corner because many Europeans have been found tinged quite red by the recent liberation. But Yugoslavia is the only nation where Communism seems to hold a majority, and still Marshal Tito promises elections in due time. But in Greece and Poland, not to speak of France, the Reds are probably a noisy minority. Let the people choose. In Poland, however, the Russians are forcing the hand with Hitlerian cynicism and in Greece the EAM chose violence to put itself in office. The general process has been one hell of a lousy augury for a peaceful and democratic future.

I hope you see my point. I will read avidly and open-mindedly anything you write or send me. But please don't hit me with a lot of Pravda hot dope on the horrible records of various opposition politicians or facts and figures on the "plebiscites" and "spontaneous elections" in the Byelo-Russia and the Polish Ukraine. Hatchet-men of the brand of David Zaslavsky present a pot-pourri of vindictiveness and calumny entirely incidental to the main issues.

Well, by the time you get this, and certainly by the time I receive your reply, much will have changed for the better, I hope. Indeed, my facts being unavoidably dated, perhaps things are altered already. Blame my facilities.

1945

U.S.S. *Snook,* Midway Island, Feb. 20, 1945

Dear Mother,

We are back again, and never did terra firma seem so good. Two months of four on, eight off, are wearying, to say the least. Besides, the last run was a stinker, physical discomfort and various other complications which tact and security regulations do not permit mention of. It was dull too—technically "unsuccessful"—and there was therefore no compensation for the affair at all.

Well, it's still the same old story with me. I just don't feel that I am fighting the war compared to the Gyrenes* and Doggies, anyway. And compared to the Roosians, the Doggies aren't fighting a war—so it is a vicious circle. The Quartermaster is strictly a fresh air man. He stands all his watches topside, which, in my opinion, is the best place to be, although this run proved an exception. The rest of the crew don't see sun or stars from the time we leave until we return to dock. The Quartermaster really doesn't have much to do but stand on his feet for four hours, moving his binoculars in occasional arcs and making brief pleasantries with the J.O.O.D., who occasionally ambles aft on the cigarette deck to see if you are awake. On some boats the Quartermasters have

* Marines.

a hand in navigation, but not on the Snook. In fact, the only break in the monotony is when they shout "Clear the Bridge!" Then there is a mad scramble, with lookouts dropping off the platform like sacks of flour, the diving alarm honking, and ballast tank vents roaring in your ear. I count the lookouts, or try to, and then, booting the J.O.O.D. in the posterior or tramping his head, drop to the conning tower, closing the hatch behind. This closing of the hatch is the supreme responsibility which the Navy has thus far placed upon my narrow shoulders. It involves some mental anxiety and a few moments of furious twisting on a wheel clamp. It is quite improbable that the hatch will jam open, although one worries about it, and rightly so, for with a Jap bomber zeroing in on you, an open hatch would be embarrassing.

I also *open* the hatch, which is less of an ordeal. Being last man down and first man up is thus far the summit of my naval career.

I got some swell letters from you, the last one from North Conway—lucky people. So Teddy is in the Navy. Well, submarines are winding up, but definitely. That is just a matter of geography and progress of the war; I guess he'll be a flat-top sailor.

Well, this time I really am going to rest and exercise. This place is well suited to it. Our last port of call wasn't. Too many material distractions. I expect to be seeing something of George Roosevelt, too. . . . George is a swell fellow and has dealt himself a good job as personal yeoman to the Base Executive Officer. . . .

Bruce Gaffney is doing soft duty somewhere in the South Pacific, he writes me. Bobby Pennoyer is on the *Pensacola,* a CA (heavy cruiser to you). Teddy, I guess, will be out here with us shortly, though from the *extremely* lurid accounts of his stay at Harvard, I can't figure why in hell he wants to come out here. But that's the old story. There are a couple of million poor guys out here who want to go stateside and a goodly number stateside who, in spite of warnings, want to come here. . . .

P.S.: The note in the Buckley Alumni Roster, "Tommy Lamont has been in the Navy two and a half years" . . . makes me feel like an old salt.

SENIOR CLASS ORATION

Class Day Exercises, Phillips Exeter Academy, June 7, 1942

It is the duty of the Class Orator, with accuracy, to interpret and give voice to the considered opinions of his classmates. Today this is no easy task. Our opinions are as the armies of the United Nations. They are flung from equator to pole, from flowered idealism to bitter cynicism. I like to think, though, we strike an intelligent medium, which is a difficult attainment for some of us in these times. But, in larger numbers than usual, we have our radicals. We have our dinner-table Fascists. We have our dreamers, our fighters, our cowards, and our boys who just don't care. Robert Frost thinks we will all mellow in time. Even a generation which has felt the awful shock of war on peace will simmer down to a contented plane. Perhaps we will—if we live long enough, and if we win.

Yet no one can easily synthesize the ideas of American youth in 1942 into concrete formulae. The war has knocked the supports from under that happy abstraction, the American way of life. It is easier for us to tell you what we do not believe in than what we do believe in. In the nineteen-twenties and thirties, when the Japanese were learning baseball from visiting American teams, when we lived in security, in peace, and in relative plenty, it was not hard then for the orator of a graduating class to outline the pattern of thought. It was not profound thought. Why should it have been? Violent death was an unreal fate. The most you had to worry about was your best girl and whether you could make $5,000 the year you graduated from college. And the orators, the spokesmen of Exeter's youth and of America's youth, would pass on their sentiment, materialistic in an optimistic way, optimistic in a blind way, and politically conservative, if not Republican, in a traditional way. Relatively speaking, unanimity of opinion, unanimity and certainty of ambition and expectation among youth was at its heydey.

In June, 1942, we think our past materialism, wondering about $5,000 a year or a car for graduation, was rather bloated, almost amusing. Now the domestic political issues of yesterday are faded and trivial. Looking back, we realize that we never honestly tried to puzzle their validity then. Six years ago only the most intellectual Exonians debated the issue of the N.R.A. Youth felt that the world would go on about the same whether the Supreme Court was New Deal or not, and whether the National Recovery Administration stood or fell. We were partially right. No force ever compelled us to solve in our minds the problems of yesterday. Well—quite simply, we are marching off to war, and we are trying to take mental stock of ourselves, to summarize the intangible forces which govern our lives. We are trying to solve, in our minds, the riddle of history and of life's purpose, for the present and for the future, and we cannot.

For the boys of the twenties and thirties, there was an easy pattern of opinion. Political concept, national destiny, personal future: These all had answer cards. Today they are the most uncertain and intangible of terms. They are hardly realities.

Why the confusion? you say. Forget the causes and effects. Look to immediate necessity. Get in and fight. Don't worry, we will. I should like to quote John Robbins, President of the *Harvard Crimson*, who says, "Those who have called us 'yellow' and 'afraid' were sadly mistaken. We were, it is true, very confused; but now most of us have emerged from the confusion of ideological conflict and have picked our path." We at Exeter have picked our path. I think most of us expect to fight, and we do not delude ourselves with hopes of a short war. We are fighting to save the country, and we are anxious to begin.

Yet, let me try and explain why some of us are in a state of mental flux and change, why of natural need our fight must bring some form of broader and more liberal, firmer and more lasting, reformation.

American youth of my generation was brought up to regard war as a far-away monstrosity. It was morally hateful, yet, at a distance, somewhat physically exciting. We were told that Socialism and Communism were evils which would deprive us and all men of initiative and the nicer fruits of labor. We were told that virtue, compassion and Christian unity were turning the tide for eternal peace. Pacifism was in the air. We drank it in. We absorbed to a degree the peace-time canards: "America was dragged into the Great War"; "Youth will never fight again." And now every one of those precepts has been refuted and shattered, including the conception of a morally distasteful war. Most of us will fight and kill without conscience.

As to the evil of Socialism and Communism, Russia has vindicated herself in our eyes by unheard-of sacrifice of blood, by heroism which has saved Russia and saved us. It is difficult indeed to see how a country can resist as Russia has, if its people are enslaved in abject poverty by a blood-smeared bureaucracy of revolutionaries. The answer is that we have been deliberately deceived, and that is why most of my classmates who have thought about it, seem to feel that a modified Socialism is inevitable in America after the war. This war, this Peoples' War throughout the world, has, through economic necessity, hastened the leveling process. In America as well as Britain, the social and economic barriers between fellow-countrymen are crumbling. The spirit of democratic cooperation, the equality of privilege, of sacrifice, and the leveling of *wealth* engendered by this conflict is going to be permanent. Some of us already feel that Socialism, or a Social democracy, would be a good thing. Youth's prejudices are not deep-set. They are easy in coming and fast in going. At any rate, the swing is definitely towards the left. In 1940, this upper-class Academy was about 85% Republican. In my class, at present, anti-Roosevelt feeling is hard to find. Of course, considerable of the switch-over to Roosevelt may be attributed to the pressure of war unity, but the appeal of the New Deal itself has grown in proportion to the popularity of Franklin Roosevelt.

And what about Socialism, or a broader economic equality, taking away the luxuries in life? We cannot wax sentimental over that. The luxury in life is gone already.

Virtue; compassion; Christian unity; pacifism. What about them? They too have been knocked from under us. For there is no religious creed strong enough to maintain any spiritual unity. There is no universal morality. Christian pacifism, the turn-the-other-cheek attitude, has failed for obvious reasons. The church has failed to outlaw war and now must needs support it. We feel, therefore, that in temporal, or shall we say, practical fields, the potency of the church, at least in America, is a nonentity.

There is one attempted explanation for the manifest indifference of youth to organized religion. In general, those who have drifted away from religion for philosophical reasons, feel simply that it is absurdly hypocritical even to talk of applying the Golden Rule in a war of survival. They feel it is impossible to practice Christian ethics in a vacuum.

But youth is not without faith. American youth has turned to nationalism—not consciously, but through necessity—for psychologically it fills the breach left by the inability of religion, or faith in science, to provide a driving, realistic credo, to satisfy our desires and aspirations. The cross, for most of us, has lost all dynamic meaning. The flag has taken its place.

I think, however, that some of us, although we have yawned and carped with justification at every sermon in the Phillips Church for the past four years, may gladly ask for salvation in Christ when death stares us in the face.

Yet we have turned to nationalism first in this crisis. What is nationalism? It is an unpleasant term, connoting to Americans the theory of racial solidarity, purity and superiority, which is the foundation of the Nazi and Japanese states. That is racial nationalism. It is a crude and brutal form of a concept which is inherent in and common to all nations.

American nationalism is political. It expresses itself through the word democracy. Its symbol is the flag. To the American form of government we owe undivided allegiance. We fight for a flag; a form of government; a way of life, detached from theology. We realize that the economic administration of this nation will and must change, but we avow that the political structure of the United States is the fairest, most liberal and most equitable yet devised. For this we will fight under the flag with as much fervor as those young men who fought for many of our principles almost a thousand years ago under the cross.

But we are realists. We do not link the word Crusade with World War II. You have not heard us flaunt the old phrases— "A war to end wars"; "Make the world safe for democracy." The gold trappings have been cut away. We do not say all we feel. But we are resolved to stamp Fascism from the face of the earth, and, rest assured, we will not leave the peace conference to the babblings of obese old men.

Some years ago, boys from England and America marched off to war. It was almost a Holy War. They burned with idealism— men like Rupert Brooke—and they died in vain. Their sacrifice was blasphemed and wasted by the inferiors who ruled the peace after the conflict. Baldwin, Chamberlain and their ilk, too old to fight, and the blind but chosen representatives of America who betrayed the League of Nations. In America, our elders had the choice between the League of Nations and national isolation. They took the latter as a path without commitments or even moral obligation to the outer world, and even up to Pearl Harbor the people of America thought they had the choice between war and peace. They thought they could choose, but they could not. War has come. And yet a choice still remains. We can choose the peace. We can build a better world order, and now is the time, if ever, or we can revert to isolationism. It would seem that a few of America's more obtuse and Fascist-minded politicians would still favor that reversion. Less dangerous men scoff at international reform as at all reform. They are only bigoted or badly disillusioned. Weak men shudder because the mere thought of a new and better world organization frightens them by its magnitude. Pessimism, cynicism, reaction, greed, and hate are all concentrated against those who even try to build. But youth is forever optimistic. Schoolboys have never been intimidated by life's terrors. We will not, in the writing of the peace to come, be discouraged or intimidated by past failures. We are cooler and more worldly than our contemporaries of the last war. If we fight as bravely as they did, we will do honor to ourselves and to our country. Yet we hope there will be a wider, finer result to our struggle. We will fight *primarily* to save the homes and soil of America, but also for the peace and freedom to create something really better, not just the same or a slight improvement on the old model. De Sales has said that as the war expands and evolves, ideas concerning the organization of the peace will change and change still more. The only denominator common to the people fighting the Axis is the will to save themselves from slavery. More constructive programs will have to wait. Wait they shall, but they *must* not be forgotten or laid aside in the hour of victory.

It is a rotten thing to die in vain.*

White Island

Composition, Exeter, 1940

The Penobscot River tumbles southward and seaward from the dark evergreen forests of the hinterland to where it meets the first salt breezes and salt water, and then, shorn of its fury, flows into Penobscot Bay. River currents join now with the ocean tides, racing southwestward down the broad reaches, past a hundred islands, until the last shade of shore recedes behind and the grey Atlantic swallows all.

---

* This Class Oration by T. W. L. II was later printed in part in a leading Scottish newspaper, *The Glasgow Herald,* of August 7, 1942. A Scottish writer then published, with comment, excerpts from the Oration in pamphlet form under the title of "What Young America Thinks."

Here where land-locked waters end and the sea begins are a dozen or more small granite islands. They are in fact the outposts of the continent. They are the last blue line of Maine coast that an eastbound sailor sees until he makes his landfall in the Azores at Fayal. Of these lonely islands my White Island is one of the outer, and unbroken ocean swells roll in against its seaweed cliffs with a dull unceasing thunder. Nothing lives on the White Island but the wild, screaming sea birds and no one ever lands except those few who love the place. To me that spot is ever tangible, for I can see and hear and smell it now.

I think of the White Island with the wind blowing—on a sou'west day when the little land clouds come drifting out from the hills of the mainland over the bay to these islands. The ocean is cold blue, flecked with a host of white caps, but by the brown ledges, where Eider duck squat on wet fronds of seaweed, the water turns to a translucent green. Foam topped, the swells pile on down Hurricane sound while we tack out to the White Island. The wind hums in the stays. The ship lays over, spanking each successive wave. On all quarters are green islands ringed with white rocks and whiter breakers. Then it's always "hard a starboard— backstays—jib-sheets," and we bring her up into the anchorage. One moment the lee rail is awash, she's tossing the biting spray across her bows—the next she rights herself and glides into the cove without a ripple. It's a snug and quiet cove with the White Island on our port as we reach in, and another little sister off to starboard. There is hardly fifty yards between the two islands, but the water is deep. We usually give her five fathoms of anchor chain. Splash—the anchor goes over stirring a swirl of bubbles and ripples that shiver the black reflections of the spruces on the shore. We haul the thumping canvas down and land.

There is often a stillness on the lee shore, only a whisper of a breeze sifting among the gnarled branches of the spectre spruces by the beach. There is a silence that doubly magnifies the dip of an oar or the rude tenor of a human voice. Great slabs of granite creep out from the moss at the wood's edge and lie white, gleaming in the sun. Occasionally on the sand bar at the far end of the cove a plover pipes. A gull cries raucously as if to mock our voices. But that is all.

Many years ago when I was very young we cut a trail across the island. I remember the shadowy, still woods, so thick I couldn't see the sky at times. There were tall spruces draped with hoary beards of Spanish moss, moist spongy moss beneath the feet, wet rocks that never saw the sun. My nostrils filled with the pungent invigorating scent of balsam and of fir. I was almost lost, awed to fear by the gloom and the solitude, when suddenly as I pushed on I caught a breath of fresh cool air and smelt the salt tang of the sea wind. Running through the last thicket I stumbled into the sunlight. The sou'west wind whipped back my hair, tore at my shirt, filled my lungs to overflowing. Booming, the surf reverberated in my ears. I looked to seaward where the blue glaring waters stretched away, tossing to infinity, until finally the blue ocean joined the blue sky, and they were one. I looked to the northwestward and saw the Camden hills faint and small and far away. I saw the distant islands and white waves breaking on rough ledges. I gazed on whitecaps, white sails, and white birds in the blue heaven. I looked down and saw a hundred feet below me the waves of the Atlantic crashing on the cliffs of my White Island.

SELECTED POEMS

Early in January, 1945, a letter from my nephew enclosing a number of his poems reached me in New York.—Ed.

U.S.S. *Snook*, Dec. 29, 1944

Dear Uncle Corliss,
I had a certain amount of time on my hands even during the last patrol. At any rate I decided a while back not to let what little verbal felicity I have fall into disuse. Hence the verse which I enclose under a separate cover.

I write you Uncle Corliss, because you are one of the few literati I know and besides my Father the only one I would dare send this trash to. I am sending these to you, because I badly want criticism of some sort. If you would look these verses over and give me your opinion on them, I would appreciate it no end.

You will probably trace my wailings to the infinitely more profound cynicism of A. E. Housman, who, incidentally, is my Bible nowadays; yea, my rock of salvation. I have, however, read some pretty awful tripe in periodicals and popular magazines. If you think—by any chance—one or two of these would be worth $5, please cut me in on how to sell the stuff. I apologize for not having it typed. But that was impossible due to circumstances.

I replied promptly to Tommy and said that I was quite favorably impressed with his poems. I told him that he had real promise as a poet and that I would be glad to try to place some of the poems for publication, if he authorized me to do so. I never received a reply. Tommy went down to his death when the submarine U.S.S. Snook was lost in action in the Pacific in April, 1945. The best of the poems follow.—Ed.

MY FATHER*

My Father is a banker,
T. S. Lamont by name;
His stamping ground is Wall Street,
And it's there he earns his fame.
He works all day from morn to night
To help finance the nation.
I wouldn't work so hard for all
The money in creation.

1934

ODE TO PEACE

Line upon line of helmets,
Line upon line of steel,
File upon file of rumbling guns
That make the foemen reel.

Wasted the happy homeland,
Blasted by fire and sword,
Ruined and racked by armies
In this world of bitter discord.

A home that once sheltered a family,
Ruins cover it still,
For the family met a choking death
From a gas bomb dropped to kill.

Thousands of suffering civilians
Desperately try to withstand
The horrible, grasping claws of war
That tear at the heart of the land.

---

* This poem was written when Tommy was ten, and originally appeared in the "Second Book of Buckley Verse," published by the Buckley School. It was later reprinted by the *New York Herald Tribune* and *The New Yorker*.

Then when the struggle is waning
And peace at last seems nigh,
A heaven-sent dove with an olive branch
Drops from a radiant sky.

Row upon row of crosses,
Silent and white as death,
Grim reminders of days gone by
And of those who no longer draw breath.

Countries are weakened and crippled,
Debts can never be paid.
Then the burden of depression and fear
On the next generation is laid.

God of the Ages, answer,
"Will it ever come true,
'Peace on Earth, Good Will toward men,'
Till Time sounds his last curfew?"

1937

COGITAVI*

When pausing in our drowsy show of life
Where bloated pigmies hold their petty sway,
The mind fights up above the tawdry play
To stages draped in courage, death, and strife,
Where man's existence, like the whetted knife,
Is keen and dangerous, edged with biting steel,
Slashing out action, turning earth's ordeal
To 'graven proof of braver, better life.
For ever there are hearts which not to be
Constrained by walls, by rules, by easy creed,
Rebel against dishonored peace and flee
The dull hypocrisy of word and deed.
Thus eager youth forever quits debate,
And fighting with brave certainty meets fate.

1941

---

* This poem was published in the *Phillips Exeter Review* and was read at the Memorial Service for T. W. L. II at North Haven, Maine, August 11, 1945.

TEACHER'S TALK

Teacher's talk is glib and easy monotony.
It flows out and belabors the hot classroom air with stickiness;
It eddies about the student's ears,
Slapping the shores of his tired mind with waves of unimportant
    words.
The student tries to think of faraway pleasures,
Salt water and the kiss of southern winds;
And then the cold piercing triviality of a date, 133 B.C., cuts in—
Behind it through the thought-gap pours the all-enveloping lecture.
You need great fortitude of mind to wall away completely
The never-ending, droning, dream cutting teacher-talk.

1942

THESE I HAVE LOVED

These I have loved:
    The shadowy wood in June, breathing
A hundred rustling sounds; the tinkling tune
Of the wood thrush calling in the brake;
The dancing sparkle of a pure mountain lake.
Blue sky; brown, towering cliffs, that in a thaw
Drop boulders down;
The excited bustle of a great town;
Scent of hemlock; biting refreshment of salt

Upon the windy sea;
Brown ledges; and white gulls dipping in the lee;
The warm, pulsating touch of a horse's back;
A boiling, fuming foam of a topsail schooner's track;
Fresh, God-given fragrance of a large meadow,
That after the shower, fills the air;
The tiny bright delicate petals of a woodland flower;
Owl's hoot in the impenetrable night;
On the mud flats, herons that make with stately gait in the dim
    light
Of evening; on your face the hot trickle of melting snow;
A hundred-thousand white-caps playing with the song of a north-
    west blow.
All these I have loved!

1942

THE SHEEP PASTURE

It runs a mile or so along the shore,
Where the thick spruces edge the grey-rocked beach,
And fish hawks' carrion-cluttered nests
Perch in dead branches, far above the reach
Of climbing boys. Inland the pastures stretch,
Laced with red hawkweed, clover, and blue vetch;
Sprinkled with junipers. The dew-wet grass
Clings to bare legs of hunters as they pass
Marking the sheep trails to the sedge-ringed pond
Where bull frogs sing. Beyond
The ferns, deep alder thickets lie,
Dark and impenetrable, hid from the bright sky,
Close foliaged, wet-leaved, silver and green
Haunted by myriad flycatchers who preen
Buff yellow plumage. But from Dyer's Hill
You look across the watered world until—
Past stone-cropped meadows, farms, isles in the bay,
The dim hills of Acadia, far away
Loom high, unending, washed with mistful blue,
Lands unexplored, mysterious to view.

1944

TO THE INTERNATIONAL BRIGADE

Would God that they could now be here,
The brave of many lands,
Who marched for us another year,
And died by Ebro's sands.

Not Ebro's surge nor Fascist lead
Can ever cleanse the stain
Of the red, hard-let blood they shed—
The men who fought for Spain.

It hurts to see a good cause fade,
While the dumb world stands by.
Better to smile at the fight you made,
And fight again and die.

But one brigade of battered ranks,
The butt of Fascist fear;
They fell on Manzanares' banks,
Belchite, Guadalquivir.

But see! They did not die in vain.
Although the world forgot,
Their furies like a cancer's pain
Have gnawed the Fascist rot.

Their dead upon the hills of Spain
Listen and hear the roar
Of cannon thundering in the same
Great cause they perished for.

Perhaps those gaunt battalions see
Among victorious hosts,
The germfire of their tragedy—
And weep—for they are ghosts.

                                        1944

IN CAMBRIDGE TOWN

When I was Freshman, fresh of face,
And lived in Cambridge town,
I drank my beer with little grace,
And all my tweeds were brown.

I spoke to those who spoke to me;
Lived strictly by the code.
My ties and shirts, impeccably,
Were always in the mode.

I wooed a maid on Chestnut Street;
I thought her rather fair.
Her words were saccharine, and faint
As perfume in the hair.

I told her she would never know
A lad so cursed as me,
And deftly set about to show
My wealth of misery.

The eldest son, unfit and cast
From out the family pale.
A rebel 'gainst the stolid past,
An aery soul in gaol.

I cried that but one close embrace
Would help me to sustain,
At least for a brief breathing space,
My burden and my pain.

And now they say another boy
Looks in those fetching eyes,
And inwardly derives great joy
From telling monstrous lies.

But from the sea could I return
To those bright college years:
I'd drink a beer in Cambridge town,
And kiss my darling's tears.

1944

IF I CAME HOME

What would you say, my darling
If I came home tonight?
Would I be brave, beloved,
And handsome in your sight?
Would you be glad and kiss me,
And say you loved me true,
And whisper that you missed me
More than I ever knew?
Or would you lie, my darling,
To give me short-lived joy,
And let your eyes betray that
You love another boy?

1944

GRINDELWALD

On Christmas Eve six years ago
The church bells pealed across the snow.
The crust was glassy with the freeze,
And blue ice cracked beneath our skis,
As we raced down the mountain mile
To white St. Anton's-by-the-stile
At Grindelwald im Berner Oberland.

Beside the ancient saints of wood,
Frost-nipped in grace, we knelt and stood
To hear the word of God and sing
Glad Christmas carols to the King.
The painted figures, green and red,
Were carved by hands a long time dead;
And candlelight suffused the air,
And lingered golden on your hair
At Grindelwald im Berner Oberland.

As we climbed back beneath the stars
It seemed this whole high world of ours
Forever would be bright and gay,
Filled with the blessings of that day:
Of you, my love, my fairest sweet,
Of peppermint and candy meat,
Of waltzes in the winter sun,
The slalom and the down-hill run.
At Grindelwald im Berner Oberland.

That Christmas morn dawned blue and clear.
The Eiger rose knife-like and sheer
Above the valley, and its peaks
Were wind-lashed, smoking fibrous streaks.
We skiied the Scheidegg and looked down
Five thousand feet to Wengen town
And saw the chalets far below
Brown nuts amid the endless snow.
We ate our chocolate and our bread
On Lauberhorn and idly said,
"Whatever comes there'll always be
Time for us to love and ski."

Where are you now? Another day,
Another year will pass, they say,
Before we two are hand in hand
At Grindelwald im Oberland.

1944

NIGHT WATCH

The fortress thunderheads arise
To hem the edges of the skies.
They lower luminous and white;
The stars are faint, the moon is bright.
Gentle the sea heaves vast and stark
To dim horizons where the dark
Is half of spirit, half of eye.
I shouldn't want to have to die
At sea and leave my watered bones
A thousand fathoms deep on stones,
In sunless bowels unseen by God.
For there is pity in warm sod.
But see!—the dawn. Horizons light;
The edges of the mind are night.

1944

24

LETTER FROM JOHN MASEFIELD

(After hearing of the death of Thomas W. Lamont II.)

Burcote Brook,
Abingdon, England, June, 1945

Dear Tommy and Ellie,

The news of your appalling loss just breaks our hearts in two with sorrow for you.

We had hoped that all of yours would be spared; that none of you, so kind, so dear, so charming, welcoming and understanding, should be stricken thus down into the depths.

One thing must console a very little: the knowledge that you had made the young life of such promise a very happy one in all ways, and one of whom all must have glad memories.

In the great closeness of human affections, there are strangenesses and stirrings often hinting at survivals of bodily death, and often beautiful with comfort. May such promptings come much to both of you and temper your dreadful grief with hope, and your desolation with companionship.

Yours in much sorrow and with many tender memories of friendship.

John Masefield

EPILOGUE
by Lansing Lamont

The special quality of the Lamonts, I have always thought, is their diversity of spirit and outlook.

Other large families thrive on their togetherness. They live year-round in a close community, often under a dominant patriarch or matriarch, and develop a pride in their oneness of outlook. The common denominator is more often the family firm or business, which becomes the engine for uniting successive generations. Or, too, a certain pattern of life determines the strong link between father, son, and grandson over the decades: public service, loyalty to some prominent institution, dedication to a particular pursuit such as teaching, medicine, music, or mountain climbing.

The Lamonts have chosen at one time or another all these patterns. We have had our patriarchs, our communes at Englewood and Sky Farm, our founders or partners in what have been essentially family-oriented firms (Lamont, Corliss & Co., J. P. Morgan Inc.) We have tasted public service in Washington and in the military; we have worked our hearts out for great institutions like Harvard and Exeter. We have pursued over several generations the worthy professions of teaching and the ministry.

One can never categorize us as merely a clan, however, nor bind us irrevocably to one course of life. That may seem a negative virtue. I happen to think it is our strength and salvation. We regenerate ourselves from decade to decade by moving into new fields of endeavor, attacking new challenges, adopting new attitudes. These are not necessarily common attributes of families as closely bound as ours.

Other clans may despair or disperse if that lone heir, on whom his relatives were depending, fails to live up to his seat in the family brokerage house or eschews a career in the family flour mill. Too often the same traditional patterns of pursuit turn a

247

family insular and dull. Even the best of clans peter out from lack of fresh exposure.

The secret of the Lamonts' success—the fact that we do persevere as a unified clan—has probably more to do with our insistence on diversity and independence than with any cloying reliance on old-fashioned togetherness.

Heresy? Contradiction? Perhaps. But look at us. I am not touting us as a tribe free of the normal pressures, strains, and fissures that other tribes undergo. We have our share, maybe more. Cousins, brothers, and sisters may have stopped speaking to each other over periods of time. Yet if there are serious mortal breaches in today's Lamont Clan, I am unaware of them. Collectively, we may no longer answer to a higher patriarch, but we continue to enjoy and communicate with each other out of prideful recognition that we share a common name and heritage. There is an affection among us that flows from the bonds of similar blood and forebears.

For all that, we are still diverse and the more vital for it. At some point way back, a wise Lamont elder refused to impose his own life style on his siblings. It was a comparatively radical concept, but a right one. Witness our own experience, watching in this century the development of the senior Lamont generation today:

They were descended from a line of merchants, farmers, and ministers. Their parents, Thomas William and Florence Corliss, were people of catholic taste and liberal outlook. Anyone who ever sat at the Palisades dining table could attest to that. It was this curiosity in matters beyond TWL's immediate calling as a banker that furnished the intellectual drive in his family. TWL of course was a remarkable example of the sort of Renaissance man who breeds diversity: a journalist in his early days, then newspaper publisher, chief angel of a literary review, international banker and economist, philanthropist for every worthy public cause, but especially education. He made his reputation in finance, but first and foremost he was a cultivated human being with a vast range of interests.

Is it little wonder that he produced and fostered children who embarked successfully on diverse careers? And children who in turn have generated lively broods with varied careers?

We all know those great American families where the dinner talk was invariably directed by the patriarch to the status of the family auto works or the condition of their racing stables. One founding father of a clan that produced a brotherhood of notable politicians demanded that money never be discussed at the table, only public affairs. TWL never indulged in those extremes, though one wished that economics had been occasionally mentioned at our gatherings. What he and his wife did was to stimulate among their sons and daughter an appreciation for good talk, good writing, and the good works of men in public life.

When Grandma Lamont once admitted in an unguarded moment that she had never heard of Babe Ruth, it seemed incomprehensible to those of us in the younger generations who took our sports pages for granted along with the editorials. The point was that she restricted her interests to only those subjects she deemed to be of lasting value. She simply was uninterested in topicalities. I doubt that the old lady was the poorer for not having known The Great Bambino. Still, it's the only incident I can recall where one of my grandparents displayed a yawning cultural gap.

I have always marveled at the litter which my grandparents produced: three sons who made their names in varied professions, and a daughter who married a captain of the arts. The men could all have accepted officerships in the bank or bought seats on the stock exchange and comfortably retired. Their sister could have pursued the exotic life of the Riviera or New York café society. The pattern of their lives could have been conventional, self-centered, and dull. And we of the next generation might have been the duller for it.

I'm not suggesting that my father, two uncles, and aunt were eccentrics. Far from it. By our standards their attitudes may often have seemed conventional. Our sons and daughters will say the same of us, and so on. But they *were* a mixed lot, and they did different and interesting things with their lives.

My father, the oldest brother, honored his father's calling and entered the bank. The next brother followed a career in philosophy, teaching, and writing. The third took to medicine and a life of rewarding research in the field of anaesthesiology. The daughter married an art museum director who stands today at the top of his profession. Not a bad score.

But look what *they* produced: sixteen grandchildren who have proved every bit as diverse and independent as the generation before.

Each has carved out a style of life that suits him or her best. Some of us are nine-to-five commuters, others free spirits unchained by office routine. Some of us worship the pastoral life, some flourish in the city's canyons. Spiritually, we march to different drums: one to the call of tall ships, another to the excitement of scholarship or public service, another to the joys of collecting fine art, still others to the exhilaration of achieving important business deals or reaching heights in some exacting and creative craft.

We have developed in our short time a third in the line of Lamonts who have entered Morgan's portals—again, appropriately, the oldest brother of this generation. He has been followed by a journalist-author, a biologist, an aspiring film maker, an already successful young financier and Rembrandt fancier, a zoologist (female!), and a budding politician who has worked in city government affairs. The women have drawn in-laws to the clan who persevere in such varied labors as city planning (one a Scot, the other English) and university teaching (Harvard and Rutgers). I should like nothing better than for the next generation to produce at least one ecologist, one performing artist, and one poet.

We Lamonts need to sustain this tradition of diversity. Not for diversity's sake, but because any great family needs the constant leavening which diversity of outlook, career, and life style offers. We become ingrown otherwise. I hope we never become exclusively a family of either poets or bankers. But I would hope we could always have at least one of each in our midst.

If we do—if we maintain individually our independence and nourish it among our children—we will stay a vital, interested clan. We will stand high within the larger community of men. Equally important, we will remain vital and interesting within our own cherished community of Lamonts.

London, England
December 1970

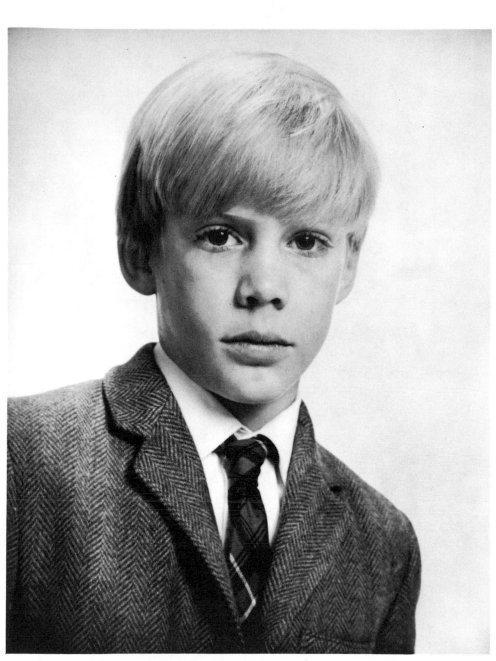

Thomas S. Lamont II, son of Lansing Lamont

APPENDIX I
ACKNOWLEDGMENTS

I wish to thank my nephew, Edward M. Lamont, for permission to reprint his essay "T.S.L.: A Happy Man, A Useful Life" and Nathan M. Pusey's "Thomas S. Lamont and Harvard" from the privately published *Thomas Stilwell Lamont* (1969), edited by Edward M. Lamont. The selections from the writings of Thomas W. Lamont II originally appeared in *Things To Be Remembered: The Record of a Young Life* (1946), another privately published book consisting of my nephew's writings and edited by me. Other portions of the book are drawn from *The Thomas Lamont Family,* also edited by me and privately printed in a limited edition in 1962. The poem "Maine Garden" in chapter 8 is reprinted by permission of Dodd, Mead and Company, publishers of *The Hawk from Heaven* by Evelyn Ames and copyright, 1957, by Evelyn Ames.

In the editing and writing of this book I wish to acknowledge especially the editorial assistance and acumen of Mrs. Virginia Marberry. I am also grateful to Edward T. Sanders, Father's able Secretary for more than twenty-five years, for supplying valuable factual information.

APPENDIX II
CLAN LAMONT NAMES
AND SEPTS

CLAN LAMONT NAMES

Lamond	La Monte	Lemond	MacLimont
Lamont	Lamound	Limond	M'Clymont
La Mont	Lawmont	Limont	MacLymont
	Lawmound	MacLamond	

CLAN LAMONT SEPTS

Black	Lyon	McIllewie	M'Sorle
Blue	M'Alduie	McIlquham	M'Sorley
Bourdon	McCaragan	McInnes	Toward
Brown	McConnochie	MacInturner	Towart
Lagman	McGildhuie	MacLucas	Turner
Lamb	M'Gilledow	MacPatrick	White
Landless	M'Gilligowie	McPhadrick	Whyte
Luke	McGillivie	M'Phorich	Yeats
	M'Gorrie	M'Queen	

APPENDIX III
FAMILY TREE